European Financial Reporting

Also by John Flower
Global Financial Reporting

European Financial Reporting

Adapting to a Changing World

John Flower

First published 2004 by
PALGRAVE MACMILLAN
Houndmills, Basingstoke, Hampshire RG21 6XS and
175 Fifth Avenue, New York, N.Y. 10010
Companies and representatives throughout the world

PALGRAVE MACMILLAN is the global academic imprint of the Palgrave Macmillan division of St. Martin's Press, LLC and of Palgrave Macmillan Ltd. Macmillan® is a registered trademark in the United States, United Kingdom and other countries. Palgrave is a registered trademark in the European Union and other countries.

ISBN 0–333–68518–0 hardback

This book is printed on paper suitable for recycling and made from fully managed and sustained forest sources.

A catalogue record for this book is available from the British Library.

Library of Congress Cataloging-in-Publication Data
Flower, John, 1934–
    European financial reporting : adapting to a changing world / John Flower.
        p.   cm.
    Includes bibliographical references and index.
    ISBN 0–333–68518–0 (cloth : alk. paper)
    1. Financial statements—Standards—European Union countries.
    2. Corporations—Accounting—Standards—European Union countries.
    3. International Accounting Standards Board.   I. Title.

    HF5681.B2F567 2004
    657'.3'02184—dc22

                                                                    2004040557

10   9   8   7   6   5   4   3   2   1
13   12   11   10   09   08   07   06   05   04

Printed and bound in Great Britain by
Antony Rowe Ltd, Chippenham and Eastbourne

Contents

List of Exhibits

Acknowledgements

The author expresses his appreciation to the Bosch Group which agreed to the use of extracts from their financial statements in the book.

Foreword

The subject of this book is the financial reporting of European enterprises. This is a vast subject and this book does not attempt to cover it comprehensively. Instead certain specific aspects have been selected for detailed examination, essentially because of their topicality and their relevance for the development of the wider subject. The following are the particular aspects of European financial reporting on which the book concentrates:

Emphasis on Western Europe

Within Europe, there is a very real division between the western and eastern halves of the continent, the dividing line between the two being the 'iron curtain' which for over forty years following the Second World War separated the countries to the west, whose political systems were based, more or less, on the principles of representative democracy and whose economic systems were based largely on capitalism and the free market, from those to the east where both politics and economics were dominated by communism. Although communism collapsed more than a decade ago, the countries of Eastern Europe differ so markedly from those of Western Europe in many important respects that it is still necessary to make a distinction between the two halves of Europe.

The emphasis in this book is on Western Europe; more specifically the fifteen member states of the European Union and two non-members, Norway and Switzerland. There are three basic reasons for this choice.

Economics

In economic terms, Western Europe is more important than Eastern Europe. The combined output (Gross Domestic Product or GDP) of the seventeen West European countries covered in this book makes up over 90 per cent of that of the entire continent.[1] The difference between the two halves of Europe is brought out dramatically by comparing the economy of the largest East European country (Russia) with those of West European countries. The GDP of Germany (the largest West European economy) is over seven times that of Russia and there are five other West European countries with a higher GDP, France, Italy, the UK, Spain and the Netherlands.[2] One consequence of the larger economies of the West European countries is that they host many more very large enterprises, which are one of the focal points of this book. Of the one hundred largest European enterprises listed in Exhibit 1.4 of Chapter 1, only two (Gazprom and Lukoil) are based in an East European country.

It is the same picture with trade. The combined imports and exports of the seventeen West European countries are more than ten times those of the East European countries. The latter point means that countries outside Europe are much more likely to have commercial contacts with countries of Western Europe than with those of Eastern Europe. For example Germany's exports to the USA are more than seven times higher than those of Russia,[3] the largest East European country. There are no less than seven other West European countries whose exports to the USA exceed Russia's.[4]

Transition

Eastern Europe is currently experiencing a period of transition, both politically and economically. The old system, based on communism, has manifestly collapsed and all the countries in the region are endeavouring to reform their economic and political systems, in most cases using as their model the countries of Western Europe. This development means that it is not particularly useful at this juncture to study the countries of Eastern Europe because there is a good chance that in the near future they will have undergone further radical change. It makes much more sense to study the countries of Western Europe, which provide an indication of the way in which Eastern Europe may well develop in the future.

Accountancy

The third reason relates to the subject matter of this book: financial reporting. The contribution of Western Europe to the development of accountancy has been much more significant than that of Eastern Europe. Double entry book-keeping was invented in the city states of Northern Italy in the thirteenth century, and the first book on the subject 'Summa de Arithmetica, Geometria, Proportioni et Proportionalita' was written by an Italian friar Luca Pacioli and published in Venice in 1494. The initial development of the accountancy profession took place in Europe. The Institute of Chartered Accountants of Scotland claims to be the world's oldest professional accountancy body tracing its origins to the Edinburgh Society of Accountants which was founded in 1853. From their beginnings in Western Europe, both accountancy and the accountancy profession have spread around the world.

Prior to 1990, accountancy in the East European countries was based on the principles of Marxist economics and on centralised state planning. Much intellectual effort went into developing a system of socialist accounting, which was of considerable academic interest. However, with the collapse of communism, it is no longer relevant. Even Russia is adopting accounting methods based on the West European model.

In brief there are two good reasons for studying accountancy as practised in Western Europe: it is the part of the world where modern accountancy developed and, given the economic importance of West Europe, it is still highly relevant today.

The national characteristics of financial reporting and its diversity

The book does not attempt to cover financial reporting in detail – for example there is no attempt to present the law and practice relating to every item in the balance sheet and profit and loss account. Instead the book aims to present the general nature and character of the financial reporting of enterprises in the different countries of Western Europe, with particular emphasis on the differences between countries. An outstanding characteristic of Western Europe, not only in financial reporting but in other matters such as politics and culture, is its diversity. This diversity certainly complicates the study of European financial reporting but also adds considerably to its interest. This diversity is analysed with respect to three aspects of financial reporting at the national level: its history, its function and the regulatory system.

History

This book does not provide a detailed history of financial reporting in Western Europe but it does set out the present situation in its historical context. A study of history provides an insight into the causes of differences between countries.

Function

It is commonplace that an enterprise's financial statements fulfil a number of different functions. However most modern textbook writers give little attention to these various functions, assuming (wrongly) that the only significant function of the accounts is to provide information for the capital market. They ignore the many other functions that accounts fulfil throughout Europe and thus overlook an important key to the understanding of the differences between European countries. This book seeks to repair this omission by devoting a whole chapter to the topic.

Regulatory systems

Each European country has its unique set of rules that governs the financial reporting of enterprises under its jurisdiction and its own national regulatory system to set these rules. Clearly differences in national regulatory systems are a major source of differences in the practice of financial reporting. For this reason, this book analyses the elements of the national systems in some detail.

The overcoming of diversity: the EU and the IASB

The diversity of financial reporting at the national level within Europe certainly makes an interesting subject of study. But diversity has a number of disadvantages, particularly in acting as a restraint on economic development. As long as economic interactions between two countries remain at a low level, it is of little consequence that each has its own unique system of financial reporting. However, at a certain stage in the development of economic relations, it becomes important that each country should at the very least comprehend the financial reporting of the other and ideally that the two countries should have a common system. That stage is reached when a significant number of persons (individuals and enterprises) in one country seek to invest in enterprises in another country or to set up a business there. With the enormous increase in international trade and international finance in the decades following the Second World War, the disadvantages of different systems of financial reporting became increasingly apparent, leading to a major effort to reduce the differences.

Two organisations have been at the forefront of this effort: the European Union (EU) and the International Accounting Standards Board (IASB). For each body, the book analyses its objectives, structure, working methods and the instruments by which it seeks to achieve its objectives: the EU's objective being the harmonisation of company accounts throughout Europe by the issue of directives and that of the IASB the development of a set of internationally accepted accounting standards. Over the last thirty years, the EU's directives and the IASB's standards have become a major influence over the financial reporting of European enterprises, as, at least for the larger enterprises, international rules have begun to supplant national rules.

The current revolution in financial reporting

The activities of these two organisations and the need for European companies to switch from national rules to international rules have resulted in the last ten years being a period of quite extraordinarily rapid and fundamental change in financial reporting. It would not be an exaggeration to describe the recent events in this field as a revolution – a revolution that is still in full swing and the outcome of which is uncertain. Three aspects of this revolution are considered in detail:

1. *The contest between the EU, the IASB and the USA*: Who is to set the rules for the financial reporting of the major European enterprises? Initially there were three candidates: the EU, the IASB and the US regulatory authorities (the source of US GAAP). The book examines how the relationships between these bodies have developed in recent years, notably why the

EU decided to ally itself with the IASB, so that currently there is an unresolved contest between the IASB's standards and US GAAP.

2. *The convergence process*: One way in which this contest might be resolved is through the convergence of the IASB's standards with national standards (including US GAAP), which is the IASB's official policy. This ongoing convergence process is considered in detail.

3. *The Enron scandals*: There is a detailed analysis of the recent accounting scandals in the USA, notably those involving Enron, WorldCom and Xerox. These scandals are not only of considerable interest in their own right but have had a considerable impact on financial reporting in Europe.

The final chapter analyses the contribution that Europe has made to the development of financial reporting. It draws on the analysis of the preceding chapters to bring out the essential characteristics of European financial reporting, noting that there is a great divide within Europe between the British approach and the Continental approach. It concludes that, at present, the British approach is dominant, at least for the financial reporting of the larger enterprises. The impact of globalisation will probably result in the disappearance of a specifically European approach to financial reporting, which will become merged with a global approach. However this will happen only with respect to the larger enterprises. The financial reporting of the great mass of small and medium-sized enterprises will continue to display national characteristics, with the consequence that, for many decades to come, European financial reporting will continue to be marked by the diversity which is at present its most conspicuous feature.

Notes

1. The combined GDP of all European countries in 2000 totalled €8844 million. That of the fifteen member states of the European Union plus the two West European countries that were not EU members (Switzerland and Norway) came to €8220 million, being 92 per cent of the total for the whole of Europe.
2. The figures for GDP in 2000 are: Russia €251 million, Germany €1873 million and the Netherlands €365 million.
3. In 2000, Germany's exports to the USA were $58 billion, compared with Russia's $7.8 billion (*Source*: US Department of Commerce).
4. The countries are: the UK ($43 billion), France ($29.6 billion), Italy ($25 billion), Switzerland ($10 billion), Belgium ($9.9 billion), Netherlands ($9.7 billion) and Sweden ($9.6 billion). The figures are for exports to the USA in 2000, same source as note 3.

1

The Enterprises of Europe

This opening chapter takes a closer look at European businesses, at the industrial, commercial and financial enterprises that form the backbone of the European economy. It considers first the various organisational forms that these enterprises may adopt.

1.1 Forms of business organisation

1.1.1 The corporation

The most common form of business organisation, for all except the smallest enterprises, is the corporation. The reasons for this are historical. During the nineteenth century, industry developed rapidly, first in Britain, where the 'Industrial Revolution' started around 1750. From there it spread to the continent, initially to Belgium and then to Germany, France and neighbouring countries. The process of industrialisation led to a significant growth in the number of large enterprises: examples were the cotton mills of Lancashire, the iron works of Lanarkshire, but above all the first railway companies. These all made use of recently invented machines, which required large amounts of capital, larger than could be provided by those who owned and managed the business. The capital requirements of these larger industrial enterprises could only be met by bringing together the savings of many individuals. The corporation was the ideal form of business organisation for these new industrial enterprises; it had two principal advantages:

1. *Legal personality*: A corporation is a separate legal entity from the individuals (the financiers and managers) who are connected with it. The corporation may own property and make contracts in its own name. This legal characteristic is known as 'legal personality'. In law a corporation is a 'person'; to distinguish it from individuals, it is often known as a 'legal person', whereas individuals are known as 'natural persons'. The corporation

1

continues to exist even if the owners (the shareholders) die or sell their interest to another person.

2. *Limited liability*: The liability of the individuals who provide the corporation's capital (the shareholders) is limited to the amount of their shares. They are not liable for the corporation's debts. This is the natural consequence of 'legal personality'. The shareholders are liable to pay to the corporation the amount stated in their contract with the corporation, which will generally be the amount payable on their shares. However they have no contract with and hence no liability towards the corporation's creditors. These debts are owed by the corporation, which is a separate person from the shareholders.

When the capital needs of an enterprise are greater than what can be supplied by the small group of people who know and trust one another and who can manage the business in partnership, then the corporate form of organisation becomes essential. The suppliers of capital can entrust their savings to the businessmen who manage the corporation on their behalf, secure in the knowledge that, because of limited liability, they will not become personally liable for the business's debts, beyond the amount of their shares. The combined effect of legal personality and limited liability is that the ownership of the corporation may be divided among several persons (each of whom owns a share of the corporation) and that these shares may be transferred independently of the corporation, thus permitting the creation of a market in the corporation's shares. Without these legal characteristics, the modern capital market could not exist.

There had been corporations in Europe before the Industrial Revolution. Examples are the Verenigde Ost Indische Compagnie (United East India Company) which was founded in the Netherlands in 1602 and the Hudson's Bay Company, founded in London in 1670, whose shares are still traded on the Toronto Stock Exchange. However the Swedes claim the oldest surviving corporation, Stora Kopparbergs Berslag ('The great copper mountain') which dates from at least 1288. In 1999 it merged with the Finnish corporation Enso Oyj to form StoraEnso Oyj whose shares are listed on the stock exchanges of Helsinki, Stockholm and New York.

However, in the past, such corporations were not common, principally because governments sought to limit their numbers. A principal reason for this reluctance was that often corporations were used as vehicles for fraud. A well-known example is the wave of speculation known as the 'South Sea Bubble' which occurred in London in 1720. Many unscrupulous promoters took advantage of an atmosphere of frenzied speculation, created by rumours of the great profits made by the South Sea Company, to set up corporations whose shares they sold at great profit, but which subsequently were found to have no substance. The authorities responded by placing severe restrictions on the formation of new corporations; for example, in

Britain, corporations could be formed only by Royal Charter or by special Act of Parliament.

However by the middle of the nineteenth century it had become evident that Britain's future economic development depended crucially on the ability of the growing industrial enterprises to organise themselves as corporations. In Britain, the necessary framework was provided by two Acts of Parliament:

1. The Joint Stock Companies Act of 1844 which greatly simplified the process of forming a corporation. Henceforth a corporation could be formed simply by registering the deeds at a government office known as the Companies Registry.
2. The Limited Liability Act of 1855 which granted the privilege of limited liability to the shareholders.

Other Western European countries followed Britain's lead in easing the restrictions on the formation of corporations. As a result of these reforms, it is now possible in all Western European countries for businessmen to set up a corporation by following certain legal formalities. In general, in order to set up a corporation, it is necessary to draw up its constitution, endow it with a minimum capital, give it a name and register all these particulars with the authorities. If all these steps are followed, the state will not normally refuse to register the corporation.

The legal terms for the basic form of corporation in the various Western European countries are presented in Exhibit 1.1. In France, the term is 'Société Anonyme'; the curious word 'anonyme' (anonymous or nameless) is meant to warn people who deal with the corporation that it is not a natural person. Many European countries have followed France in using this term or a translation, including Belgium, Greece, Netherlands, Spain and Portugal. In Germany, the term is 'Aktiengesellschaft' (literally 'share certificate society') where the emphasis is on how the company's ownership is defined: similar terms are used in Austria, Denmark, Italy, Norway, Sweden and Switzerland.

The term in Britain and Ireland is 'Public limited company'; here the emphasis is on the limited liability of the shareholders. In strictly legal terms this is a nonsense, since it is the shareholders and not the company that enjoy limited liability (a corporation is liable for its debts up to the full extent of its assets) and the limited liability of shareholders follows logically from incorporation which endows the corporation with its own separate personality. The use of the term 'limited company' in Britain stems from the historical accident that, when the corporate form of business organisation was first made generally available by the Joint Stock Companies Act of 1844, it was specifically provided that, as an exception to the general rule with corporations, the liability of shareholders was unlimited. Only eleven years later, with the Limited Liability Act of 1855, were shareholders permitted to

Exhibit 1.1   The basic corporate form

	Legal name	Initials	Date*
Austria	Aktiengesellschaft	AG	1899
Belgium	Société Anonyme	SA	1873
Denmark	Aktieselskab	A/S	1917
Finland	Osakeyhtiö	OYJ	1895
France	Société Anonyme	SA	1867
Germany	Aktiengesellschaft	AG	1870
Greece	Anonymi Etairia	AE	1920
Ireland	Public Limited Company	PLC	1855
Italy	Società per Azioni	SpA	1882
Luxembourg	Société Anonyme	SA	1915
Netherlands	Naamloze Vennootschap	NV	1928
Norway	Aksjeselskap	AS	1910
Portugal	Sociedade Anónima	SA	1888
Spain	Sociedad Anónima	SA	1869
Sweden	Aktiebolag	AB	1895
Switzerland	Aktiengesellschaft	AG	1881
United Kingdom	Public Limited Company	PLC	1855
European Union	Societas Europaea	SE	2001

* Date of the law by which this corporate form became generally available.

limit their liability. In fact, in Britain, it is still possible to form a company in which the liability of the shareholders is unlimited, although this is rarely done as it brings few benefits to offset the increase in risks.

Exhibit 1.1 gives two further items of information concerning European corporations:

1. The dates of the laws by which the corporate form of business organisation became generally and easily available to businessmen. It was possible to form a corporation in most Western European countries before the dates listed in Exhibit 1.1. For example, as is pointed out by Mikol (1995), the French Commercial Code of 1806 created the société anonyme, which possessed the twin characteristics of a corporation: legal personality and limited liability. However official permission was necessary for the forma-tion of a société anonyme and this official permission was not a mere formality. The application was checked at the local level by the prefect, it was then examined by the minister and finally submitted for approval to the head of state. The great change brought about in France by the act of 1867 was that official permission was no longer required; article 21 of the 1867 act provided: 'In the future, sociétés anonymes will be able to be formed without government authorisation. They can be formed, irrespective of the number of shareholders, by a private deed under seal

executed in duplicate.' In the generation following Britain's Limited Liability Act of 1855, all of the major European countries reformed their laws to make incorporation generally available to business: France in 1867, Spain in 1969, Germany in 1870, Belgium in 1873 and Italy in 1882. The exception was the Netherlands which did not succeed in reforming its law until 1928, despite a first proposal having already been made in 1871.

2. The last column in Exhibit 1.1 indicates for each country the letters that are attached to the corporation's name. These initials warn everyone that they are dealing with a corporation and not with a natural person. There is a general requirement throughout Europe that the corporation's full name, including these letters, must be given on all documents issued by the corporation (contracts, letters, orders, invoices and so on) and displayed at the corporation's offices. In theory customers and others should be put on their guard; in practice most people, perversely, consider that the letters SA, AG or PLC add a note of solidity and respectability!

Included in Exhibit 1.1 is the 'Societas Europaea', which is a form of corporation set up under the law of the European Union. However it was only recently (October 2001) that the EU enacted the laws that regulate this form of corporation, after more than thirty years of discussion. Therefore, at the time of writing, the first Societas Europaea has still to be formed.

1.1.2 Smaller corporations

Although at the outset the corporation was conceived principally as a form of organisation suitable for larger businesses, it was often adopted by smaller businesses which sought to secure the two principal advantages of incorporation: legal personality and limited liability. However the corporate forms of organisation that were initially made available to businessmen and which are listed in Exhibit 1.1 were found in certain respects not to be completely suitable for small businesses. Many of the laws relating to this corporate form were appropriate only to large enterprises with many shareholders. Since these corporations offered their shares for sale generally, it was considered necessary to subject these corporations to relatively strict rules to prevent the investing public being defrauded. These rules covered such matters as the minimum capital and the formalities to be observed in setting up and operating the corporation, including the information to be provided to the public at large. It was felt that many of these rules were inappropriate for the smaller corporations which had only a few shareholders and which did not offer its shares for sale to the general public.

In general governments were sympathetic when smaller businesses demanded that they should not be subject to the full rigour of the rules that were designed to protect the investing public; however as a quid pro quo they insisted that the smaller businesses should not be allowed to offer their shares for sale publically. Hence in all European countries, except in Scandinavia (Norway, Sweden and Finland), the law provides for a second form of corporation which is designed specifically to meet the needs of smaller businesses. Exhibit 1.2 sets out the legal terms used to denote this second corporate form and the identifying letters. In France the term is société à responsibilité limitée (company with limited liability) and most countries have adopted a close translation of this term; the German term 'Gesellschaft mit beschränkter Haftung' has the identical meaning as the French term. Only in Denmark does the legal term not include the words 'limited liability'. Hence it would be convenient to apply the general term 'limited liability company' to this corporate form. Unfortunately this term is used in the United Kingdom and Ireland to denote both corporate forms: the first form is termed 'public limited company' and the second 'private limited company'. It should be noted that the word 'public' is used to denote that the shares are publicly available and not that the company is owned by the state. Because of this wider usage of the term in Britain, one cannot apply the term 'limited liability company' to this corporate form. Exhibit 1.2 uses the term 'alternative corporate form' which is correct but not very informative. One cannot use the term 'smaller corporation' because many of the enterprises that have adopted the alternative form are quite large. The most convenient way to refer to this corporate form is by the identifying initials (SARL, GmbH and so on).

The specific rules that govern this form of corporation differ somewhat from country to country, but, in broad general terms, most of the following characteristics apply throughout Europe:

Exhibit 1.2   The alternative corporate form

Country	Legal title	Initials
Austria	Gesellschaft mit beschränkter Haftung	GmbH
Belgium	Société privée à responsibilité limitée	SPRL
Denmark	Anpartsselskab	ApS
France	Société à responsibilité limitée	SARL
Germany	Gesellschaft mit beschränkter Haftung	GmbH
Greece	Etaria Periorismenis Efthinis	EPE
Ireland	Private limited company	Ltd
Italy	Società a responabiltà limitata	Srl
Luxembourg	Société à responsibilité limitée	SARL
Netherlands	Besloten vennootschap met beperkte aansprakelijheid	BV
Portugal	Sociedade por quotas de responsbilidade limitada	Lda
Spain	Sociedade de responsbilidade limitada	SRL
Switzerland	Gesellschaft mit beschränkter Haftung	GmbH
United Kingdom	Private limited company	Ltd

1. The minimum capital which must be subscribed on the formation of the corporation is set at a lower figure. Under EU law, a corporation of the basic form (SA, AG and so on) must have a minimum capital of €25,000, but there is no such requirement for corporations of the alternative form. In fact in certain countries there is no minimum capital requirement; thus, in Britain, it is perfectly legal for a private limited company to be formed with only a derisory capital, as was demonstrated by the students of the London School of Economics when they set up 'The Tuppenny Company Ltd' whose capital consisted solely of two shares of one penny. In France, the minimum capital for an SA is €40,000 but for an SARL only €8000; in Germany the equivalent figures are AG, €50,000, and GmbH, €25,000.

2. The rules relating to the formation and operation of the corporation are less strict. The shareholders may, in adopting the corporation's constitution, decide not to include certain rules (obligatory for larger corporations) which are designed to protect the interests of shareholders but which add to the costs and difficulties of administration.

3. As a quid pro quo, these corporations are generally prohibited from offering their shares for sale to the general public. Often their constitution places limitations on the right of shareholders to sell their shares to outsiders, in order to protect the other shareholders from having to accept as a shareholder someone not to their liking. Such a provision makes this corporate form very suitable for closely held enterprises where the suppliers of capital know one another, perhaps being members of the same family. On the other hand it makes it completely unsuitable for businesses that seek a wider share ownership, such as those whose shares are listed on a stock exchange.

4. The information that these corporations are obliged to disclose in their financial statements is somewhat reduced. However they are not exempted from the general rule (at least in the countries of the EU) that all corporations must file a copy of their financial statements at a government office, where they can be inspected by any member of the public.

Although the alternative corporate form is designed principally for the smaller family enterprise, the laws of the European countries generally place no limit on its size. In France, there is a rule that a société à responsibilité limitée may not have more than fifty shareholders, but there is no limit on the amount of the share capital. In fact some enterprises are very large; French government statistics show that in 1989 there were fifteen SARLs which each employed over 2000 workers. In Germany, many of the larger enterprises adopt the alternative corporate form; in 1986 there were over 2000 GmbHs with a subscribed capital of over DM 10 million in West Germany alone.

The relationship between corporate form and size is brought out clearly in the statistics presented in Exhibit 1.3. In France, in 1989, there were over

Exhibit 1.3 The relative importance of large and small corporations

France – 1989

	Small corporations (<10 employees)		Medium-sized corporations (<10–2000 employees)		Large corporations (>2000 employees)		All corporations	
	Number	%	Number	%	Number	%	Number	%
SA's	70,441	13.66	74,577	53.21	354	95.93	145,372	22.15
SARL's	445,311	86.34	65,575	46.79	15	4.07	510,901	77.85
Total	515,752	100.00	140,152	100.00	369	100.00	656,273	100.00

Germany – 1986

	Small corporations (capital <DM1 million)		Medium-sized corporations (capital: DM1–10 million)		Large corporations (capital >DM10 million)		All corporations	
	Number	%	Number	%	Number	%	Number	%
AG's	396	0.12	809	7.23	985	30.77	2,190	0.63
GmbH's	333,779	99.88	10,376	92.77	2,216	69.23	346,371	99.37
Total	334,175	100.00	11,185	100.00	3,201	100.00	348,561	100.00

Germany – Analysis by amount of capital*

	Small corporations (capital <DM1 million)		Medium-sized corporations (capital: DM1–10 million)		Large corporations (capital >DM10 million)		All corporations	
	Total capital (DM millions)	%	Total capital (DM millions)	%	Total capital (DM millions)	%	Total capital (DM millions)	%
AG's	127	0.48	3,105	10.21	113,166	54.72	116,398	44.12
GmbH's	26,496	99.52	27,301	89.79	93,625	45.28	147,422	55.88
Total	26,623	100.00	30,406	100.00	206,791	100.00	263,820	100.00

* Total amount of capital of corporations in each category.
Note: average capital per corporations – AG's   53,149,772 DM
                                                    GmbH's   425,619 DM.

650,000 corporations, including over 500,000 SARLs and nearly 150,000 SAs. Most of these corporations (over 500,000) were very small (less than 10 employees), and of these very small corporations, most (86 per cent) were SARLs. However, of the large corporations (more than 2000 employees), the great majority (over 95 per cent) were SAs, despite the fact that less than a quarter of all corporations were of this form.

In West Germany in 1986, there were almost 350,000 GmbHs but only some 2000 AGs. As in France, the great majority (over 95 per cent) were very small (capital of less than DM 1 million): almost all these very small corporations were GmbHs. Of the larger corporations (capital greater than DM 10 million), only 30 per cent were AGs, but these accounted for 54 per cent of the total capital of corporations in this category. The average AG is more than one hundred times larger than the average GmbH: the AG's average capital is DM 53 million, compared with DM 425,000 for a GmbH.

There are significant differences between France and Germany: there are almost twice as many corporations in France compared with Germany, and, in Germany, the alternative corporate form (GmbH) is relatively more important than in France. However certain broad generalisations can be made with respect to these countries, which apply, to a greater or lesser extent, to all the countries listed in Exhibit 1.1:

- Most corporations are small and most are of the alternative corporate form (SARL and GmbH).
- Most of the larger businesses are organised as basic corporations (SA and AG), but most SAs and AGs are not large. The reason why many smaller enterprises are organised in the form of SAs and AGs is that there are certain fiscal disadvantages attached to the alternative corporate form, particularly when the enterprise is controlled by a single person. These disadvantages are more pronounced in France than in Germany, which explains the relatively higher proportion of SAs compared with AGs.[1]
- The great majority of SARLs and GmbHs are small, but there are a few that are large, relatively more in Germany than in France.

Finally mention should be made of the large number of corporations in both countries: 650,000 in France and 350,000 in Germany. The corporate form of business organisation is very popular. In both countries businessmen responded very positively to the liberalisation of the process of incorporation that occurred in the nineteenth century and in fact the number of corporations has grown steadily since then. The position in the other European countries is very similar. The European country which has the most corporations is Britain: in 1994 there were over one million limited companies of which only some 12,000 were public limited companies. In Britain there is one 'legal person' for every 50 'natural persons'.

1.1.3   A third corporate form: the limited partnership

There is a third corporate form, the limited partnership, which has been of historical importance in some European countries and which may well become important again in the future, but, at present, is little used. The limited partnership is similar to the alternative form of corporation in that it has legal personality, with shareholders (or limited partners) who have limited liability. The important difference is that there is, in addition, at least one general partner who assumes unlimited liability. The limited partners are entitled to a share in the profits of the corporation but are forbidden to play any role in its management. The limited partnership is permitted by the laws of most European countries but is not common because it offers few advantages over the alternative corporate form. However it is significant in two countries:

1. *France*: The société en commandite par actions, where the general partner, who assumes unlimited liability and who manages the corporation, is termed the commandite, was the most common form of incorporated business enterprise before the société anonyme was made generally available to business by the act of 1867. Thereafter almost all major enterprises adopted this latter form. An exception is Michelin, a very large tyre manufacturer, whose shares (representing the interests of the limited partners) are quoted on the Paris stock exchange. The general partners (the 'commandites'), who control the enterprise, are all members of the Michelin family and they are prepared to accept unlimited liability, because it carries with it the advantage that they cannot be removed by the limited partners who are prohibited by law from interfering in management. In effect, the Michelin family is able to retain control of the business even though it provides a minority of the corporation's capital; the enterprise is immune from takeover.

2. *Germany*: The Kommanditgesellschaft, where the general partners (the Komplementäre) accept unlimited liability, also has a long history, but, as in France, it has been largely supplanted by the other corporate forms (AG and GmbH). There are, however, some half dozen Kommanditgesellschaft listed on the Frankfurt stock exchange, where they are identified by the letters KGaA. Moreover it still survives as a curious hybrid corporate form, the GmbH & Co. KG, which is in essence a combination of a GmbH and a Kommanditengesellschaft, the GmbH being the general partner. This particular corporate form offers certain tax advantages.

It is not impossible that, in the other European countries, limited partnerships may become more popular in the future, especially as a means of thwarting potential takeover bids. The United Kingdom recently revised its law to permit the formation of limited liability partnerships, identified by the initials LLP. Certain major audit firms, such as KMPG LLP, have turned themselves into limited partnerships as a way of protecting the private wealth of their partners, whilst preserving the partnership form.

1.1.4 Other corporate forms

Finally mention should be made of three other corporate forms that are of considerable importance in Western Europe: state corporations, cooperative societies and mutual societies:

1. *State corporations*: In many European countries, the government assumes responsibility for organising certain economic activities, such as public transport, water supply and electricity generation. Frequently a state corporation is set up under a special law, to manage this activity. The powers of the state corporation are defined in the special law and not in the general law. Examples of state corporations are Société National de Chemins de Fer Français (French state railways) and Instituto Nacional de Industria, which manages the industrial enterprises owned by the Spanish government. On occasions, state enterprises are organised as corporations under the general law with the government owning all the shares; an example is Deutsche Bahn (German railways) which is an AG.
2. *Cooperative societies*: Cooperative societies exist in all European countries and are particularly common in Scandinavia, Germany and the Netherlands. They have the twin characteristics of the other corporate forms (legal personality and limited liability), but differ from them in the rules for the distribution of profits. Generally shareholders are paid only a fixed rate of interest on their shares and the remaining profit is added to the society's reserves. It is common for cooperative societies to distribute part of their profits to their members in the form of a rebate on their purchases from or sales to the society.
3. *Mutual societies*: Mutual societies are similar to cooperative societies in that profits are not distributed as dividends on shares but retained for the benefit of members. Insurance businesses are often organised in this way; their profits, after allocations to reserves, are divided among their members in proportion to the premiums that they have paid. In Britain, a form of mutual society, known as a building society, which specialises in the financing of house purchases, is particularly common.

The emphasis in this book is on the larger enterprises, and therefore on the basic form of corporation as presented in Exhibit 1.1, with only occasional references to the alternate corporate form.

1.2 The separation of ownership from management

Many of the first corporations were large enterprises that were attracted to the corporate form of organisation as a means of securing the large funds needed for their activities. Typically such corporations had many shareholders, as the requisite amount of capital could be raised only by combining the resources of many investors. Most of these investors did not concern themselves with the management of the corporation in which they held shares; there was no strong necessity for them to do so, as their private wealth was protected by limited liability. Instead they delegated the task of managing the corporation (which formally they owned) to one or more managers. The function of managing the corporation became separated from the ownership of the corporation. Over the past hundred years or so, this separation has become increasingly prevalent, until today all the major European corporations (as well as those of the USA and Japan) are managed by individuals who, at most, own only an insignificant proportion of the shares. This has the great advantage that the persons appointed as managers may be those most competent at the job and not simply those with the most money.

The way in which the separation of management from ownership is achieved in the different European countries varies according to the terms of the national laws as do the terms applied to the corporation's managers: in Britain they are termed 'directors', but in France 'administrateurs'. However the following points generally apply:

1. The managers are formally appointed by the shareholders. In certain countries, such as Germany, the appointments are made indirectly. The shareholders appoint the members of a supervisory board, which in turn appoint the managers. Also certain other groups, such as the corporation's workers, may have the right to appoint some members of the supervisory board, but the majority of the members are generally appointed by the shareholders.

2. The shareholders have no power to intervene in the management of the corporation – that is the responsibility of the directors/administrateurs. In general, the shareholders' powers are limited to appointing and dismissing the directors/administrateurs, which is done by a vote at the general meeting of shareholders. Such meetings are held once a year and more frequently if demanded by a sufficient number of shareholders. Essentially the relationship between the shareholder and the director/administrateur is analogous to that between principal and agent or between landowner and steward. The directors/administrateurs have the authority to manage the corporation, and for most of the year they occupy themselves with this task free from the attentions of the shareholders. Only periodically, normally once a year, do the shareholders have the opportunity of checking that the directors/administrateurs have been doing their job properly.

3. The directors/administrateurs are obliged to make periodic reports to the shareholders. The purpose of these reports is to enable the shareholders to assure themselves that the directors/administrateurs have managed the

corporation's affairs honestly and efficiently, preserving and, if possible, increasing the funds entrusted to them by the shareholders.

An important element of these periodic reports of the managers to the shareholders are the financial statements which are the principal subject matter of this book.

1.3 The corporation's financial statements

Corporations in all European countries are required to prepare and issue financial statements, consisting of, as a minimum, a balance sheet and a profit and loss account, together with appropriate notes. However many corporations supplement these basic statements with further reports, such as cash flow statements.

Almost all larger corporations own subsidiaries, which are other corporations that they control, generally because they own, directly or indirectly, more than half the shares and can thus assure that their nominees are appointed as the subsidiaries' managers. In effect, the typical larger business consists not of a single corporation but of a group of corporations. The group consists of a parent company at the head of the group, which owns shares in and controls a number of other corporations. Such groups are very common in modern business; for example, the German corporation, DaimlerChrysler AG, controls over nine hundred subsidiaries.[2] DaimlerChrysler AG and its subsidiaries form the DaimlerChrysler Group which is managed as a single economic unit although it is made up of a myriad of legal entities.

Under German law, DaimlerChrysler AG and every other German corporation in the DaimlerChrysler Group are each required to prepare financial statements that present the position of the separate corporation; these financial statements are known as the 'individual accounts' because they refer to the individual corporation and not to the group as a whole.[3] In addition, in order to present the financial position and performance of the DaimlerChrysler Group, accountants prepare group accounts which combine the assets, revenues and so on of DaimlerChrysler AG and its subsidiaries. These group accounts are sometimes termed 'consolidated accounts' because they are created by combining or consolidating the information contained in the individual accounts of DaimlerChrysler AG and of each subsidiary. It is important to distinguish these group accounts or consolidated accounts from the individual accounts, since they refer to quite different entities: for the group accounts the entity is the group, for the individual accounts, the entity is the separate corporation, say DaimlerChrysler AG or one of its subsidiaries, treated separately.

In the DaimlerChrysler Group, the general public owns shares in the parent company, DaimlerChrysler AG. A shareholder in DaimlerChrysler AG receives from the corporation two sets of financial statements:

1. The 'individual accounts': the balance sheet and income statement of DaimlerChrysler AG.
2. The 'group accounts', consisting of a consolidated balance sheet which presents the assets and liabilities of the whole group (DaimlerChrysler AG and its subsidiaries) and a consolidated profit and loss account.

For the shareholder, both sets of accounts provide important but different information: the individual accounts provide information about the legal entity in which the shareholder owns shares; the group accounts provide information about the economic entity, which this legal entity controls.

1.4   The top one hundred European enterprises

1.4.1   Data

Exhibit 1.4 presents information relating to the one hundred largest European enterprises, based on the author's own investigation of their financial statements, notably the following items:

1. *Name of the group*: All the enterprises that are listed in Exhibit 1.4 are in fact groups that consist of a parent corporation and many (sometimes many hundred) subsidiaries.
2. *The parent corporation*: Two items of information are given concerning the parent corporation at the head of the group:
   (a) the corporate form, as indicated by the abbreviation, AG, SA, PLC and so on;
   (b) the country of registration. The country of registration has a very important influence over the form and content of the financial statements (both the parent corporation's individual accounts and, more importantly, the group accounts) because, in preparing these accounts, the parent corporation is obliged to follow the law of the country in which it is registered. For example the group accounts of the DaimlerChrysler Group (Europe's second largest enterprise) are prepared by the parent corporation (DaimlerChrysler AG) in accordance with German law.[4] Similarly the group accounts of the HSBC Group (Europe's third largest enterprise) are prepared by HSBC Holdings PLC in accordance with British law. Since German law and British law are not identical, there are significant differences in the way that particular items and transactions are treated in these accounts. It is these national differences that make the study of financial reporting at the international level such a complex and fascinating subject.
3. *Group statistics*: Three separate pieces of information are given concerning the group, all of which give an indication of the group's size. The three

Exhibit 1.4 The top one hundred European enterprises

Rank	Name of group	Parent corporation		Group statistics			Size statistic	
		Corporate form	Country of registration	Assets €M	Revenue €M	Employees	Absolute	Relative (%)
1	Allianz	AG	D	852,056	73,536	181,651	224,941	100.00
2	DaimlerChrysler	AG	D	187,327	150,377	365,571	217,563	96.72
3	HSBC Group	PLC	GB	724,017	40,464	177,475	173,241	77.02
4	ING	NV	NL	716,370	50,571	115,815	161,287	71.70
5	BP	PLC	GB	151,742	193,216	115,250	150,059	66.71
6	Royal Dutch/Shell	NV/PLC	NL/GB	145,606	192,397	116,000	148,119	65.85
7	Volkswagen	AG	D	108,896	87,466	324,892	145,724	64.78
8	Siemens	AG	D	77,939	85,077	445,100	143,442	63.77
9	Deutsche Bank	AG	D	758,355	46,615	77,442	139,892	62.19
10	BNP Paribas	SA	F	710,319	37,766	87,685	132,992	59.12
11	UBS	AG	CH	813,200	41,112	69,061	132,170	58.76
12	Deutsche Post	AG	D	156,701	39,175	371,912	131,676	58.54
13	Crédit Suisse	AG	CH	657,969	42,073	78,457	129,503	57.57
14	Royal Bank of Scotland	PLC	GB	633,368	29,695	111,800	128,114	56.95
15	ABN Amro	NV	NL	556,018	32,791	107,416	125,113	55.62
16	Deutsche Telekom	AG	D	125,821	55,641	255,969	121,463	54.00
17	HVB Group	AG	D	691,157	37,180	65,926	119,210	53.00
18	AXA	SA	F	444,657	38,574	78,142	110,256	49.02
19	Fortis	SA/NV	B/NL	485,765	40,069	65,989	108,701	48.32
20	Barclays	PLC	GB	619,633	25,964	77,200	107,492	47.79
21	Electricité de France	State	F	144,839	49,095	171,995	106,941	47.54
22	FranceTélécom	SA	F	106,587	46,630	240,145	106,075	47.16
23	Carrefour	SA	F	38,924	69,162	396,662	102,212	45.44
24	Total	SA	F	85,329	102,896	121,469	102,169	45.42

Exhibit 1.4 (Continued)

Rank	Name of group	Parent corporation		Group statistics			Size statistic	
		Corporate form	Country of registration	Assets €M	Revenue €M	Employees	Absolute	Relative (%)
25	Fiat	SpA	I	92,521	55,886	190,405	99,481	44.23
26	Nestlé	AG	CH	60,142	61,266	254,199	97,841	43.50
27	Santander Central Hispano	SA	E	324,208	27,001	104,178	96,975	43.11
28	HBOS	PLC	GB	545,864	29,662	56,081	96,836	43.05
29	Vodaphone	PLC	GB	251,010	48,834	66,667	93,492	41.56
30	Suez	SA	F	84,151	46,090	202,402	92,249	41.01
31	Société Générale	SA	F	501,441	17,688	88,278	92,169	40.97
32	Zurich Financial Services	AG	CH	272,592	40,928	67,824	91,125	40.51
33	Lloyds TSB	PLC	GB	388,565	21,406	79,537	87,135	38.74
34	Peugeot	SA	F	56,008	53,353	198,600	84,035	37.36
35	RWE	AG	D	100,273	43,523	131,765	83,157	36.97
36	Unilever	NV/PLC	NL/GB	44,598	49,007	258,000	82,616	36.73
37	Banco Bilbao Vizcaya	SA	E	279,542	20,801	93,093	81,498	36.23
38	La Poste	State	F	51,279	31,637	315,445	79,987	35.56
39	E.ON	AG	D	113,065	37,130	107,856	76,789	34.14
40	Aviva	PLC	GB	284,282	24,227	64,562	76,326	33.93
41	Rabobank	NV	NL	374,720	20,314	58,107	76,192	33.87
42	Gazprom	JSC	RUS	72,001	17,975	322,200	74,710	33.21
43	Ahold	NV	NL	24,738	62,742	254,279	73,352	32.61
44	Assicurazioni Generali	SpA	I	234,724	26,712	59,753	72,090	32.05
45	Banca Intesa	SpA	I	280,733	16,640	71,501	69,383	30.84
46	Veolia Envoronnement	SA	F	42,018	30,221	257,177	68,864	30.61
47	Crédit Agricole*	SA	F	505,718	27,432	22,878	68,212	30.32
48	Commerzbank	AG	D	422,134	20,448	36,566	68,086	30.27
49	Groupe Caisse d'Epargne	SA	F	357,133	19,265	43,092	66,680	29.64

50	Telefónica	SA	E	68,041	28,411	152,845	66,605	29.61
51	Olivetti	SpA	I	83,384	31,829	106,620	65,652	29.19
52	Vivendi Universal	SA	F	69,200	58,150	61,815	62,890	27.96
53	ENI	SpA	I	62,736	48,423	80,655	62,575	27.82
54	Renault	SA	F	53,228	34,733	132,351	62,547	27.81
55	BMW	AG	D	55,511	42,907	101,395	62,274	27.68
56	Tesco	PLC	GB	25,367	45,132	203,766	61,560	27.37
57	Metro	AG	D	22,923	51,648	191,512	60,978	27.11
58	ThyssenKrupp	AG	D	31,160	36,824	191,254	60,318	26.81
59	Bosch	GmbH	D	27,475	35,272	225,897	60,269	26.79
60	Unicredito	SpA	I	208,388	15,555	66,555	59,975	26.66
61	SNCF	State	F	39,620	22,182	242,163	59,705	26.54
62	Munich Re	AG	D	196,441	26,127	41,396	59,671	26.53
63	Dexia	SA	B	350,924	27,909	21,009	59,036	26.25
64	Almanij	NV	B	252,780	13,878	52,969	57,064	25.37
65	Deutsche Bahn	AG	D	44,231	15,765	259,241	56,542	25.14
66	Philips	NV	NL	32,289	31,856	170,087	55,929	24.86
67	Saint Gobain	SA	F	30,148	30,343	171,256	53,908	23.97
68	Bayer	AG	D	41,692	30,083	122,600	53,574	23.82
69	EADS	NV	NL	47,400	29,988	103,967	52,870	23.50
70	Abbey National	PLC	GB	316,255	14,029	32,364	52,365	23.28
71	ENEL	SpA	I	71,204	27,861	71,501	52,152	23.18
72	BT	PLC	GB	43,378	30,440	104,700	51,707	22.99
73	Crédit Lyonnais*	SA	F	244,886	12,651	40,950	50,247	22.34
74	DZ Bank	AG	D	338,255	14,538	25,247	49,887	22.18
75	GlaxoSmithKline	PLC	GB	34,323	33,383	104,499	49,288	21.91
76	Nordea	AB	S	249,619	12,288	37,322	48,556	21.59
77	San Paolo-IMI	SpA	I	203,773	12,160	46,103	48,522	21.57
78	Anglo-American	PLC	GB	32,023	19,283	177,000	47,812	21.26
79	BASF	AG	D	35,086	32,536	89,389	46,730	20.77
80	Compass Group	PLC	GB	14,117	16,737	392,352	45,258	20.12

Exhibit 1.4 (Continued)

Rank	Name of group	Parent corporation		Group statistics			Size statistic	
		Corporate form	Country of registration	Assets €M	Revenue €M	Employees	Absolute	Relative (%)
81	Pinault-Printemps-Red.	SA	F	30,024	27,474	108,423	44,720	19.88
82	Aegon	NV	NL	238,206	12,987	26,659	43,528	19.35
83	ABB	AG	CH	28,163	19,770	139,051	42,620	18.95
84	Novartis	AG	CH	43,515	22,600	72,877	41,538	18.47
85	Bouygues	SA	F	24,783	22,258	128,278	41,362	18.39
86	Landesbank Baden-Würt	State	D	320,454	15,312	14,228	41,176	18.31
87	Auchan	SA	F	17,631	27,562	142,956	41,108	18.28
88	Arcelor	SA	Lux	25,836	24,718	105,556	40,698	18.09
89	Roche	AG	CH	44,061	20,584	69,659	39,828	17.71
90	Prudential	PLC	GB	233,917	11,559	21,930	38,995	17.34
91	Alstom	SA	F	24,787	21,351	109,671	38,718	17.21
92	Lukoil	JSC	RUS	20,980	16,568	150,000	37,359	16.61
93	Foncière Euris	SA	F	17,744	23,980	122,043	37,308	16.59
94	Aventis	SA	F	31,073	21,271	78,099	37,234	16.55
95	Bayerische Landesbank	AG	D	341,297	15,029	9,390	36,384	16.17
96	Royal & Sun Alliance	PLC	GB	43,739	21,118	50,479	35,993	16.00
97	Vinci	SA	F	20,282	17,570	127,380	35,671	15.86
98	Danske Bank	A/S	DK	235,759	10,465	17,808	35,286	15.69
99	Repsol YPF	SA	E	38,064	35,563	30,110	34,414	15.30
100	Volvo	AB	S	26,087	20,354	70,546	33,459	14.87

* In mid-2003, Caisse d'Epargne and Crédit Lyonnais announced plans to merge.

items have been chosen because they are the criteria of size chosen by the EU. The EU's Fourth Directive defines a large company as one that exceeds two of the following three criteria: total assets of €14.6 million, turnover of €29.2 million and 250 employees.

(a) *Assets*: This figure is the amount at which the group's assets are reported in its group balance sheet. It relates to gross assets before deducting liabilities and provisions, but taking into account deductions for depreciation. It is expressed in Euros; for groups for which the Euro is not the reporting currency (for example the HSBC Group) the reported figure is translated into Euros at the exchange rate ruling at the balance sheet date. The figures were extracted from the group accounts for the fiscal year that ended between 1 July 2002 and 30 June 2003; for most groups this was the balance sheet as on 31 December 2002.

(b) *Revenue*: This figure is taken from the group income statement for the fiscal year ending at the balance sheet date. It is the sum of:

  (i) the sales of the group's products and services;

 (ii) interest received; this is the principal source of revenue for banks and, to ensure comparability between banks and other enterprises, revenue for both includes interest received;

 (iii) in the case of insurance companies, revenue includes premiums on accident insurance (fire, motor and so on) but not life assurance premiums, which are considered to be akin to deposits received;

Other sources of income are not included in revenue; for example capital gains, profits on sale of fixed assets and extraordinary items. There is no general agreement on how to measure an enterprise's revenue and not everyone agrees with the measure used in Exhibit 1.4; in particular *Fortune* magazine uses a different measure in determining the Fortune 500, notably in including life assurance premiums in the revenue of insurance companies. The author considers that his measure is logical and defensible, in treating life assurance premiums as transfers of capital, akin to deposits in a bank account.

(c) *Employees*: This figure is taken from the notes to the annual accounts.

Each of these three figures is a measure of the group's size. However it is desirable to have a single overall measure of size. This is given by the size statistic, given in the next column.

4. *Size statistic*: The size statistic is the geometric mean of the figures relating to assets, revenues and employees (given in the three previous columns). It is an overall measure of the size of the group: the larger this statistic, the larger the group. The annex to this chapter presents a fuller explanation of the theory behind this statistic, setting out the assumptions on which it is based and explaining how (given these assumptions) it presents

a valid measure of the size of the group. The size statistic provides a relative measure of size. For example it can be used to compare two groups: if the size statistic of one group is 10 per cent larger than that of the other group, then the first group may be considered to be 10 per cent larger. In Exhibit 1.4, the relative measure is given as a percentage of the largest enterprise; this shows that Volvo, number 100 in the list, is 15 per cent (33,459/224,941) of the size of Allianz, number 1 in the list. This measure is meaningful. However the absolute (as opposed to the relative) value of the size statistic has no meaning: it is dimensioned in units of $\unicode{x20AC}^2$ men, which defies interpretation.

1.4.2 Analysis of the top one hundred

The analysis of the information contained in Exhibit 1.4 provides a fuller picture of the top European enterprises.

Corporate form

In all one hundred groups, the parent enterprise is a corporation. This is even the case for the four enterprises that are formed under special laws applicable to state enterprises: Electricité de France, SNCF and La Poste in France, and the Landesbank Baden-Württemberg in Germany.

Country of registration

Exhibit 1.5 analyses the national origin of the top one hundred European enterprises, based on the country in which the parent corporation is registered.

Exhibit 1.5 The home country of the top one hundred

Country of registration of the parent corporation	Number of enterprises
France (F)	25
Germany (D)	22
United Kingdom (GB)	17
Netherlands (NL)	8½
Italy (I)	8
Switzerland (CH)	7
Spain (E)	4
Belgium (B)	2½
Russia (RUS)	2
Sweden (S)	2
Denmark (DK)	1
Luxembourg (L)	1
Total	100

Note: The two Anglo-Dutch groups (Royal Dutch/Shell and Unilever) have been split 50/50 between the Netherlands and the UK; similarly Fortis has been split between Belgium and the Netherlands.

The most noteworthy feature of this analysis is not so much the dominance of the larger countries (France, Germany and the UK) but the relatively large number of enterprises from two smaller countries, the Netherlands and Switzerland. The country of registration of the parent enterprise is of considerable significance as it governs the form and content of the group's financial statements.

Global scope

Almost all the groups listed in Exhibit 1.4 have very considerable interests and operations outside their home country. For example, Europe's second largest enterprise, the DaimlerChrysler Group consists, in addition to the parent corporation (DaimlerChrysler AG), of over 900 subsidiaries in over 60 countries. The group has sales organisations in all major countries and in most smaller countries. Only 15 per cent of its sales are in Germany, its home country. It has production facilities in five continents. For example, its Mercedes cars are produced in Stuttgart (Germany), Tuscaloosa (USA), Pretoria (South Africa), Poona (India) and Sao Bernardo do Campo (Brazil). Of its global workforce of 365,571 only just over half (51 per cent) are located in Germany.

Industrial sector

Exhibit 1.6 presents an analysis of the top one hundred enterprises by industrial sector. The analysis is rather crude as many of the enterprises cover more than one sector; for example Royal Dutch/Shell is both an oil company and a producer of chemicals. In Exhibit 1.6, it has been classified as 'Oil, natural gas and mining', rather than 'Chemicals and pharmaceuticals' on the basis that 90 per cent of both its assets and its sales are in the former

Exhibit 1.6 The top one hundred enterprises analysed by sector

Sector	Number of enterprises
Oil, natural gas and mining	7
Automobiles	7
Other manufacturing (engineering, electronics, etc.)	9
Chemicals and pharmaceuticals	7
Food and drink	3
Construction	2
Retailing	7
Telecommunications and media	6
Finance: banking and insurance	41
Utilities: electricity, water, railways, post	11
Total	100

sector. The most striking feature of Exhibit 1.6 is that almost half (41 per cent) of the top one hundred are financial institutions (banks and insurance companies); the enterprise at the top of the list, the Allianz Group, is a financial conglomerate that covers both banking and insurance. In fact five of the top ten enterprises are financial institutions. It is a striking fact that, in all but three of the countries that figure in Exhibit 1.4, the largest enterprise is a financial institution; the exceptions are Italy (Fiat), Russia (Gazprom) and Luxembourg (Arcelor).

1.4.3   Comparison of Allianz with DaimlerChrysler

However, is it possible to compare in a meaningful way a financial institution with other enterprises? This question will be considered with reference to the top two enterprises in Exhibit 1.4: the Allianz Group, which is a financial conglomerate, and the DaimlerChrysler Group, which is principally a motor manufacturer. They are very different enterprises as is brought out very clearly in certain salient facts set out in Exhibit 1.7. The balance sheet value of Allianz's assets is over four times that of DaimlerChrysler, but, on the other hand, DaimlerChrysler's revenue is over twice that of Allianz as is also the number of its employees. The difference between the two enterprises is brought out most clearly in the breakdown between tangible assets and financial assets.

The two enterprises have fundamentally different asset structures. Daimler-Chrysler has many more tangible assets – these are assets with a physical existence which one can touch, such as land and buildings, equipment and merchandise. In fact its tangible assets, at €80,154 million, are more than ten times higher than those of the Allianz Group. Allianz is strong in financial assets – these are assets that represent a monetary claim on another person or enterprise. They comprise (in addition to cash) bank balances, accounts receivable, loans to customers, bills of exchange and other financial instruments issued by governments and enterprises, including debt securities,

Exhibit 1.7   Allianz compared with DaimlerChrysler

	Allianz Group	DaimlerChrysler	Ratio	Ratio
Balance sheet	€ millions	€ millions	Allianz/DC	DC/Allianz
Tangible assets	7,384	80,154	0.092	10.855
Financial assets (including monetary and intangible assets)	844,672	107,173	7.881	0.127
Total assets	852,056	187,327	4.548	0.220
Total revenue	73,536	150,377	0.489	2.045
Employees	181,651	365,571	0.497	2.012

bonds and shares. Allianz's financial assets are enormous; at €844,672 million, they represent more than €10,000 per head of the German population.

There is a temptation to consider that tangible assets are in some way more significant than financial assets. The ordinary man in the street would probably consider that DaimlerChrysler is a larger enterprise than Allianz because it has more tangible assets. DaimlerChrysler's factories, machines and inventories are much more extensive and impressive than the offices which are the only significant tangible assets of Allianz. However financial assets should not be ignored; Allianz is an important enterprise because, through its loans and investments, it exercises enormous influence not only over the German economy but, through its subsidiaries, the entire world.

According to the size statistic, Allianz and DaimlerChrysler are virtually the same size: DaimlerChrysler is 96.72 per cent the size of Allianz. Allianz's assets are over four times greater than those of DaimlerChrysler, whereas, in terms of both revenue and employees, DaimlerChrysler is over twice the size of Allianz. The precise ratios are 4.548 for assets, 2.045 for revenue and 2.012 for employees. In order to compare the two enterprises, it is necessary to combine the last two ratios; their product is 4.115, which shows that, in respect of revenue and employees combined, DaimlerChrysler is 4.115 times larger than Allianz. This is just smaller than the ratio by which Allianz's assets are larger and hence Allianz is shown to be the larger enterprise. The above analysis demonstrates that the size statistic is a meaningful measure of size which takes into account three different dimensions of the size of an enterprise. In the author's view, because the size statistic incorporates both assets (in which financial institutions are dominant) and revenue and employees (according to which other enterprises are larger), it is reasonable to use it as a means of comparing the two very disparate types of business.

This concludes the general analysis of European enterprises. The rest of the book concentrates on their financial reporting, starting in the next chapter with the analysis of the functions of their financial statements. The Annex to this chapter explains the theory behind the statistic that is used in this chapter to measure the size of an enterprise.

Annex: How to measure the size of an enterprise

How to combine disparate measures: a simple example

This annex explains how it is possible to combine three different disparate measures of the size of an enterprise into a single combined measure, using a simple example, given in Exhibit 1.8 which presents the figures for the three criteria for three enterprises: A, B and C.

Exhibit 1.8 Data of the enterprises to be compared

	Criterion 1 Total assets at 31 December 2002 (€ millions)	Criterion 2 Employees average over 2002 (number of people)	Criterion 3 Turnover during 2002 (€ millions)
Enterprise A	10	1,300	20
Enterprise B	12	1,000	21
Enterprise C	8	1,200	25

It is apparent that there is no trivial answer to the question as to which enterprise is the larger. Each of the three enterprises is larger than the other two on one criterion but smaller than at least one other on the other criteria.

As a first step towards answering the question, it is necessary to make four assumptions:

1. that each of the chosen criteria is an appropriate measure of the size of an enterprise;
2. that equal weight is given to each criterion; this condition will be relaxed later;
3. that each criterion is measured in units that are linear, which means that, for any criterion, the amounts may be added together to give a meaningful sum. For example, if enterprise A merged with enterprise B, the amounts for the three criteria for the merged enterprise are the sum of the amounts for the individual enterprises: capital €22 million, employees 2300, turnover €41 million,[5] all of which are meaningful amounts. Ratios and rates are not linear; for example if A's profit rate is 10 per cent and B's 15 per cent, then the rate for the merged enterprise is not 25 per cent;
4. that for each enterprise the value for each criterion is positive and non-zero.

The case of two enterprises and two criteria

It is easier to consider initially only two enterprises (A and B) and two criteria (1 and 2). Using the notation A_1 to denote the value for enterprise A for criterion 1 (and so on for enterprise B and C, and for criteria 2 and 3), it is reasonable to state that, considering only criterion 2, A is larger than B since $A_2 > B_2$ ($A_2/B_2 = 1.3$). In respect of criterion 1, B is larger than A: $B_1 > A_1$ ($B_1/A_1 = 1.2$). Hence, considering the two criteria separately, one cannot decide which of the two enterprises is the larger. However, when the two criteria are considered together, it is reasonable to state that A is larger than B, for A is 30 per cent larger than B on criterion 2 whereas B is larger than A on criterion 1 by only 20 per cent. As 30 per cent is greater than

Exhibit 1.9   Why the square root is used as the size statistic

	Criterion 1	Criterion 2	Product	Square root (size statistic)
Enterprise J	16	4	64	8
Enterprise K	16	4	64	8
Enterprise L	32	8	256	16
Ratio L/J	2	2	4	2

20 per cent, A is larger than B. This is the logical conclusion to draw from the two assumptions that the two criteria are equally important and are measured in linear units.

In mathematical terms, A is greater than B, if $A_2/B_2 > B_1/A_1$ which can be rearranged as:

$$A_1 \times A_2 > B_1 \times B_2 \qquad \text{(Formula 1)}$$

Similarly, A is equal to B if

$$A_1 \times A_2 = B_1 \times B_2 \qquad \text{(Formula 2)}$$

and A is smaller than B, if

$$A_1 \times A_2 < B_1 \times B_2 \qquad \text{(Formula 3)}$$

In simple terms, the product of the values of the criteria gives an indication of whether one enterprise is larger, equal to or smaller than another enterprise.

In fact, it is more appropriate to use the square root of the product, that is $\sqrt{(A_1 \times A_2)}$ rather than the product itself. The use of the square root does not affect the inequalities shown above (because it is applied to both sides) and it provides a more intelligible measure of the size of the enterprise. This is demonstrated in Exhibit 1.9 above. It is assumed that two identical enterprises (J and K) merge to form a new enterprise L. Clearly L is twice the size of J. This relationship ($L = 2 \times J$) is only indicated when the square root is used; the product indicates that L is four times larger than J. As the square root gives an indication of the relative size of an enterprise, it is termed the 'size statistic'. With three criteria, the cube root should be used. In general terms, the size statistic is the geometric mean of the criteria values.

Extension to three criteria

Considering only criteria 1 and 2, A is larger than B. However, on criterion 3, B is larger than A. How can the third criterion be brought into the calculation?

Exhibit 1.10   Using enterprise Q to compare A and B

	Criterion 1	Criterion 2	Criterion 3	Product	Cube root (size statistic)
Enterprise A	10	1,300	20	260,000	63.83
Enterprise B	12	1,000	21	252,000	63.16
Enterprise Q	12	1,050	20	252,000	63.16
		$(1,000 \times 21/20)$			
		$(B_2 \times B_3/A_3)$			

To do this, it is necessary to invent a dummy enterprise (Q) that is equal in size to B, but has the same value as enterprise A for criterion 3. The values for all the enterprises concerned are given in Exhibit 1.10.

Enterprise Q is equal to enterprise B, because they are equal for criterion 1 and, in respect of criteria 2 and 3, $Q_2 \times Q_3 = B_2 \times B_3$ (see formula 2 above). The value of Q_2 was deliberately calculated so as to make the equality hold. Since A and Q are equal with respect to criterion 3, it is possible to compare them solely in respect of criteria 1 and 2. Furthermore, since B is equal to Q, by comparing A and Q, one is at the same time comparing A and B. From formula (1) above, A is greater than Q (and B), if $A_1 \times A_2 > Q_1 \times Q_2$. However, $Q_1 = B_1$ and $Q_2 = (B_2 \times B_3/A_3)$. Hence, by substitution, A is greater than Q (and B) if $A_1 \times A_2 > (B_1 \times B_2 \times B_3/A_3)$, which can be rearranged as:

$$A_1 \times A_2 \times A_3 > B_1 \times B_2 \times B_3 \qquad \text{(Formula 4)}$$

Hence, with three criteria, one arrives at exactly the same measure as with two criteria: the product of the criteria values indicates whether one enterprise is larger than another. In fact, the measure of relative size (the size statistic) is given by the cube root of the product.

It is easy to extend this analysis to any number of criteria; for *n* criteria, the measure of the size of enterprise A is:

$$A_1^{1/n} \times A_2^{1/n} \times A_3^{1/n} \times \ldots A_n^{1/n}$$

The size statistic shown in the last column of Exhibit 1.10 has no meaning when considered alone; it is denominated in '€²-men' which defies meaningful interpretation. The number only makes sense when it is compared with another number in the same column. Thus the ratio of the numbers for enterprises A and B indicates that enterprise A is slightly larger than B (by about 1 per cent).

Unequal weights for the criteria

The assumption that all the criteria are equally important (have equal weights) will now be relaxed. Assume, for example, that it is decided to give criterion 2 twice the weight of criterion 1 (which has the same weight as criterion 3). In effect criterion 2 is to be given the same weight as criteria 1 and 3 combined. This can be achieved by inputting the values for criterion 2 twice. The size statistic for enterprise A becomes:

$$(A_1 \times A_2 \times A_2 \times A_3)^{1/4}$$

which can be rewritten as

$$(A_1 \times A_2^2 \times A_3)^{1/4} \text{ or alternatively } A^{1/4} \times A^{1/2} \times A^{1/4}$$

The weights do not have to be whole numbers. The general formula is:

$$\prod A_i^{w_i} \text{ where } \sum w_i = 1$$

The combination of total assets, turnover and number of employees

In respect of the three suggested measures of the size of the enterprise (total assets, turnover and number of employees), all are appropriate criteria (for example used by the EU to define a large enterprise) and none was negative or zero in the set of enterprises considered. Therefore it is appropriate to use the method of combining these measures that has just been described. All three measures are given the same weight. The size statistic for each enterprise (presented in Exhibit 1.4) is therefore calculated as the cube root of the product of total assets, turnover and number of employees.

Characteristics of the size statistic

The size statistic measures the relative sizes of enterprises; it only makes sense when the size statistic of one enterprise is compared with that of another enterprise. Its absolute value (for example, 217,563 for DaimlerChrysler) has no meaning. However when two size statistics are compared, the comparison is meaningful. It has already been established that when one enterprise's size statistic is larger than that of another enterprise, then the first enterprise is larger. However it is possible to be more precise. The degree to which the size statistic is larger gives a measure of the degree to which the first enterprise is larger. For example, if the size statistic is 10 per cent larger, then overall the first enterprise is 10 per cent larger. This would occur if it were exactly 10 per cent larger on all three criteria. However it holds for more complex situations; for example where the two enterprises are equal according to one criterion, the first enterprise is 10 per cent larger according to the second criterion and twice 10 per cent[6] larger according to the third criterion. In effect, the twice 10 per cent on the third criterion compensates for the equality on the first criterion. It holds for all cases where the geometric mean of the percentages for the three criteria is 10 per cent. Thus where the two enterprises are equal on two criteria and the first enterprise is three times 10 per cent (that is 33.1 per cent being $1.1^3 - 1$) according to the third criterion, then the first enterprise is shown as being 10 per cent larger according to the size statistic.

Notes

1. For more information on the relative advantages of the different corporate forms in France and Germany, see McGee, Cerfontaine and Williams (1998).
2. In many cases, there is a chain of control: DaimlerChrysler controls corporation A which itself controls corporation B. In effect DaimlerChrysler controls corporation B through its control over corporation A, and therefore both corporation A and corporation B are subsidiaries of DaimlerChrysler AG.
3. DaimlerChrysler's subsidiaries that are based in foreign countries are generally obliged to draw up their individual accounts in accordance with that country's law.
4. German law permits German listed corporations to draw up their consolidated accounts according to US GAAP or the IASB's standards, and, in fact, DaimlerChrysler uses US GAAP. However this is simply a particular instance of the general principle that, in financial reporting, a corporation is obliged to follow the law of the country in which it is registered, coupled with the considerable liberalism of the German legislator in this matter.
5. In drawing up the consolidated accounts, it is possible that the turnover of the merged enterprises (as measured by accountants) may be less than the sum of the turnovers of the constituent enterprises. However this does not invalidate the argument that the sum is meaningful.
6. The percentages should be calculated in the same way as compound interest. Thus twice 10 per cent is 21 per cent, being $(1.1^2 - 1) *100$.

References

McGee, A., Cerfontaine, A. and Williams, C. (1998). *Business Start Up in Europe*. London, ACCA.
Mikol, A. (1995). 'The history of financial reporting in France' in Walton (1995).
Walton, P. (1995). *European Financial Reporting: A History*. London, Academic Press.

2
The Functions of the Financial Statements: Different European Approaches

It is a fact that corporations in all European countries prepare and issue financial statements, consisting, as a minimum, of a balance sheet and a profit and loss account. This chapter considers the functions of these financial statements; the next chapter covers how the rules that govern their form and contents are set.

2.1 The information function of the financial statements

Why do corporations spend resources on the preparation and publication of financial statements? The short answer is that they are obliged to do so by law. But this only begs the second question: why do governments consider it appropriate to subject corporations to this requirement? To answer this question, it is necessary to consider the functions that are performed by the corporation's financial statements. Although one can conceive of bizarre functions that may be performed by a corporation's financial statements (such as acting as a door stop or being used as a fly swatter), there is general agreement that their function is to provide information (and occasionally disinformation) about the corporation. However, although there is, within Europe, a broad consensus on this basic point, there are considerable differences of viewpoint on the matters of detail, particularly:

- who are considered to be the principal users of this information; and
- for what purpose they will use the information.

Different opinions on these matters explain the subtle differences in the functions attributed to the corporation's financial statements by accountants in different European countries. This chapter presents the different functions that have been attributed to the corporation's financial statements at various times in different European countries, notably:

- The maintenance of capital – the regulation of dividends
- The monitoring of management – stewardship
- Information for investors
- Information for the state
- Information for employees
- Information for the general public
- Computation of tax.

2.2   The maintenance of capital: the regulation of dividends

When, in the nineteenth century, the governments of most European countries changed the law to make it easier for businesses to organise themselves as corporations, they generally included a requirement that corporations should each year present a balance sheet. In most countries, this was the sum total of the legal obligations relating to financial reporting; there was no requirement to present a profit and loss account, whereas the other reports that today make up a full set of financial statements (such as the cash flow statement) had not been invented. Why was there this emphasis on the balance sheet?

The principal reason for the requirement to present a balance sheet was to check that the corporation had maintained its capital. The need for the corporation to maintain its capital stemmed from the limited liability of its shareholders. A person who was owed money by the corporation (a creditor) could not sue the shareholders for the repayment of his debt; he could only sue the corporation. The only resources that were available for the repayment of these debts were the corporation's assets. In order to protect their position, creditors sought to ensure that the corporation's assets were not dissipated through making unwarranted payments to shareholders. Governments agreed with them and therefore made it illegal for a corporation to pay any dividend that would reduce its net assets below a certain minimum amount – normally set at the amount raised by the corporation through the issue of shares, that is the corporation's share capital. In effect, the corporation's share capital represented a reserve fund available for the repayment of creditors which could not be drawn upon for the payment of dividends. A corporation was only allowed to pay a dividend to the extent of the increase of its net assets over its share capital, that is to the extent of its profits, profits being defined as increase in net assets. Hence, a corporation that sought to pay a dividend, should first draw up a balance sheet in order to check that it had sufficient profits – the existence of the distributable profits being demonstrated by the surplus of the net assets over the corporation's share capital. In theory any person who was considering lending money to the corporation would first check that the corporation's share capital was sufficiently large to provide an adequate margin out of which the creditors would be repaid, even in the event of a large fall in the value of its assets.

The principle that dividends should only be paid out of profits was also in the interests of shareholders. A common fraud in the early days was for an unscrupulous promoter to set up a corporation, raise money through the issue of shares and then pay high dividends, claiming that the corporation's business was being successful. The public impressed by the high dividends was often persuaded to subscribe for additional shares, unaware that the dividends were being paid out of capital and not out of profits. Hence the rule that dividends should be paid only out of profits was in the interests both of creditors and of shareholders. This coincidence of interests probably explains why most governments were ready to legislate.

However, in reality, the rule that dividends should only be paid out of profits offered very little protection to creditors, for two reasons:

1. In many corporations, the amount of the share capital was very low in relation to their debts, offering a quite inadequate cushion for creditors. Although generally corporations were required to have a certain minimum amount of share capital, the legal minimum was generally not large and there was no requirement that a corporation should increase its share capital in line with the growth of its business and of its debts.[1] Hence, for many corporations, the level of capital that they are legally obliged to maintain before they may pay a dividend is derisory in relation to the size of their debts. This is particularly the case with corporations that have been in existence for some time and have built up a balance of accumulated profits.
2. There was no way in which the law could prevent a corporation's share capital being eroded through losses (as opposed to dividends). Hence creditors had no assurance that a corporation's share capital would be maintained. In some European countries there is a rule that a corporation should be dissolved if it loses half its share capital, unless the shareholders resolve otherwise. However, this rule offers more protection to shareholders (in bringing the corporation's plight to their attention in a forcible manner) than it does to creditors.

However, although the concept of maintenance of capital has had little practical value in protecting creditors, it has had very considerable impact on financial reporting. This was because capital maintenance, which was essentially a legal theory and never a practical reality became, in many European countries, the basis for the law's approach to financial reporting. The idea that a principal function of the balance sheet was to protect creditors became established in the minds of judges and, through court judgments and judicial dicta, in the practice of accountants. Accountants appreciated that, if they drew up a balance sheet in which assets were stated at unrealistically high values and/or liabilities at unrealistically low values and the corporation paid a dividend on the basis of this balance sheet, this dividend might later be shown to have been unlawful (as having been paid out of capital), when subsequently the true value of assets and liabilities became apparent. There would be a distinct danger that the accountants would be held responsible for the unlawful dividend, with possibly severe financial and professional consequences; for example they might be ordered by the court to compensate the corporation for the wrongly paid dividend and their reputation would suffer from their being publicly shown to have prepared faulty accounts. On the other hand the consequences of understating assets or overstating liabilities seemed far less severe. In these circumstances, accountants came to understand that it was in their best interests to err on the side of caution; that it was less dangerous to understate assets than it was to overstate them. Hence they adopted the principle of prudence, which has been defined in the following terms: 'Prudence is the inclusion of a degree of caution in the exercise of the judgements needed in making the estimates required under conditions of uncertainty, such that assets and income are not overstated and liabilities or expenses are not understated' (IASB Framework, paragraph 37).

The principle of prudence has had a very great influence on the practice of accountants in certain European countries; in fact one may characterise it as the guiding principle in Germany and countries with close cultural and economic ties to Germany, such as Austria and Switzerland. German accountants consider that it is a far more serious error to overstate assets than it is to overstate liabilities; in fact many German accountants consider that the overstating of liabilities is almost desirable, because it provides an additional cushion against failing to maintain the corporation's capital. The reasons for this attitude are rooted in history. When the corporate form was made generally available to German enterprises through the Aktiengesetz of 1870, there was a rush of creations of new corporations. Between 1871 and 1873 the number of Aktiengesellschaft increased fivefold. Many of these newly formed corporations failed, causing serious losses to shareholders and creditors. The slack laws of the time made it easy for unscrupulous promoters to commit fraud, for example, by overvaluing the assets that they contributed to the newly formed corporation. Corporations were able to report profits (when in reality they were making losses) by stating their assets at inflated values. Dividends were paid out of these fictional profits to the detriment both of shareholders (who were often encouraged to subscribe for additional shares in the mistaken belief that the corporation was flourishing) and of creditors (whose security was being reduced by the dissipation of the corporation's funds). As a reaction to these frauds and at the demand of aggrieved shareholders and creditors, the government changed the law to make prudence the guiding principle of financial reporting in Germany. In recent years, the principle of prudence has been criticised in Germany, principally because it was found to conflict with certain other functions of financial reporting, which are considered later, particularly the provision of information for investors. Nevertheless prudence is still one of the fundamental principles of German financial reporting, although not so dominant as it was even so recently as a decade ago.

In England the principle that, in paying dividends, a limited company should maintain its capital intact, was initially applied by the law courts, which agreed that this was necessary in order to protect creditors. However, in the last decade of the nineteenth century, the courts, in a series of cases,[2] greatly modified the previous rule which they found placed unnecessary and undesirable restrictions on the freedom of companies to pay dividends. The reasoning followed by the courts can be explained with reference to a hypothetical example[3]: a company, whose principal assets are four ships, loses three of them when they flounder during a hurricane. The fourth ship survives and continues to be operated profitably. Should the company be forbidden to pay a dividend until such time as its capital had been restored to its former level through the retention of the profits earned by the fourth ship? This would inflict unreasonable hardship on the shareholders, for many of whom the dividend might be their only income. Moreover, the company might have no profitable outlet for the liquid funds accumulated through the retention of profits. Furthermore, with only one ship operating, the company would not need the level of capital that it required when it had four ships; for example its operating costs would be less, leading to a lower level of creditors. Hence at the reduced level of operations, it would be unreasonable to require the company to maintain the same level of capital as it had when it had four ships. In effect, to demand that the company maintain its initial level of capital would provide an unnecessarily high level of protection for creditors, whilst inflicting unreasonable hardship on the shareholders. The courts accepted this argument and held that, provided that the company had sufficient funds, such that the payment of a dividend did not threaten its solvency and its ability to pay its creditors, it should not be prevented from paying a dividend by the rigid application of the capital maintenance rules. Thus it was decided that companies do not need to take into account the fall in value of fixed assets in determining the amount of profits available for dividend. These court decisions were criticised by the British accountancy profession[4] which considered that the principle of prudence required that the fall in the values of all assets (both current assets and fixed assets) should be reported in the balance sheet and continued to base its practice on this principle. Hence, in England, a difference arose between profit, as defined by the law (at least for dividend purposes) and that calculated by accountants. In effect the accountancy profession still adopts an approach to capital maintenance which has long been rejected by the law courts.

In most other European countries, the law placed the same emphasis as in Germany on the need for corporations to maintain their capital and accountants were faced with the same asymmetric punishment function as their German counterparts, that is, the penalties for overstating assets were much more severe than those for overstating liabilities. Hence, throughout Europe, prudence was an important principle of financial reporting. However in recent years the influence of prudence has declined as other functions of financial reporting have increased in importance.

2.3   The monitoring of management: stewardship

As already explained in the previous chapter, the growth of large corporations led to a separation between ownership and management. In larger corporations, the relationship between the shareholders (the owners) and the directors (the managers) became similar to that between a principal and his agent. The classical way for a principal to assure himself that his agent has acted correctly according to his instructions is to require the agent to render periodic accounts. For example when, in the fourteenth century, a Flemish merchant gave his London agent one thousand florins to buy wool, the merchant would periodically demand an account from the agent, which would demonstrate what he had done with the money: some spent on buying wool, some spent on necessary expenses such as port dues and an unspent balance. If the total equalled one thousand florins, the merchant could be assured that the agent had not stolen or lost his money. However for the total to agree, assets and expenses had to be reported as the amount of money expended, that is at historical cost. When accounts serve the purpose of demonstrating that someone has properly cared for the resources entrusted to him, they are said to fulfil the stewardship function of accounts, by analogy to the accounts rendered by a steward to his lord in medieval times.

In the larger corporation, the interests of the shareholders are very similar to those of the medieval merchant; they want to be assured that the directors have not stolen or lost the funds entrusted to them. For this reason, the constitution of most of the first corporations provided that the directors should periodically render accounts to the shareholders, generally in the form of a balance sheet. Initially a primary function of these accounts was for the directors to demonstrate that they had not lost or stolen the funds entrusted to them by the shareholders. This aim could be quite effectively achieved with the aid of a balance sheet in which the assets were stated at historical cost. However it soon became clear that this aim was too limited. The shareholders were interested not only in the directors' honesty but also in their efficiency – whether they had been successful in putting the corporation's funds to profitable use. However adding the aim of monitoring efficiency to that of checking honesty greatly complicates the accounts – a profit and loss account becomes essential and valuation much more problematical since historical cost is no longer the uncontested valuation basis. For example, the London agent of the Flemish merchant can effectively demonstrate his honesty by rendering accounts that report inventory at a cost of one thousand florins; however to demonstrate his efficiency as a buyer, it is more relevant to know the current market price of the wool that he had bought.

The question arises as to what the shareholders should do, if the accounts demonstrate that the directors have been inefficient or dishonest. As indicated in the previous chapter, under the law of most European countries, shareholders have no right to interfere in the management of the corporation. Therefore the only effective action that they can take is to vote for the replacement of the unsatisfactory directors. However the shareholders must take some decision on receiving the accounts, even if it is only to decide to take no action because they consider the directors' performance to be satisfactory. There is no point in a corporation spending resources on financial reporting if the shareholders take no notice of the information contained in the accounts that they receive.

2.4   Information for investors

With the stewardship function of accounts, the principal should take some action with respect to the agent when the latter's performance is demonstrated to be unsatisfactory. In the case of corporations, the appropriate action is for the shareholders to dismiss the directors, which they can do through an adverse vote at the meeting of shareholders. This remedy is set out in the law of most European countries. However, in the case of a large corporation with many shareholders, it is very difficult, almost impossible, for the individual shareholder to achieve a change in the composition of the management through the voting process. The individual shareholder would have to secure the support of other shareholders, possibly numbering many thousands, in order to secure a majority of votes – a process that would involve much effort, time and expense. Hence the only realistic alternative for the individual shareholder who is dissatisfied with the performance of the directors is to sell his shares.

The position where the individual shareholder has no effective way of influencing the management is the norm for all large corporations. In this situation, the shareholder does not consider himself to be a part owner of the corporation with a concomitant responsibility for assuring that it is managed efficiently, but rather as an investor, who takes the management as a given fact that he cannot change. This change in the shareholder's status also affects the way in which he uses the financial statements that he receives from the corporation. They no longer provide the basis for deciding how he should vote at the shareholders' meeting, but rather supply input for his investment decision concerning his shareholding: as to whether he should sell his shares, buy more shares or simply keep his existing holding. When the accounts provide information to be used for investment decisions, they may be said to be fulfilling the investment function.

There is a subtle distinction between the stewardship function of accounts and the investment function. With the stewardship function, the emphasis is on the past performance of the management. Certainly the basic reason why a shareholder would want to dismiss a dishonest or inefficient director is because he wants to avoid further losses in the future; 'bygones are for ever bygones' and past losses may only be made good by future actions. However the basis of the shareholder's decision to dismiss the director is his evaluation of his past performance. Stewardship accounts present what has happened in the past. They are based on solid facts.

However when making investment decisions, the shareholder is essentially interested in the future – the level of the corporation's future profits and dividends will determine the value of his shares in the future. Of course any forecast of the future is subject to a great degree of uncertainty and the only solid facts that the shareholder has available relate to the past. Hence, as regards the accounts, the shareholder, for the want of anything better, may be obliged to make use of financial statements that present the past position. But these financial statements only have any value in aiding investment decisions in so far as they form a basis for forecasting the future.

There is another important difference between the stewardship function and the investment function. With the stewardship function, it is clear that the persons to whom the corporation's financial statements are addressed are the shareholders – only they have the power to dismiss the directors. However, with the investment function, the set of addressees has to be widened to include potential shareholders, that is persons who are considering buying shares, and also their advisors, such as stock brokers and financial journalists. Furthermore the set of investors should be widened still further to include, in addition to shareholders, persons who invest in the corporation's bonds and debentures, for their information needs are very similar to those of shareholders. Even suppliers who provide goods and services on credit (that is trade creditors) are helping to finance the enterprise and hence should be considered as investors, even if normally only for the short term. Hence the group of people to whom the accounts are addressed when they fulfil the investment function is very wide indeed.

There is general agreement that, in recent years, increasing emphasis has been placed on the investment function of financial statements. In fact one distinguished academic, William Beaver, has characterised the supplanting of the stewardship function of accounts by the investment function as 'an accounting revolution' (Beaver, 1998).

2.5   Information for the state

The state, as the guardian of the public good, has a considerable interest in the financial reporting of corporations. Most governments consider that they have a responsibility to protect shareholders and creditors from being defrauded by dishonest company managers and therefore have enacted laws regulating the accounts that corporations must prepare.

However the state needs information about enterprises for its own purposes. An important function of the modern state is the management of the economy. All parties agree that the state should aim to manage the overall level of activity in the economy, so as to avoid excessive cyclical fluctuations and to achieve the highest possible level of employment. For this purpose it requires information about the performance of the business sector. The level of business profits is a particularly important indicator of the state of the economy. If profits are unusually high or increasing rapidly, this may indicate that the economy is 'overheating', with the attendant danger of the boom culminating in a depression. On the other hand, if profits are too low, then this may indicate that the state should take action to stimulate overall demand, perhaps by lowering interest rates or reducing the level of taxation. Hence the state has a clear interest in ensuring that business firms report their profits in a timely and accurate fashion. The same considerations apply to other items in the financial statements that are significant for the management of overall demand; for example, the level of inventories: if they are declining rapidly, this may be a sign of excessive demand.

The state also has a role to play in preventing a financial crisis, such as that which would follow the failure of a major bank. Hence financial institutions, such as banks and insurance companies, are in all European countries subject to close supervision by the government, which includes detailed regulations on the financial reports that must be presented regularly. The governments of certain countries go much further in intervening in economic matters. Many offer subsidies to encourage activities that are considered to be socially desirable, for example to stimulate employment in depressed regions or to boost investment in research. The government in order to assess whether, before their being granted, such subsidies are necessary and whether, after payment, they have been effective, requires information from enterprises, both overall (from all enterprises in a particular region or sector) and from individual enterprises.

Finally the state requires information in order to assess what contribution the individual enterprise should make to government revenues, that is the amount of tax that it should pay. The simplest and most straightforward way for the enterprise to inform the state on all the above matters is through the financial statements that it prepares for the benefit of other users (shareholders and creditors). This has two considerable advantages: the enterprise saves resources by preparing only one set of reports and it assures consistency in the information that it provides to the different users. However, it has the great disadvantage that the information needs of the state and of other parties, notably investors, are not identical. Hence it may be more efficient for the state's information needs to be met by special reports that are additional to and different from the financial statements that the enterprise prepares for shareholders and investors. This is particularly the case with the information that is used to compute the tax payable by the enterprise. Given the importance of tax, notably in the great impact that it has on the enterprise's cash flow, it is dealt with at greater length in Section 2.8 below. However, in most other matters, it is the common practice of European governments to meet their information needs concerning enterprises from their regular financial statements, notably in the following areas:

1. computation of macroeconomic data relating to national income and its components (profits, investment, inventories and so on);
2. assessment of the need for and the effectiveness of government intervention in the following fields: underdeveloped regions; depressed industrial sectors; desirable economic activities (for example research); and employment (either overall or of particular target groups, for example young people).

As already indicated, the function of the financial statements in providing information for governments conflicts with their other functions, particularly the investment function. European countries differ in the relative importance that they give to the two functions. It is possible to divide them into two groups: those that give more weight to the investment function and those who consider that information for the state is more important. Countries with a large and active capital market belong to the first group: the principal examples are Great Britain and the Netherlands. However where the stock exchange is weak, the other functions are given more importance. This has clearly been the case with France and Germany. Nobes (2002) summarises the position very well: 'In most Continental European countries..., external financial reporting has been largely invented for the purposes of protecting creditors and for governments as tax collectors and controllers of the economy.' Note that Nobes mentions, correctly, both the government information function and the protection of creditors, that is the maintenance of capital. However, in recent years, even France and Germany have begun to give increasing importance to the investment function of accounts. This matter is considered further when the regulatory systems of the various European countries are considered in Chapter 4.

2.6   Information for employees

Employees have a vital interest in receiving information about the enterprise for which they work, since, to a greater or lesser extent, their future welfare depends on their employer's continued prosperity. Employees need information to help them with the following decisions:

1. To decide on what should be the proper distribution of the enterprise's income between the various parties, who are principally, in addition to the employees, the shareholders and the management, or, to put it more crudely, to decide on the level of wages that they should claim, backed up, if necessary, by strike action.
2. To decide whether to seek alternative employment. If there are doubts about the employer's ability to offer stable and remunerative employment in the future, the employee might be better advised to leave.

The enterprise's financial statements can provide highly relevant information on these matters. It should be noted that the interest of employees in the enterprise is often far more fundamental than that of the shareholders as measured in the following ways:

1. *Proportion of income*: Generally the employee's wage represents a far higher proportion of his total income compared with the shareholder's dividend.
2. *Proportion of wealth*: The shareholder is able to divide his investment between several corporations; typically the employee has only one employer.
3. *Strength of attachment*: The shareholder, when he has doubts about the corporation's viability, can get out by selling his shares on the stock exchange and investing in another corporation. It is far more difficult for the employee to find another job and therefore he is more strongly bound to the employer.
4. *Length of relationship*: It is common for shareholders to change their investments frequently, whereas generally employees stay with their employer for years. Generally the rate of shareholder turnover is higher than employee turnover.

The above remarks apply with particular force to corporations whose shares are listed on the stock exchange and are held principally by investors for short periods in diversified portfolios.

For all these reasons, one would expect that corporations would give greater weight to reporting to employees than to shareholders. However, in most European countries, enterprises attach little importance to reporting to employees. In some countries there is no legal obligation on a corporation to provide its employees with information, except in certain relatively unusual situations defined under EU law, for example when the enterprise is planning a major reorganisation. In those countries, where there is an obligation, corporations generally fulfil it by providing their employees with copies of the reports that they have prepared for the benefit of shareholders, that is, reporting to employees is treated as a by-product of reporting to shareholders. Only in Belgium is reporting to employees treated with the importance that it deserves. On this matter see Chapter 8 of Lefebvre and Flower (1994).

2.7 Information for the general public

Enterprises impact on the welfare of the general public in both positive and negative ways. Thus people in the immediate proximity of the enterprise's plant may be affected by the noise and smoke that it emits. However these disadvantages may be offset by benefits, for example employment provided for local workers and donations to local charities. Air and water pollution generated by the enterprise may affect not only local people but those living at considerable distances. For this reason, pressure groups, such as Friends of the Earth, seek information about the enterprise's policy and actions on environmental matters. However this is not the only field in which the general public needs information. For example, it would like to know if the enterprise has sought to influence political decisions through making donations to political parties.

The financial statements are an important source of information about the enterprise and so the role of providing information to the general public has to be added to the other functions of financial statements. In recent years European enterprises have become increasingly responsive to the demand from the general public for more information about matters that affect the general welfare. This is particularly true of enterprises in Britain and Scandinavia which regularly include in their annual reports supplementary information on such matters as the enterprise's policy and actions in relation to the environment and the employment of minorities.

2.8 Computation of tax

All European governments levy taxes on the income of corporations. The rates of tax vary but on average they come to about one-third of the enterprise's profits. The question arises of how to measure the profits on which the amount of tax payable is computed. There are very strong arguments in favour of basing the tax computation on the profits reported in the corporation's financial statements, which implies that income and expenses for tax purposes should be identical to those recorded in the enterprise's books of account. The principal arguments are:

1. *Economy of effort*: The enterprise does not have to make special calculations of income and expenses for tax purposes. The figures recorded in its books of account provide the basis for both the tax computation and the financial statements.
2. *Prevention of tax fraud*: The fiscal authorities' audit of the tax computation is rendered easier.

3. *Equality between stakeholders*: Since it takes about one-third of the profits, the state may be considered to be a partner in the enterprise, alongside the shareholders. In the interests of consistency, all partners' share of the profits should be calculated in the same way.

However there are disadvantages, which stem from the unfortunate fact that the information needs of the fiscal authorities and of the shareholders are not identical. The government's interest is principally in a measure of profit that will enable it to collect an amount of tax with reasonable certainty, with the minimum of administrative cost and with the least opportunity of evasion by the taxpayer. The government is not primarily interested in an accurate measure of the corporation's profits (which is the principal interest of the shareholders) but in one that facilitates the collection of the most revenue. Furthermore, on occasions the governments fix the rules for the computation of taxable profit with the aim, not of raising revenue, but rather of stimulating some action which it considers desirable. For example, it may decide to stimulate investment in a particular region and, with this aim in view, it may permit corporations that set up a factory there to charge the full cost of the factory as a tax deductible expense in the first year. The government is prepared to accept lower tax revenues because it gives greater priority to the stimulation of investment. However, from the viewpoint of the shareholders, to charge the full cost of the plant in the first year leads to an understatement of profits in that year and an overstatement in later years. Hence, in deciding how to calculate profit, there is a clear conflict between the information needs of the government and of the shareholders.

The governments of European countries have differed in their approach to this conflict between the needs of shareholders and those of the fiscal authorities. In many countries there is a legal rule that the computation of taxable income must be based on the figures reported in the corporation's financial statements, that taxable profit is the same as reported profit. In order to prevent corporations from charging excessive expenses in those areas where accounting conventions allow the preparers some discretion (such as the estimation of depreciation and of the level of the provision for doubtful debts), this rule has to be backed up by further more detailed rules in these areas. The result is that the financial statements are 'tax-driven': many of the more important items, such as the depreciation expense, are determined on the basis of the tax rules. This is the case even when the tax rules allow some discretion, for the preparer is motivated to report the highest permitted level of expenses.

In Britain, there is no rule that taxable income is computed on the basis of the figures reported in the financial statements. The same is true of Ireland, the Netherlands and the Scandinavian countries. However, in most Continental European countries, there is such a rule and hence the financial statements are considered to be 'tax-driven'. This is the case in the major countries (France, Germany, Italy and Spain) and in most smaller countries, such as Belgium and Switzerland. In these countries, the tax function of the financial statements is given precedence over the investment function. However it is an oversimplification to divide Europe into two camps (those countries where accounts are tax-driven versus the others), for the following reasons:

1. In all European countries, the taxable entity is the separate corporation and not the group. Hence it is principally the financial statements of the individual corporation that are tax-driven. In principle, the consolidated accounts are not influenced by tax, except to the extent that they are based on the tax-driven individual accounts. Even in those countries where the individual accounts are tax-driven, corporations are permitted to draw up their consolidated accounts according to different rules. Hence a rough division of functions has arisen: the individual accounts fulfil the taxation function and the consolidated accounts the investment function.
2. Even in those countries where there is no basic rule that the taxable income is computed on the figures reported in the accounts (that is principally Britain, Ireland, the Netherlands and the Scandinavian countries), many corporations follow the tax rules in drawing up their financial statements. There are two reasons for this:

   (a) Economy: it saves the expense of two calculations of profit, one for the financial statements and one for tax.
   (b) Where there are doubts about the tax-deductibility of an item of expense, the corporation's case is weakened if it does not report the expense in its financial statements.

2.9   Synthesis

This chapter has identified no less than seven different functions of the corporation's financial statements:

1. The maintenance of capital
2. The monitoring of management – stewardship
3. Information for investors
4. Information for the state
5. Information for employees
6. Information for the general public
7. Computation of tax.

It is possible to simplify the above list. The computation of tax is clearly a particular aspect of the provision of information for the state. Of the remaining six functions, two are of much less importance than the others: information for employees and information for the general public. In no European country are they considered to be primary functions and in practice the information needs of employees and of the general public are met through the provision of financial statements prepared principally for other purposes. Furthermore the maintenance of capital is no longer a principal function of financial statements; it was included in the analysis because of its importance in the past and as helping to explain the current approach to financial reporting in certain countries.

Finally there are clear affinities between the stewardship function and the investment function, since both involve providing information for shareholders. For this reason, many commentators include the stewardship function as an aspect of the investment function. This is not the author's position. He considers that the shareholder's decision to replace the management (based on the information contained in stewardship accounts) is sufficiently different from the decision to sell his shares (based on accounts that fulfil the investment function) to justify considering the two functions as separate. The author attaches great importance to the stewardship function; many corporate scandals (such as the Enron debacle in the USA) can be traced to the inadequate control of management. In the author's view, treating the stewardship function as an aspect of the investment function tends to belittle its importance, but he admits, with regret, that stewardship seems to play a very minor role in modern thinking on financial reporting.

Hence the two principal functions of the financial statements are to provide information for investors and to provide information for the state. The two functions have the common characteristic of providing information; they differ as to whom the information is to be provided and the use made of this information. European countries differ as to the relative importance that they give to the two functions. In very crude terms, Britain and Ireland place more emphasis on the investment function, whereas, in most countries of Continental Europe, the provision of information for the state (including for the computation of tax) is considered more important. However, in recent years, even the latter countries have begun to put more emphasis on the investment function, with the increasing importance of the capital market as a source of finance. This has been achieved by developing the consolidated accounts as a source of information for investors. Historically, in many Continental European countries, the government information function was performed by the individual accounts. Governments were primarily interested in the activities of the individual corporation and tended to ignore the group. Hence in many Continental European countries, consolidated accounts were neglected until quite recently. In fact it would seem that, in these countries, consolidated accounts were developed especially to perform the investment function.

2.10   Comparison with the USA

What have been presented in this chapter are the European approaches to the function of the financial statements. The position in the USA is fundamentally different. In effect, in that country, only one function is recognised: the investment function. As will be explained in Chapter 7, in the USA the rules of financial reporting are set principally by the Financial Accounting Standards Board (FASB). The FASB sets out the objectives of financial reporting in the following terms: 'financial reporting should provide information that is useful to present and potential investors and creditors and other users in making rational investment, credit and similar decisions' (FASB, 1978, paragraph 34). The reference to 'creditors' is to their decision to extend credit and not to the protection of creditors through the limitation of dividends. In fact the FASB does not even mention this latter function. Although the FASB refers to 'other users' it is clear that their needs are secondary to those of investors. One reason why the FASB gives priority to investors is that it considers that 'information provided to meet investors' and creditors' needs is likely to be generally useful to members of other groups', that is, as is the practice in much of Europe, the information needs of employees and the public may be met as a by-product of reporting to investors. However in contrast to the position in much of Continental Europe, the FASB considers that the information needs of the state and the tax authorities should be met by special purpose statements that are separate from the regular accounts.

The consequence of only one function of the financial reporting being recognised in the USA is that there is far less diversity of practice there compared with Europe. The converse that in Europe several functions are recognised with different European countries placing differing degrees of emphasis on each function, is the root cause of the great diversity in financial reporting practice throughout Europe.

2.11   The preparers' viewpoint

So far this chapter has considered only the demands and needs of the users of financial statements. However financial statements are drawn up, not by the users, but by the enterprise's accountants under the authority and control of the enterprise's management. These persons are known collectively as the 'preparers'. Ideally the preparers should take as their objective the fulfilment, to the best of their ability, of the users' needs and demands. However the preparers have their own objectives, which often are quite different from those of the users. The most fundamental objective of an enterprise's directors is survival – to avoid losing their jobs, as a result of being dismissed through an adverse vote of the shareholders or following a successful takeover bid. The financial statements can play a very important role in helping the enterprise's management to achieve its objective of survival. If the accounts show that the enterprise is doing well, for example they report a steadily increasing profit, the shareholders will be happy and not be inclined to vote out the management; also the market price of the company's shares will remain high, deterring a takeover bid. However the accounts are prepared by the management (or at least under their direction). Hence there is a temptation for the management not to present the full truth about the enterprise in the financial statements, particularly when the company is doing badly. They will manipulate the financial statements so that they present an unduly rosy picture. This is exactly what happened with Enron and WorldCom in the USA, as is analysed in detail in Chapter 9. In those countries where the amount of tax that a company pays is based on its published accounts, there is the opposite tendency: to present the enterprise's performance as worse than it is in reality. Rarely is it in the preparers' interest to present the full truth about the entity. This was what was meant by the statement, at the start of this chapter, that one possible function of the financial statements might be to present disinformation about the enterprise. Clearly this is not in the interest of the users. How this danger is averted is the principal subject of the next chapter.

Notes

1. In certain European countries, the law requires that corporations make transfers out of profits to a legal reserve. A common rule is that 10 per cent of each year's profit should be so appropriated until the legal reserve amounts to 10 per cent of share capital. However there is no requirement to build up reserves in proportion to the corporation's debts.
2. These cases are analysed in French (1977).
3. This example was used by a lawyer in one of the court cases, Dovey v. Cory, 1901 – see French (1977, p. 315).
4. The position of the British accountancy profession is set out in Yamey (1962).

References

Beaver, W. (1998). *Financial Reporting: An Accounting Revolution.* Englewood Cliffs, Prentice-Hall.

FASB (1978). Statement of financial accounting concepts No. 1, Objectives of financial reporting by business enterprises, FASB, Stamford.

French, E. (1977). 'The evolution of the dividend law of England'. *Studies in Accounting.* W. T. Baxter and S. Davidson. London, The Institute of Chartered Accountants.

Lefebvre, C. and Flower, J. (1994). *European Fiancial Reporting: Belgium.* London, Routledge.

Nobes, C. (2002). 'Causes of international differences'. *Comparative International Accounting.* C. Nobes and R. Parker (eds). Prentice-Hall, London.

Yamey, B. (1962). 'The case law relating to company dividends'. *Studies in Accounting Theory.* W. Baxter and S. Davidson. London, Sweet and Maxwell.

3
Regulation

It is a fact that, throughout Europe and indeed the world, financial reporting is governed by rules which prescribe, in varying degrees of detail, the form and content of financial statements. This chapter and the following chapter consider these rules, not so much their content, but rather the nature of the rules themselves, the authority attached to the rules and the bodies that issue them – the rule-makers. Within Europe, there is great diversity in these matters. The rules that govern financial reporting range from laws, enacted by the state, which must be obeyed under threat of sanctions imposed by the courts, to recommendations issued by professional associations. Even though such recommendations may not be backed by any formal authority and have only persuasive force, they are nevertheless relevant, if they are followed in practice and have thus have become a form of self-imposed rule. Before considering these rules in more detail, it is proposed first to consider the question: 'Why, in financial reporting, are rules necessary or desirable?'.

3.1 Why are rules needed

In European countries the need for financial reporting by the enterprise to persons outside the enterprise arose in two rather different situations: to satisfy the needs of the suppliers of capital and to provide the state with information that it demanded, notably in order to raise taxes. As explained in Chapter 2 the first scenario applied principally in Britain and the second on the Continent. The theory of regulation has been developed almost entirely by economists from the USA and Britain, countries where the principal function of financial reporting is perceived to be the provision of information for the capital market. For this reason the theory neglects the taxation function of financial reporting and concentrates almost exclusively on the capital market function. It is this theory that is discussed here.

The nineteenth century, in both Europe and the USA, was marked by the growth of large industrial and commercial enterprises which required more capital than could be provided by a small number of owner-managers. Hence corporations were formed which drew their capital from a large number of persons. It was impractical for all these providers of finance to be involved in the management of the corporation; hence the shareholders were obliged to delegate the running of the enterprise to one or more managers, whose stake in the capital of the corporation might be relatively small. Commonly, as part of the arrangement, the managers were required to report periodically to the providers of finance on how they had fulfilled the delegated task; the principal means of reporting were the financial statements. As a result of this development, the major industrial and commercial corporations, both in Europe and other developed regions of the world, are now controlled by professional managers over whom the shareholders, the formal owners of the corporation, have only tenuous and, at best, sporadic control.

In this situation, there is a danger that the managers will take decisions that are not in the best interests of the shareholders, such as to pay themselves excessive salaries or, more subtly, to invest in projects that increase their power and status ('empire building') but which yield little in the way of profit for the shareholders. More significantly, the managers, who control the form and content of the financial statements issued by the corporation, will make sure that these portray a picture that is favourable to themselves; for example, they will not provide full and frank information on investment projects that have failed; this is 'bad news' which must be kept from the shareholders. In fact there is no incentive for managers to give any meaningful information at all in the financial statements. This is because 'knowledge is power'; a person who possesses information has a certain power which is greatly diminished if the information is shared with other people. In particular managers will be most reluctant to disclose voluntarily any information that may be used by the shareholders and other providers of finance to monitor and assess their performance. The managers will make sure that the financial statements are bland and uninformative, although no doubt with the aid of much creative and artistic skill, they will succeed in painting a very rosy picture of the corporation.

There is general agreement that the managers of enterprises need to be induced by outside forces to produce financial statements that contain the information required by users. However there is no general agreement on the nature of these outside forces. On the one hand, there is an academic school that holds that market forces are sufficient. On the other hand, there are those who contend that the market fails to exercise sufficient discipline on corporate management and that, given this failure of the market, rules must be imposed by outside rule-makers.

3.2   The case for the market

The principal advocate of the market school is Benston, who argues (Benston, 1980) that it is unnecessary and undesirable for rule-makers to intervene by setting rules, because market forces alone will ensure that enterprises voluntarily disclose the information demanded by investors. The enterprises that did not issue meaningful financial statements would find themselves at a competitive disadvantage compared with those that did. His line of reasoning runs as follows:

1. Investors are aware that there is a danger that managers may run enterprises in their own selfish interests and not in the interests of shareholders, and that the managers are unlikely to inform the shareholders of their self-seeking activities.
2. To adjust for the losses that are expected to arise from the dishonest and inefficient behaviour of managers, investors will reduce their estimates of the future profits to be earned by *all* enterprises.
3. However, some enterprises will be managed honestly and efficiently. The managers of these enterprises have an incentive to inform investors of this 'good news'. This information will allay some of the investors' suspicions and remove some of the uncertainty surrounding the enterprise's future profits. Hence investors will revise upwards their estimates of the profits of these enterprises and revise downwards their discount rate, leading to a rise in the share price.
4. Among the other enterprises, that is those that do not report fully, there will be some that are better managed than others. However, unless they disclose this good news, they will be classified in the same category as the worst enterprises. Hence these enterprises also have an incentive to report fully.
5. This process should continue until the only enterprises not to report fully are those with really bad news – that is even worse than the investors suspect.

Benston acknowledges that managers may be motivated to report false or misleading information and that therefore investors may have no confidence in the financial statements issued by corporate management. He accepts that the financial statements have to be validated by a person or organisation trusted by the investors. Hence it is in the interest of both managers and investors that the financial statements are certified by an independent auditor, who has an established reputation for honesty and competence. Investors will believe the auditors (whereas they distrust the managers); they reason that the auditors will not certify a financial statement that is false or misleading, because this would damage the auditors' reputation for integrity which is their principal business asset.

Benston develops his theory principally in relation to the information needs of investors. The enterprise that issues full and frank financial statements will be able to raise funds more easily and more cheaply. Its share price will be maintained at a high level, which has two advantages: it keeps the cost of capital low and it deters potential takeover bids. On the other hand, the corporate management that failed to provide investors with the information that they demanded would find that the share price would stagnate. The enterprise would be unable to raise new funds (or only at excessive cost) and it would be vulnerable to being taken over. In fact it would seem that market forces would lead ultimately to the elimination of enterprises that did not provide the information demanded by investors. Such an enterprise would not grow and finally would be taken over by a more efficient enterprise – a case of 'survival of the fittest' or 'virtue rewarded' in the market place.

According to Benston, the provision of financial statements should be the object of a private contract between the enterprise and the supplier of finance, which should specify in detail the form and content of the reports to be supplied, covering both the rules on which they are to be based and the means by which they are to be validated. It is in the interests of both parties that the rules are so formulated that they assure the supply of the information that will enable the supplier of finance to reduce to a minimum the uncertainty which she attaches to the outcome of her investment. In this way, the premium that she adds to her required rate of return to compensate for risk and uncertainty will be reduced and the cost of capital to the enterprise will be minimised.

The above analysis applies equally well to other outside parties who would be reluctant to enter into contracts with an enterprise that provided little information about its financial position and performance. Such outside parties would include:

- lenders and banks who would refuse to extend credit;
- suppliers who would refuse to sell goods on credit;
- customers who would refuse to enter long-term contracts, particularly when these involve outlays on their part which can only be recovered in the longer term;
- workers who would be reluctant to accept employment with an enterprise whose future prospects are impossible to gauge with any confidence; this would be a particular concern for skilled workers and middle management.

In all the above cases, the enterprise would find itself at a disadvantage in comparison with those of its competitors that provided the necessary information.

Benston (1976) cites, as evidence for his theory, the behaviour of enterprises which, in the past, published financial statements before there was any legal or contractual obligation to do so, and which, in the present, disclose more than the legal minimum.

3.3   The case against the market

3.3.1   Financial statements as 'public goods'

The case against the market is well presented by Bromwich (1992, Chapter 10). He points out that, in general, enterprises make their financial statements available to all those who request them, either freely or at only a nominal charge. Also, in most countries, enterprises are obliged to file a copy of their financial statements with a state agency where they may be inspected by anyone for a small fee. This is a requirement of EU law. In these cases the financial statements become what are termed by economists 'public goods'. A public good has two important characteristics:

1. If the good is supplied to one person, its benefits may be enjoyed generally and indiscriminately by all other people in society.
2. Its consumption or enjoyment by one person does not reduce the amount of the goods available for consumption by others.

Public service broadcasting and nuclear deterrence are often cited as examples of public goods. The general view of economic theorists is that, in the case of public goods, the market does not assure with complete efficiency the supply of the amount demanded by society. Some of the demands of consumers who would be willing to pay the incremental cost of additional supply will not be met.

Financial statements are clearly public goods. They are available to all for, at most, a small fee, and the process of reading a financial statement does not cause it to be used up. Also there is a danger that the demands of individuals for additional information may not be met. From the viewpoint of the individual, it is not economic to offer to pay the enterprise to include additional information in the financial statements if these are to be made available to all simultaneously at no charge. The individual would have to bear the costs; the other users would enjoy the benefits but would have paid nothing. They would be 'free-riders'.

It is easy to demonstrate that making information available to all greatly reduces its value to the individual who paid for its provision. For example, an individual may believe that the release by the enterprise of a certain item of information (say whether or not the enterprise has been awarded a particular contract) would lead to a change in the share price from €10 to either €11 or €9 , depending on whether it was good news or bad news. If the individual received the information before the rest of society, she would be able to make a profit by buying the shares or selling them short. However, if the information is released to everyone at the same time, the market price would adjust immediately, offering no opportunity for speculative trading. Certainly it is likely that shareholders in general would benefit from the reduction in the uncertainty surrounding the enterprise's future profits, but the degree to which any individual shareholder would benefit is small. It is limited to the increase in the expected value of the shareholding, which, for any individual shareholder, is likely to be less than the cost of obtaining the information.

The problem with public goods is that each individual is faced with the decision of paying for the entire cost of providing the goods for the whole of society. In deciding on the supply of the goods, the total social cost is compared with the benefits accruing to a single individual, whereas, to achieve the optimal supply, the social cost should be compared with the total social benefit (the aggregate of the benefits of all individuals). Hence it is very likely that the good will be supplied at a level below the social optimum. The situation is aggravated by each individual holding back from paying for additional supply in the hope that some other individual will do so instead.

3.3.2 The problem of insider trading

The problems that arise from financial statements being public goods could be alleviated if the individual were to insist that the information for which she has paid should be supplied to her alone and not released generally. However most countries have enacted 'insider trading' laws which make it an offence for an individual to use, for her own profit, information about an enterprise that has been obtained privately. These laws remove, in principle, the economic rationale for the individual to pay for additional information.

There is no doubt that the prohibition of insider trading makes the market less efficient than it would be otherwise. Since certain information is disregarded in setting the market prices, the latter are, to this extent, incorrect, which can lead to a misallocation of resources. For example, assume that a pharmaceutical enterprise has developed a new drug which is expected to be highly profitable. For competitive reasons, the enterprise does not immediately disclose the discovery. The profits from the drug are expected to lead to an increase in the price of the enterprise's shares from €10 to €15. A director of the enterprise, using his inside knowledge, buys a large bloc of shares in the anticipation of making a profit from the expected increase in the share price. The director's purchase, since it represents additional demand, will probably lead to an immediate increase in the share price, from say €10 to €11. This increase is desirable as it brings the share price closer to €15 which is the optimal price from the viewpoint of society for two reasons:

1. It leads to a better allocation of resources. At the price of €15 the enterprise's cost of capital is lower, which correctly reflects the profitability of its activities.

2. It assures equity between successive generations of shareholders. Consider the case of a shareholder who sold her shares after the enterprise discovered the drug but before the discovery was announced. The price of €10 received from the sale was set in ignorance of the discovery and does not fairly represent the real value of the shares. The fundamental event that led, ultimately, to the increase in the share price from €10 to €15 was the discovery of the drug and not the announcement of this discovery. The shareholder who, after the discovery of the drug, sells at €10, does not receive a fair price.

The director, who, on the basis of inside knowledge, bought the shares at a price of €10, makes a profit which most people would consider to be unjustified; he has exploited both his position of trust and the ignorance of the shareholder. However the director's action in buying the shares causes the market price to come closer to the 'correct' price, that is, the price that would be set if all information were generally available. That is certainly in the general social and economic interest. Furthermore the greater the extent of insider trading, the closer the market price will be to the correct price.

The phenomenon of insider trading creates a nice dilemma for society. Many are outraged by the profits made by insiders which arise solely from their exploiting the ignorance of others; to them insider trading is socially unacceptable. On the other hand insider trading improves the efficiency of markets, which is clearly in the general interest. In this conflict between social acceptability and economic efficiency, it would seem that economic efficiency has lost, for most countries have passed laws that prohibit or severely restrict insider trading – but perhaps the cause of economic efficiency is not completely lost, for it is notorious that these laws are very difficult to enforce and are therefore often ineffective.

The above analysis demonstrates that, on the demand side, there is no mechanism by which the demand of users for information can cause enterprises to be motivated to provide that information. The supply of information will now be considered.

3.3.3   The supply of information

On the supply side, conditions tend to aggravate the problem. There are two important points to be made about the cost of financial reporting:

1. *High costs*: The preparation of financial statements is a costly process, involving the capturing, storing and processing of data. Economies may certainly be possible because of the overlap between the financial statements and the internal management accounts. However the cost of transforming information that has been prepared initially for management purposes may be considerable. Also many of the items in the financial statements may have no direct counterpart in the management accounts and, for

their calculation, separate arrangements have to be made; examples are the historical cost of fixed assets and the provision for deferred taxes.

2. *Cost structure*: Most of the costs are fixed; it costs only slightly more to produce a thousand copies of the financial statements than it does to produce the first copy. The cost of the first copy comprises the entire cost of the accounting system that was established to produce the necessary data, the costs of specific calculations and the printing set-up costs. The cost of subsequent copies is, largely, the paper on which they are printed. This cost structure reinforces the character of financial statements as public goods. Not only are enterprises supposed to make their financial statements available to all on demand, but they are not inhibited, on grounds of cost, from doing so.

Financial reporting costs enterprises money which they cannot recoup by charging the users. It is to be expected that enterprises would react to this situation by minimising the costs involved. Since most of the costs are occasioned by the capture and processing of data, costs can only be curtailed by reducing the quantity and quality of the information contained in the financial statements.

This analysis of the supply side reinforces the conclusion that has already been made in respect of the demand side: the market is so imperfect that it cannot be relied upon to induce enterprises to issue financial reports that meet the information needs of users.

3.4   The verdict

The cases for and against the market have been presented above. Which is correct? Of course, as generally happens, there are valid points in both arguments and the truth lies somewhere between the two extremes. However most commentators tend to come down against the market. They admire the intellectual rigour of Benston's arguments but conclude that his theory does not accurately represent the real world. In reality the market is so imperfect that it does not perform the function that Benston assigns to it. This view is well expressed by Solomons (1983, p. 107): 'The market cannot be depended upon to discipline promptly enterprises that are left free to choose what to report and how to report to their investors and creditors. Even if good accounting can be relied upon to drive out bad in the long run too much damage may be inflicted in the short run to make freedom from regulation in this field an acceptable policy.'

Given this failure of the market, there is no force that inhibits corporate management from providing only that information which it considers in its interest to supply. In this situation enterprises must be compelled to provide appropriate information by the imposition of rules by outsiders. The position has been well captured by Burggraaff who, in a very readable paper

(Burggraaff, 1983) which covers the whole field of this chapter, states that the major function of rules is 'to reduce the freedom of preparers, in order to satisfy some of the demands of the users'.

This judgement does not mean that the earlier analysis of the advantages of the market is without relevance. On the contrary, it provides a valuable frame of reference with which to judge the efficiency of the rules that are imposed to counteract the imperfections of the market. Although most commentators accept that rules are necessary, they also regret this necessity and point out the following limitations of rules.

- The imposed rules should be the minimum that are required to counteract the imperfections of the market. There are strong reasons for believing that the allocation of resources achieved through market forces is the best for society as a whole and that there is a danger that any interference with the market may lead to a reduction in the general welfare. Hence any imposed rules must be clearly directed towards and limited to the correction of proved market failures.
- The costs of regulation should always be borne in mind. Regulation, like any other economic activity, is only worthwhile if its benefits exceed its costs. Some of the costs are obvious, such as those incurred by enterprises in maintaining appropriate accounting systems. However the less obvious, indirect costs are probably much more significant. One such indirect cost has already been mentioned: the danger of misallocation of resources through interference with the market. Others are mentioned below.
- Even if the market is not completely effective as a means of disciplining enterprises, this does not mean that the alternative, say government regulation, will be any more efficient. Against 'market failure', there should always be set the possibility of 'government failure'.
- Any system of imposed rules leads to the danger that innovation and progress will be stifled. Enterprises will be restrained from experimenting in new forms and methods of financial reporting. One may legitimately doubt that the rules imposed by authority are the very best conceivable. The dangers have been well expressed by Baxter, who in a cogent article (Baxter, 1981), sets out the arguments for and against rules, coming out finally strongly against. He is highly sceptical of man-made rules – 'Only god-like creatures know where the truth lies. It follows that ex cathedra pronouncements by human authority are tendentious and inevitably sometimes be wrong. The most eminent authorities erred persistently on, for instance, the shape of the earth, the origins of life, and the circulation of the blood . . . We cannot with complete confidence expect infallibility in the future.' He cites two famous historical figures in support: Sir Francis Bacon, the philosopher statesman of Elizabethan England, 'Truth is the daughter, not of Authority, but of Time' and Isambard Kingdom Brunel, the nineteenth-century engineer and entrepreneur, 'rules will embarrass

and shackle the progress of improvement tomorrow by recording and registering as law the prejudices and errors of today'. Accountants should never accept that their principal function is to apply the rules set by authority; they should always treat these rules with scepticism and be prepared to exercise their own intelligence and judgement. Above all they should not be beguiled by an apparently comprehensive and formidable structure of laws and rules into giving up thinking.

The dangers and drawbacks of rules should always be kept in mind. However, for the reasons given earlier, it is generally accepted that in financial reporting some imposed rules are a regrettable necessity.

3.5 Uniform rules versus relevant rules

In deciding on what specific rules to impose, the rule-maker is faced with a choice between uniform rules and relevant rules.

3.5.1 Uniform rules

There are clearly considerable advantages to be gained if the financial statements of all enterprises were to be based on the same rules. Solomons (1983) refers to three arguments in favour of the imposition of uniform rules:

1. *Credibility*: Where the current accounting rules allow discretion to the preparers of accounts, it can happen that two enterprises that are essentially similar in all respects can, by using different rules, report quite different figures for assets and profit. A notorious example occurred in 1967 when the British company GEC took over AEI, when two quite different figures for profit were issued in respect of the *same* company. In October 1967, prior to the takeover, the AEI directors forecast a profit of £10 million for the calendar year 1967. Since this forecast was made so late in the year, it was to a large extent a statement of actual profits. Later, after the takeover (when GEC, having won control of AEI, could dictate its accounts), AEI reported a loss of £4½ million for 1967, that is a difference of £14½ million compared with the previous estimate. In effect, the public was presented with two fundamentally different figures for AEI's profit for 1967. It subsequently transpired that most of the difference was attributable to the use of different accounting rules notably for the valuation of assets. As is common in takeovers, the incoming management had an incentive to paint as gloomy a picture as possible, so as to be able to claim that any subsequent improvement was the result of their superior abilities. The whole incident lead to a loss in the public's confidence in accounting figures, which was not limited to GEC and AEI but applied to enterprises in general. The general public accepts a figure as creditable only if there is general agreement among experts as to its

magnitude. For example, a patient would lose confidence in doctors in general, if one told him that his cholesterol level was 205 and another that it was 300. The measurement of profit is more complicated than the measurement of cholesterol, but the general public does not appreciate such niceties.

2. *Comparability*: The information provided by an enterprise is more valuable if it can easily be compared with that provided by other enterprises. This comparison may provide an indication of possible weaknesses or ineffi- ciencies; for example, a certain cost category may be significantly higher than the industry average, or inventory turnover may be slower than with competitors. Comparability can be achieved by requiring that all enterprises follow the same rules. A by-product of uniform rules (that are also stable over time) is that, for any particular enterprise, the financial statements of the current year are completely comparable with those of preceding years.

3. *Efficiency of communication*: In the absence of an agreed set of rules governing financial reporting in general, it would be very difficult for the user to understand and interpret the financial statements of any particular enterprise. To assist comprehension, the enterprise would have to include with the accounts a lengthy and detailed explanation of the rules that had been followed in their preparation. This procedure imposes costs both on the preparer and on the user, who has to read and understand these explanations, which will be different for every enterprise. These costs may be avoided if a common set of rules (available to and understood by all) were used by all enterprises.

It is important to understand that the benefits claimed for a common set of rules depend entirely on the characteristic of uniformity and on no other characteristic of the rules, such as the value, relevance or quality of the information provided. For example, a rule that required that all fixed assets be depreciated over ten years (regardless of their economic life) would lead to all enterprises reporting comparable information that would be easily understood by users and would avoid the GEC/AEI type scandal of identical enterprises reporting different profits. In fact to maximise the benefits, absolute uniformity is necessary; no discretion at all should be given to the preparers of financial statements. This is rather like the rule that all vehicles should drive on the right-hand side of the road. There is no moral or qualitative argument in favour of using the right-hand side rather than the left-hand side, but there are very substantial advantages in all vehicles using the same side. Of course the British, in their perverse fashion, drive on the left-hand side, but only in Britain. On the Continent, they soon discover that it pays them to drive on the right-hand side. This example illustrates perfectly that it is solely the fact of uniformity that counts, not the nature of the rule (that is right or left).

A major argument against leaving the form and content of financial statements to be determined by a private contract between the enterprise and the supplier of finance (as suggested in Section 3.2) is that this will result in undesirable diversity. Each enterprise would draw up its financial statements using a unique set of rules, being those that it has agreed with its shareholders and other suppliers of finance.

3.5.2 Relevant rules

However the quality of the information provided by financial statements cannot be ignored. Information by itself has no intrinsic value. It is only valuable if it is useful to someone. Like any other economic goods, the value of information depends ultimately on the preferences of consumers. It is generally assumed that people and organisations need information in order to make decisions and that the principal objective of financial reporting is to provide this information. Accountants use the term 'relevance' to describe information that is useful. So in deciding the relevance of rules, the information needs of the users of financial statements must be considered.

In Chapter 2, four groups of users were identified: investors (including shareholders and lenders), the state, employees and the general public. In effect the users of financial statements form a very wide and diverse group and their information needs are very diverse. In general, they all demand some form of information on the financial position and performance of the company relating to the past, the present and (as far as is feasible) the future. Some user groups may require non-financial information (for example, the trade unions would like information on employment levels), but this is beyond the scope of this book.

3.5.3 The conflict between uniformity and relevance

It might be felt that it would be relatively easy to achieve both uniformity and relevance. All that needs to be done is to devise the rules that best meets the information needs of users and then impose this single set of rules on all enterprises. However this approach ignores the great diversity among enterprises on such matters as the nature and size of the business, and the number and relative importance of shareholders, employees and other user groups. In fact each enterprise is essentially unique, both in what it reports (the structure of its assets and so on) and to whom it reports (the composition of the users of its accounts). If the same rules were to be imposed on all enterprises, this would inevitably result in the financial statements of some enterprises failing to satisfy fully the information needs of its particular users. In effect the desirable qualities of uniformity and relevance are incompatible and rule-makers have to make a choice between them or, at least, find an acceptable compromise.

3.5.4   Multi-base reporting

Given the diversity of the users' needs, it would seem improbable that these would all be satisfied by the publication of financial statements based on a single set of rules. For example, it is often claimed that asset values based on historical cost are the most useful for stewardship purposes, but that market value is more appropriate when assessing credit risk. Hence it has been suggested that enterprises should provide not a single figure for asset values, profits and so on, but rather a number of alternative figures based on different concepts. This information could be provided in footnotes, supplementary statements or in adjacent columns. In this way, the information needs of each user group would be met. There have been experiments in this direction; for example, the 1980 financial report of Royal Dutch/Shell gave no less than five different figures for profit based on different concepts.

However both accountants and users have rejected this approach as confusing. Most agree with Burggraaff (1983) who concludes: 'For sophisticated users this type of reporting may have merit, but for the general public it is, in my view, confusing. The ordinary reader is at a loss to determine what figure is relevant to him and his confidence in the ability of the profession to prepare relevant and reliable figures will be eroded.' The author agrees. The essential task of the accountant is to distil the mass of information available about an enterprise into a form that is easily understood and assimilated by the ordinary reader. Although there is certainly a good case for supplying supplementary information, for example in the notes, this does not absolve the accountant from exercising her skill and judgement in reporting figures for such fundamental measures as profit and net worth. The accountant who shrinks from this responsibility is not fulfilling the function that society expects of her.

The current position is that enterprises issue a single set of financial statements, which set out single measures of asset and liability values (in the balance sheet) and of revenues and expenses (in the profit and loss account). Much additional information is given in the notes; for example the market value of assets that are presented in the balance sheet at historical cost. One suspects that the ordinary reader looks only at the two principal statements, whereas the sophisticated reader concentrates on the notes. Both law and practice insist that enterprises publish a single set of accounts, which, as they have to satisfy the diverse information needs of many different categories of users, are known in the literature as 'general purpose financial statements'.

3.6   The role of law

Since the market cannot assure the provision of the information, both in quantity and in quality, that is demanded by important groups in society, the government, at the instigation of these groups, is obliged to intervene. This result is made all the more inevitable in that the government itself is an important user of information. Hence governments pass laws that regulate financial reporting. At the heart of every regulatory system laws can be found.

3.6.1 The politics of law-making

The making of law by the legislature is essentially a political process, for two reasons:

1. The actual rules that are laid down will influence the distribution of wealth among social groups. For example, the rules may be changed to allow enterprises to capitalise research and development expenditure; this change in the rules would probably lead to enterprises reporting higher profits, at least initially, which would benefit shareholders (who may expect higher dividends), managers (who may receive larger bonuses based on reported profits) and the state, as tax collector (which may expect to receive more taxes computed on the basis of reported profits). Also manufacturers of research equipment and research departments of universities may be expected to benefit, as enterprises are no longer deterred from undertaking research by its effect on reported profits. But the change is very likely to be to the detriment of other groups, such as lenders, creditors and employees, who would all suffer in that cash would have left the company (in the payment of dividends, bonuses and tax) thus diminishing the resources at the company's disposal and rendering its financial and economic future somewhat less secure. This subject is dealt with in the literature on 'the economic consequences of financial reporting', which is well summarised in Blake (1992).
2. The balancing of the interests of the different social groups in setting the rules involves the normal political processes of consultation, lobbying, bargaining, debate and, in the end, voting. The enactment of laws by the legislature after the customary political process, is the normal way in which society settles questions involving the distribution of wealth among its members.

3.6.2 The advantages of law

The setting of the rules of financial reporting by law has a number of advantages which have been well analysed by Bromwich (1992), who sets out two incontrovertible advantages:

1. The legitimacy and social acceptance of the rules are assured, at least when they have been set by a democratically elected legislature.
2. Compliance with the rules may be enforced through society's usual procedures, the ultimate sanction being penalties imposed by the courts.

Bromwich also claims that governments by using their taxation and subsidy powers may be able to mitigate the undesirable side effects of an accounting rule that, in other respects, is socially desirable. However this seems rather improbable, as it presupposes a fundamental change in government behaviour. Normally governments set the rules of financial reporting to achieve tax objectives, not vice versa.

Over the past century, the extent to which law regulates financial reporting has increased significantly in all European countries, accelerating in recent years. A major cause has been the activities of the EU which are dealt with in Chapter 5.

3.7 The need for additional rules

The advantages of law are clear cut. However, generally the legislator prefers to limit the role of law to the laying down of the objectives and the more important principles of financial reporting and to leave the development of the detailed rules to other bodies. There are a number of good reasons for such behaviour which have been analysed exhaustively by Baldwin and McCrudden (1987). They may be summarised as follows:

- *Detail*: Financial reporting is simply too detailed for every aspect of it to be covered in the law.
- *Priorities*: Compared with all the other matters that compete for the legislature's time and attention, financial reporting is rarely the most important or the most urgent. Hence there is a danger that the legislature will neglect the subject and that the necessary laws will be enacted only after considerable delays, so that, by the time they come into force, they are already out of date. Law is rarely an effective way of dealing with urgent problems or with new developments in financial reporting. Hence it is reasonable for the legislator to leave these tasks to other bodies, which may be expected to act with greater expedition and efficiency.
- *Technical complexity*: Much of financial reporting concerns highly technical matters. It is likely that the typical member of the legislature will not be well informed on these matters and will not be unhappy to pass the responsibility to another body, which, possessing the necessary technical competence, is likely to do a better job. The legislator is probably glad to be relieved of an uncongenial and boring task.
- *Cost*: Given the low priority that it gives to financial reporting, the state may decide that it is not economic to allocate resources to the development of detailed rules, particularly as it would be costly to acquire or hire the necessary technical expertise.
- *More democratic*: Given the typical legislator's lack of interest and expertise in financial reporting, there is a danger that, if the law seeks to regulate financial reporting in detail, the source of its provisions will be some

anonymous civil servant and not the democratically elected representatives of the people. Therefore it may be more democratic to leave the setting of the detailed rules to a body that either better represents the people concerned or has the time and resources to consult them fully. This may lead to more open and better informed rule-making.

- *Political considerations*: The decision not to legislate may be influenced by political considerations. The government may decide that a particular issue is so controversial and divisive that whatever decision it takes it will be criticised. It prefers not to be involved and is very happy to 'pass the buck' to some other body. This has four advantages: it relieves the government of the problem, it gives the impression that the problem is being tackled, it furnishes a perfect scapegoat when the problem is not solved and it deflects the activities of lobbyists and pressure groups which the government may find embarrassing.
- *Continuity*: Since the political composition of the legislature may change quite frequently and since it only legislates on financial reporting sporadically, there is a danger that the laws that it enacts will be inconsistent and lack any basic principles. It is possible that the rules developed by other bodies may be more consistent, since their composition may be more stable and they give sustained attention to their task.

3.8   The hierarchy of rules

For all these reasons, it is very common throughout Europe that the laws enacted by the legislator tend to be limited to laying down the objectives and the more important principles of financial reporting. The legislature provides the framework and leaves it to other bodies to fill in the detail. Hence, in the regulatory system, the law is supplemented by a whole range of other rules, set by other bodies. The set of rules may be considered as a hierarchy. The principal elements of this hierarchy are presented in Exhibit 3.1, which, following Ordelheide (1999), shows the hierarchy in the form of a pyramid.

3.8.1   Law

Law is at the top of the hierarchy; it is the dominant element, for two reasons:

1. The other rules must be consistent with the law, both with its general principles and its specific provisions. In virtue of the authority given by society to the legislature, any conflict between the law and a rule lower down in the hierarchy must be resolved in favour of law.
2. Law provides the criteria by which it can be judged whether the other rules are to be accepted as valid and authoritative, that is whether they may be included as proper elements in the hierarchy of rules.

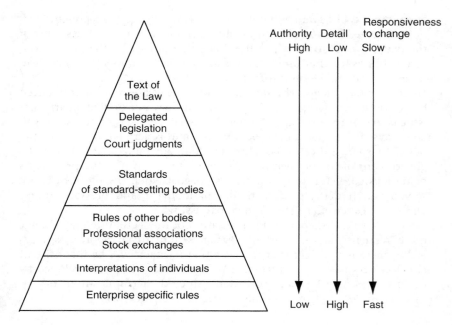

Exhibit 3.1   The hierarchy of rules

The second level of the hierarchy is composed of delegated legislation and court judgments. This level derives its authority from law; its rules may be considered to be part of the body of law – elaborations and clarifications of law – and they are enforced by the state's law enforcement agencies.

The rules of the remaining levels of the hierarchy (standards, recommendations and interpretations) do not form part of the law; they are included in the system of rules because, to varying degrees, they are complied with by the preparers of accounts, essentially because of the prestige and expertise of the bodies and individuals involved. However the authority attached to standards is more complex, as is explained later.

Ordelheide (1999) makes three general remarks about the hierarchy of rules. They are illustrated by the vertical lines in Exhibit 3.1.

1. *Authority*: The authority attached to a rule decreases as one descends through the levels of the hierarchy, that is the further the rule is removed from law.
2. *Detail*: The rules become more detailed and more concrete as one descends through the levels of the hierarchy, with incomplete and unclear rules established at one level being further elaborated at a lower level. There is a development from general principles to particular rules.

3. *Responsiveness to change*: The responsiveness to change increases as one descends through the levels of the hierarchy. When a new accounting issue arises (for example, how to report a newly invented financial instrument), the accountant who prepares the accounts has to find a solution immediately. She can seek advice from individuals, who will generally be able to respond more quickly than the bodies higher up the hierarchy, whose rule-making procedures are generally more formal and therefore slower. It is possible that the solution adopted by the preparer will be challenged in the courts, so that eventually, perhaps after several years, the courts will issue a definitive judgment on the matter. But it may be many more years before the law is amended to take into account the changed circumstances.

The levels in the hierarchy will now be considered.

3.8.2   Delegated legislation

It is very common for laws enacted by the legislature to contain provisions that empower other government bodies, such as ministries and state agencies, to enact rules within laid-down limits. These rules are given a variety of names: government decrees, ministerial orders, statutory instruments and so on. Such rules have the same authority as laws and, as with laws, compliance is achieved through the courts of law. There is one government department that, in most European countries, is very active in issuing regulations that have a great influence over company accounts: the fiscal authorities who are responsible for raising taxes.

3.8.3   Court judgments

The courts of law have a major role to play in the functioning of the system of rules. They issue judgments on the acceptability of the rules. The courts may be asked to rule on the constitutionality of a law enacted by the legislature, but their more common task is to decide on the legality of the rules lower down in the hierarchy. Thus the courts may declare that a particular rule is invalid, as not being in conformity with the law. In principle this rule should no longer be considered to be part of the system of rules. This also applies to delegated legislation (such as government decrees), for if the court decides, in a particular case, that the government does not possess the necessary authority, it will declare the decree to be illegal. Alternatively, the courts may decide that a rule does conform with the law and thus enhance its authority as when, for example, it confirms the interpretation of the law given by a particular individual. In fact, in certain circumstances, the courts by endorsing a particular rule may thereby incorporate it into the body of the law.

However it is comparatively rare for the courts to rule on the legality of financial reporting rules. Hence only a small fraction of the rules lower down in the hierarchy owe their authority to the endorsement of the courts. The great majority of such rules owe their presence in the system of rules to the simple fact that they are followed in practice.

3.8.4   Standards

Standards are a peculiar feature of almost all systems for the regulation of financial reporting. They specify, in greater or lesser detail, how particular aspects of financial statements should be dealt with. Essentially standards supplement and extend the legal rules in areas where these are inadequate. Hence they may be regarded as:

- providing authoritative interpretations of the law where this is ambiguous or unclear;
- expanding the legal rules when these do not cover a point in sufficient detail;
- supplementing the law, by providing additional authoritative rules on matters not covered by the law.

Standards are set by organisations which, in this book, are termed 'standard-setting bodies'. Standard-setting bodies are a very common feature of the regulatory systems of the European countries. However there is great variety among the European countries in the status and importance of their standard-setting bodies, particularly in respect of two matters:

1. The extent to which the body is instituted, controlled and/or recognised by the government; that is the extent to which the body may be regarded as an extension of the state.
2. The degree of authority attached to the standards that it issues, for example the extent to which they are recognised by the courts as valid interpretations or extensions of the law.

Within Europe, one finds examples of standard-setting bodies that, at one extreme, are clearly organs of government and whose standards are accepted by the courts as part of the law, and, at the other extreme, bodies that have an exclusively private status and whose standards have no formal legal authority (although often followed by accountants). But most bodies fall between these two extremes.

The variety within Europe in this matter is further illustrated by the terms employed. The word 'standard' is used only in English-speaking countries and Germany; in other countries, different terms are used, such as Richtlijnen ('Guidelines', Netherlands) and Principi ('Principles', Italy). The complexities of standard-setting in the European countries are considered in detail in the next chapter.

3.8.5 Rules of other bodies

Many other bodies set rules. In general, the authority of the rules extends only to the members of the bodies; in respect of non-members, the rules have, at most, persuasive force. Three such bodies are important in the field of financial reporting.

Stock exchanges

Corporations that seek to have their shares and other securities listed on a stock exchange have to agree to observe the rules of that stock exchange. These rules may contain detailed provisions relating to financial statements, for example requiring the disclosure of information additional to that prescribed in the law, and they may be a very important influence on the financial reporting of the small number of corporations to which they apply. However, although listed corporations may be small in number, their economic importance is often considerable. Listed corporations generally observe these rules, because the stock exchange authorities have a very effective means of assuring compliance: they can suspend the listing of the corporation's shares and, as an ultimate sanction, expel the corporation from the exchange.

Professional associations of auditors

In all European countries there is a legal obligation for the accounts of enterprises to be audited by a qualified auditor and there exist professional associations which represent those who are so qualified. Commonly these associations issue guidance to their members on the conduct of audits and, in particular, on the accounting rules that should be respected in the financial statements that they audit. Occasionally the professional associations seek to compel their members to follow these rules by threatening disciplinary measures; the ultimate sanction is exclusion from the association. However this happens rarely. More commonly, the rules are in the form of recommendations, which the members are not strictly obliged to follow but often do, because of the prestige and moral authority of their professional body.

It is to be expected that the recommendations of professional audit bodies would have considerable influence on the financial reporting of enterprises. The preparer of the accounts (the enterprise accountant) may lack knowledge and experience of how to deal with complex accounting issues and may turn for advice to the auditor. This is often the case with smaller enterprises. Moreover the auditor may seek to ensure that the accounting principles prescribed by her professional body are applied in the financial statements by threatening to qualify or withhold the audit opinion. However, if the enterprise management resists, the auditor faces a quandary: she is faced with the choice of either disregarding the rules of the professional body or losing the client. The choice is often governed by the consequences of disregarding the professional rules, which are rarely severe.

A distinction should be made between the accountant (who prepares the accounts) and the auditor (who checks them). In some (but not all) European countries, there are professional associations that represent the accountants and they issue recommendations to their members. However their influence is rarely significant, because the accountant's primary responsibility is to her employer (the enterprise) and not to the professional association.

Industrial associations

These are loose associations of enterprises in specific industrial sectors. They often issue guidance to their members on accounting matters, frequently on management accounting, less frequently on financial reporting. There is rarely any attempt to enforce compliance. Nevertheless the industrial association's guidelines may be widely followed in matters specific to the industry because they are perceived as being technically competent and relevant to the particular problems of enterprises in that industry.

Clearly there are many similarities between the rules referred to in this paragraph and standards. In fact the term 'standard' is never applied to the rules issued by stock exchanges and industrial associations. Possibly this is because the term is considered to imply that the rule has a general application, which is not the case with the rules of stock exchanges (only listed corporations) or of industrial associations (only enterprises in the specific sector). However, in the case of rules issued by professional associations of auditors, the term 'standard' is sometimes used, particularly where they are intended to be mandatory on members of the association.

3.8.6 Writings of private individuals

The weakest forms of rule are interpretations and opinions of individuals, such as learned professors and distinguished lawyers, in the form of books and articles. They are binding on no one, unlike the rules of other bodies which may be binding on their members. Nevertheless they may be very influential, particularly where the law is ambiguous or lacking, and these lacunae have not been filled by the issue of rules by a body higher up the hierarchy.

3.8.7 External bodies

In addition to those elements of the regulatory system that were described in the previous sections, there are two bodies that are outside the national system but which set rules that have had an increasingly significant influence over the financial reporting of European companies. They are the European Union (EU) and the International Accounting Standards Board (IASB). Both bodies play a significant role in the overall regulatory system; they are considered further in the succeeding chapters.

3.9 Conclusion

The preceding sections have presented in general terms the various categories of rules that govern financial reporting, and the various bodies that make these rules. In the following chapter, these general concepts are applied to an analysis of the system for the regulation of financial reporting at the national level.

References

Baldwin, R. and McCrudden, C. (1987). *Regulation and Public Law*. London, Weidenfeld & Nicholson.
Baxter, W. (1981). 'Accounting standards – boon or curse?' *Accounting and Business Research* **12**(1): 3–10.
Benston, G. (1976). *Corporate Financial Disclosure in the UK and the USA*. London, D.C. Heath.
Benston, G. (1980). 'The establishment and enforcement of accounting standards: methods, benefits and costs'. *Accounting and Business Research* **11**(1): 51–60.
Blake, J. (1992). 'A classification system for economic consequences issues in accounting regulation'. *Accounting and Business Research* **22**(4): 305 ff.
Bromwich, M. (1992). *Financial Reporting, Information and Capital Markets*. London, Pitman Publishing.
Burggraaff, J. (1983). 'The political dimensions of accounting standard setting in Europe'. *Accounting Standard Setting: An International Perspective*. M. Bromwich and A. Hopwood. London, Pitman: 184.
Ordelheide, D. (1999). 'Germany'. *Accounting Regulation in Europe*. S. McLeay. Basingstoke, Macmillan.
Solomons, D. (1983). 'The political implications of accounting and accounting standard setting'. *Accounting and Business Research* **13**(2): 107–18.

4
The National System for the Regulation of Financial Reporting

This chapter analyses the system for the regulation of financial reporting. Enterprises, in preparing their financial statements, are obliged to follow the rules of the country under whose jurisdiction they fall – in the case of groups, this is the country in which the parent enterprise is registered. In each European country the financial reporting of the enterprises under its jurisdiction is governed by a unique mix of the rules that were analysed in the last chapter: laws, decrees, standards, recommendations and interpretations. The bodies that set these rules are also specific to the country; that is, each country has its own unique system for the regulation of financial reporting. The importance of the bodies varies. In fact, in some European countries, certain categories of bodies are not present; for example, there is no standard-setting body in Ireland. The same applies to rules; for example, the writings of academics have no significant influence in many European countries, and, in fact, were only mentioned in the last chapter, because of their importance in a few countries. Also the authority of the different bodies and of their rules varies from country to country. The different categories of rule-makers will now be considered, beginning with the state.

4.1 The state as rule-maker

In all European countries the most important rule-maker is the state. The three principal functions of the state are:

1. the legislative function, which is fulfilled by the legislature in enacting laws;
2. the executive function, which is performed by the government; it executes the law but also, in fulfilling this function, it makes rules;
3. the judicial function, which enforces compliance with the law through penal sanctions and resolves disputes concerning the law.

All three functions play an important role in all national regulatory systems. But the importance of these functions and, in particular, the way in which they interact, vary considerably across Europe.

4.1.1 Commercial codes

In nine European countries there is a commercial code which sets out in one volume all the laws relating to business, including accounting. These codes, to a greater or lesser extent, trace their origins to the 'Code Napoléon' which was introduced in France in 1807. During the nineteenth century, the countries of Southern Europe, Spain, Portugal, Italy and Greece, all introduced commercial codes following the French model. Also Austria and Switzerland have commercial codes. There are two Northern European countries with commercial codes: Germany (Handelsgesetzbuch) and the Netherlands (Wetboek van Koophandel). In all countries, the commercial code, like all laws, is enacted by the legislature, which periodically passes laws that amend its text.

In the European countries that do not have a commercial code, the law is set out in a series of separate acts of the legislature. Hence in all countries, the law is set out in instruments enacted by the legislature. The principal advantage of a commercial code is one of convenience in that it combines all the laws in one document.

4.1.2 National accounting plans

Four European countries (France, Spain, Portugal and Greece) have a national accounting plan. This is a massive document that sets out in great detail the rules governing the form and content of the financial statements of enterprises, including matters of format, valuation and disclosure. The plan also specifies the accounts to be maintained within the enterprise's accounting system and how particular transactions are to be recorded in these accounts. The use of the plan is, in general, obligatory for certain categories of enterprise.

The following advantages have been claimed for imposing a uniform plan of accounts on all enterprises:[1]

1. It is an indispensable means of standardisation in accounting theory, terminology and practice. As a result, endless misunderstanding, confusion and controversy will be avoided or at least reduced in the management of enterprises, public administration and taxation. It promotes equality between taxpayers by ensuring that they all record expenses and revenues in the same fashion.
2. It allows a uniform approach to the financial management of enterprises, facilitating the application of scientific management.
3. It simplifies both internal and external control (audit) and hence makes accounting fraud more difficult.

4. It facilitates the preparation of national accounts. The calculation of national income is based on measures that are uniform for all enterprises.
5. It simplifies and speeds up the education of accountants.
6. It assures the provision of correct and comparable information for third parties.

Most of these advantages are based on the premise that there exists a best accounting system and that everyone will benefit if all enterprises were to apply it. However some advantages arise simply from the fact of uniformity. The advantages of uniformity and the conflict between uniformity and relevance were discussed in Section 3.5 of the previous chapter.

The intellectual basis for accounting plans was developed in the early years of the last century by a Belgian accountant, Paul Otlet. But it was a German academic, Eugen Schmalenbach, who was most influential in promoting them and Germany was the first country to introduce a national accounting plan, the 'Reichskontenrahmen', in 1937. During the Second World War, France, then under German occupation, developed its own plan, which however was never formally implemented (Standish, 1990). After the war, Germany abolished its plan, as part of a general movement to sweep away the institutions of the former regime, but France, more pragmatically, developed its plan further. In 1947, France introduced the Plan Comptable Général (PCG), which over the years has been substantially modified and expanded, notably in 1957 and 1983. Although the use of the PCG was not made mandatory for enterprises until 1982, in fact it was almost universally applied by French enterprises long before then, principally for tax reasons (see Lande and Scheid, 1999).

The national plans of the other three countries have clearly been influenced by the French PCG; in fact French officials assisted all three countries in developing their plans: Spain's Plan General de Contabilidad (PGC) of 1973 and 1990, Portugal's Plano Oficial de Contabilidade (POC) of 1977 and 1989, and Greece's General Accounting Plan of 1980.

In these four countries, the national accounting plan is the single most important influence over financial reporting. In the other European countries the position is as follows:

- *Germany*: German law does not impose a national accounting plan, for reasons already mentioned. However industrial associations publish accounting plans which are widely used by enterprises. The position in *Austria* and *Switzerland* is similar to that in Germany.
- *Italy*: Given its close proximity to France and the influence of that country on its legal system, it is rather surprising that Italy has no national accounting plan (see Olivero, 1997). However, as in Germany, many enterprises use standardised accounting plans, some based on a plan published by the association of professional accountants.

- *Belgium*: In this country, there is a standard chart of accounts imposed by law on all enterprises (except the smallest). However this specifies only the codes and the titles of the accounts in the enterprise's accounting system. It therefore covers only part (and a relatively unimportant part) of what is included in the national plans of France, Spain, Portugal and Greece.

In the other European countries, in the past, the state did not consider that it was its function to regulate the financial reporting of enterprises in detail and has therefore never considered it appropriate to develop a national accounting plan.

4.1.3 Laws versus decrees

Law is the foundation of all regulatory systems. Under the constitution (whether written or unwritten) of every European country, the authority to make rules that are binding on individual citizens resides with the legislature. However it is common for the legislature to delegate to the government the authority to enact binding rules in specific defined areas. The rules that are issued by the government under this delegated authority are designated by a number of different terms: decrees, orders, regulations, instruments and so on. For simplicity, in this chapter, the term 'decree' is used to cover all forms of binding rules issued by the government.

It is common for the law that is enacted by the legislature to set out the general principles and the more important rules of financial reporting and to include a provision that the government has the authority to issue decrees that set out the detailed rules. This represents a sensible division of tasks, since the legislature has neither the time nor the expertise to deal with the detail of technical matters.

All European countries make use of decrees but to a varying extent. The relative importance of laws (enacted by the legislature) and decrees (issued by the government) may be gauged from an examination of the rules for the implementation into national legislation of the EU's Fourth and Seventh Directives. The EU member states may be classified according to the extent that the rules in these areas are set by law or by decree.

1. In two countries, *Germany* and the *United Kingdom*, virtually all of the rules relating to the implementation of the EU's Fourth and Seventh Directives were set in laws enacted by the legislature: Germany's Bilanzrichtliniengesetz of 1985 and the UK's Companies Acts of 1981 and 1989. There were a very few government decrees, on such relatively minor matters as: the recognition of consolidated accounts of other countries (Konzernabschlußbefreiungs verordnung of 2 October 1991) and the use of the ECU in the accounts (Statutory instrument no. 2452 of 16 November 1992).

2. In three countries, *France, Spain* and *the Netherlands*, there was a relatively balanced use of laws and decrees:

   (a) In *France*, the principal provisions of the Fourth Directive were enacted by the law of 30 April 1983; the remaining details were filled in by the decree of 29 November 1983. The Seventh Directive was implemented by the law of 1 March 1985 and the decree of 17 February 1986.

   (b) In *Spain*, Law 19/1989 which amended the Spanish commercial code was followed by Royal Decree 1564/89 for the Fourth Directive and Royal Decree 1815/91 for the Seventh Directive.

   (c) In *the Netherlands*, Law 663/83 enacted the main provisions of both directives; Decree 665/83 set out the detailed rules for formats and Decree 666/83 those for valuation.

3. In *Denmark* and *Ireland* there has been a movement over time towards a greater use of decrees, the Fourth Directive was implemented in both countries through a law (the Årsregnskabloven of 1981 and the Companies Act of 1986), but the Seventh Directive was implemented by means of a decree – in Ireland entirely (the European Communities – Companies, Group Accounts – Regulation) and in Denmark largely (Årsregnskabs-bekendtgoerelsen). On Ireland, Ole Sørensen remarked, 'the issues were regarded as technical accounting matters of minimal public interest which did not require legislative provision' (see Quinn and Sørensen, 1997). On Denmark's choice of a decree in place of a law, Christiansen commented: 'The implications of this change may be considered either centralistic and undemocratic...or professionally acceptable if the Ministry involves those who use and prepare financial statements in the regulatory process' (Christiansen and Elling, 1993, p. 72).

4. In the remaining countries, *Belgium, Greece, Italy* and *Portugal*, both the principal provisions and the detailed rules relating to the EU directives were enacted by decree. In all cases, the decrees were either based on a previous law which gave the government the necessary authority or were subsequently ratified by the legislature. *Belgium* provides a good example of the relationship between laws and decrees. Almost all the rules relating to financial reporting are set by decrees which are based on the law of 17 July 1975. Article 10 of this law states: 'The King shall prescribe the form and content of the balance sheet, the income statement and the notes required to be filed by law.' Of course the Belgian King knows little of balance sheets; it is the government which acts on his behalf. However the decree has to be signed by the King for it to be valid. Furthermore the law specifies the matters that may be regulated by decree: the balance sheet, the income statement and the notes. For example, if the Belgian government were to issue a decree on the contents of the cash flow statement, this would be declared invalid by the courts of law.

In all European countries it is the practice that the government prepares the draft of any law relating to financial reporting and submits it to the legislature for enactment. It is comparatively rare for the legislature to reject the government's proposed text. Hence it might be felt that the distinction between laws and decrees is more apparent than real – that the texts of both are determined by the government and thus the legislature has no real say. However the legislature has both the power and the opportunity of amending the government's draft law (which it does not infrequently), whereas it is much more difficult or impossible to amend decrees. Hence there is a real distinction between laws and decrees.

4.1.4 Tax regulations

Taxation is an important influence on financial reporting, but there are great variations among the European countries as to the degree of this influence. However two important broad generalisations may be made:

1. *Small and medium-sized enterprises*: In all European countries, the tax rules have a major impact on the accounts of small and medium-sized enterprises. This is because these enterprises prepare formal financial statements principally for tax purposes, that is, as the basis for computing the amount of tax to be paid on profits and/or asset values. These enterprises have no other significant need for financial statements; for example, they do not require them for the purpose of informing their shareholders, as they can do this by more direct and informal means. Financial reporting is an expense to be minimised, which is achieved by preparing only one set of accounts whose principal, even sole, function is the computation of tax.
2. *Consolidated accounts*: The influence of tax rules on the consolidated accounts is far less marked by comparison with their impact on the individual accounts. The reason is that, in general, the taxable entity is the individual corporation – not the group. The figures that are reported in the consolidated accounts do not, as a general rule, have any effect on the amount of tax paid by corporations in the group which is calculated on the basis of their individual accounts. Nevertheless the tax rules may influence the consolidated accounts, because these are an aggregation of the individual accounts, which are, to a greater or lesser extent, influenced by tax. Almost all European countries permit corporations to eliminate the influence of tax for the purposes of the consolidated accounts, but generally only the larger corporations are motivated to do so.

Bearing in mind these general considerations, it is possible to divide the European countries into three groups, depending on whether the influence of taxation on financial reporting is very strong, strong or moderate.

1. *Very strong tax influence: Germany, Austria, Greece, Italy and Portugal*:   In these countries there is a fundamental rule that the amount of tax to be paid is calculated on the basis of the figures in the entity's published financial statements. This rule has the effect that, if an enterprise wishes to claim an expense as a deduction from taxable income, it must record it in its financial statements. Thus the financial statements are distorted by items included solely for fiscal purposes, for example, accelerated depreciation. Similarly all increases in asset values are taxable, unless exempted by special tax rules. Since enterprises seek to minimise the tax payable, assets are only revalued on the basis of tax rules (see Ebbers, 1997). Enterprises, both large and small, draw up their accounts principally with the aim of minimising the tax charge; financial reporting, at least at the level of the individual enterprise accounts, is 'tax-driven'. The position in the two largest countries in this category may be summarised as follows:

   (a) In *Germany*, the basic principle is that the computation of the tax payable is based on the figures in the accounts. This is known as the 'authoritative principle' ('Maßgeblichkeitsprinzip') – the accounts form the authoritative basis for the tax computation. In theory this would seem to imply that the accounting rules 'drive' the tax computation. But the reverse is the reality. The reason is that enterprises draw up their accounts with a view to minimising the tax burden by selecting the options (in both the tax and the accounting rules) that lead to the lowest reported profits. This reverse influence of tax on financial reporting is known as the 'reverse authoritative principle' ('umgekehrtes Maßgeblichkeitsprinzip').

   (b) In *Italy*, the situation is very similar to that in Germany. There is the same general rule that tax is based on the accounts and the same reverse influence of tax. In 1991, an attempt was made to mitigate the impact of tax on the accounts by requiring enterprises to report the tax-driven elements of revenues and expenses in a final section of the profit and loss account known as the fiscal annex. However enterprises complained that the calculations were too complex and the fiscal annex was abolished when the law was revised in 1984. Zambon (1998) judges that 'the effect of this regulation change is that virtually no value in the company income statements is now free from fiscal influence'.

2. *Strong tax influence: Belgium, Finland, France, Spain and Sweden*:   In these five countries, financial reporting in the past was certainly 'tax-driven' but, in recent years, there has been an attempt to reduce the influence of tax. By and large, these efforts have been less than completely successful.

   (a) In *Belgium*, the government has stated that its aim is fiscal neutrality and that in principle the fiscal authorities should accept the financial reporting rules for the purpose of computing taxable income. However, in practice, enterprises still chose, from among the rules acceptable to the tax authorities, those which lead to the lowest profit. Thus enterprises invariably use the completed contract method for valuing long-term contracts and charge depreciation on assets under construction, both of which are accepted by the tax authorities although not generally considered to be the best accounting practice (Jorissen and Block, 1995, p. 397).

(b) In *Finland*, there is a basic rule that taxation is based on the financial accounts. Hence depreciation is commonly reported at the maximum permitted by the tax authorities. Majala (2004) reports that tax law defines many accounting concepts and has a profound influence on the profit and loss account. There are many conflicts between tax law and accounting law, which creates a dilemma for companies that wish to reduce their tax bill.

(c) In *France*, the financial statements still include items of a purely fiscal character, for example accelerated depreciation. However these items have to be shown separately in the accounts, – in the profit and loss account as an exceptional item and, in the balance sheet between equity and provisions. In this way, accounting law seeks to limit or, at least, isolate the impact of tax on the presentation of the financial statements.

(d) In *Spain*, prior to the implementation of the EU's Fourth Directive, financial reporting was strongly 'tax-driven'. But a major change was effected by Law 19/1989 which stated clearly that financial reporting and taxation were mutually independent. Nevertheless tax is still a major influence, particularly in relation to the revaluation of assets. It is the invariable practice of Spanish enterprises to revalue their assets (in their published balance sheet) in accordance with the rules issued periodically by the fiscal authorities.

(e) In *Sweden*, there is a general prescription that tax should be based on the commercial accounts. However, in recent years, the question of whether financial accounting and financial reporting should be separated has been widely discussed. There have been three committee reports on the subject: the first in 1987 decided that the advantages of maintaining the tax link outweighed the disadvantages; however, two later reports (in 1991 and 1995) came to the opposite conclusion. But, at the time of writing, the law has not been changed.

3. *Moderate tax influence: Denmark, Ireland, the Netherlands and the UK*: In these countries there is no formal rule that, for an expense to be tax deductible, it must be recorded in the accounts. However undoubtedly all except the larger corporations chose the rules that are acceptable to the fiscal authorities in drawing up their accounts. This facilitates the computation of tax and simplifies the negotiations with the authorities.

Furthermore, in Denmark, taxation also influences the financial statements in that many enterprises restate the value of land and building in their accounts at the values periodically determined by the fiscal authorities.

4.1.5   The courts of law

In all countries, the courts of law deal with cases involving the financial statements of enterprises. In their judgments the courts often deliver interpretations on points of law that are unclear and these judgments become a source of law for enterprises, which naturally do not want to prepare accounts that may be found by the courts to be invalid. Hence, in principle, the courts should be an important rule-maker. However, it would seem that in only three European countries have the courts been particularly active in issuing judgments in cases involving financial reporting.

The Netherlands

This country is unique in having a special court solely for company law cases: the Ondernemingskamer (OK). Buijink (1999) characterises the OK as 'the element providing "official closure" in Dutch financial reporting regulation'. This court has issued judgments that have influenced financial reporting in the Netherlands, for example in accepting that deferred tax may be an asset. However in the thirty years of its existence, the OK has ruled on only some fifty cases involving financial reporting and the number of cases has declined in recent years. It would seem that plaintiffs are reluctant to take cases to the OK because of the high costs and the delays involved. Hence the OK has not fulfilled all that was expected of it when it was set up in 1973.

Germany

In this country, the Bundesfinanzhof, the Federal Tax Court, has issued a number of judgments that interpret the principles of regular accounting that underlie both financial reporting and taxation. The regular commercial courts rarely deal with cases involving accounts. This would seem to confirm the assessment made in the previous section that taxation is a very strong influence on financial reporting in this country.

Italy

In Italy the courts occasionally rule on financial reporting matters. Olivero (1997) refers to a judgment of the Tribunal of Bologna, which cancelled the financial statements of a enterprise because full information had not been given. However, from the facts given of this case, it would seem that the Italian courts base their judgments almost entirely on the observance of formalities. Riccaboni (1999) gives details of a number of court judgments which have clarified the law.

4.1.6 Common Law versus Roman Law

Nobes and Parker (2002) suggest that a major factor of influence over financial reporting is a country's legal system, particularly whether it is based on Common Law or Roman Law. An analysis of the situation in Europe does not confirm this proposition. There would appear to be very little difference in the role that law plays in the regulatory system of Great Britain (a Common Law country) compared with Germany (a Roman Law country). In both countries the statute law regulates financial reporting to very much the same degree of detail. The Companies Act is very similar to the Handelsgesetzbuch. Furthermore the courts in Britain have played hardly any role in developing the law on financial reporting through decided cases – the defining characteristic of Common Law. There have been virtually no cases in the last hundred years on the detailed rules of financial reporting such as the valuation of assets or the calculation of profits, whereas there have been a number of influential cases on auditing, particularly on the liability of the auditor. It would seem that judges feel more confident on questions of liability than they are on valuation.

4.2 Standard-setting bodies

Standard-setting bodies are a central element of the regulatory system in most countries and a full understanding of their role and functioning is also central to a comprehension of the whole system.

4.2.1 Data

The principal standard-setting bodies of the European countries as at the end of 2003 are listed in Exhibit 4.1. which gives, for each official body, its name (in both the original language and an English translation), the initials by which it is invariably known, the date of the body's foundation and, where applicable, the founding date of the earliest predecessor body. This gives an indication of how long the body has been involved in the country's rule-making process. France led the way in setting up the first standard-setting body in any European country in 1947: the Conseil Supérieur de la Comptabilité, later to be transformed into the Conseil National de la Comptabilité (CNC). France was followed a generation later, in the decade 1965–75 by Spain, the UK, Finland, Italy, the Netherlands and Belgium. There were further foundations in the 1980s involving Denmark, Greece, Norway, Portugal, Sweden and Switzerland. The most recent foundations were the Deutsche Rechnungslegung Standards Committee (DRSC) founded in 1998 and the Organismo Italiano de Contabiltà (OIC), founded in 2001. There are two countries missing from the list: Ireland and Austria. In these countries, there is no institution that may reasonably be described as a standard-setting body.

Exhibit 4.1 National standard-setting bodies

Country	Initials	Title (English translation)	Date of foundation	Status
Belgium	CBN/ CNC	Commissie voor Boekhoudkundige Normen/Commission des Normes Comptables (Accounting Standards Commission)	1975	State body
Denmark	RR	Regnskabsrådet (Accountancy council)	1994	State body
Denmark	RP	Regnskabspanelet (Accounting panel)	1992 1988*	Private body
Finland	KILA	Kirjanpitolautakunta (Accounting Standards Board)	1974	State body
France	CNC	Conseil National de Comptabilité (National accountancy council)	1957 1947*	State body
Germany	DRSC	Deutsche Rechnungslegung Standards Committee (German Accounting Standards Committee)	1998	Hybrid body
Greece	ESL	Ethniko Sumvoulio Logistikis (National council of accounting)	1988	State body
Italy	CSPC	Commissione per la statuizone dei principi contabili (Commission for the establishment of accounting principles)	1975	Private body
Italy	OIC	Organismo Italiano de Contabilità (Italian Accountancy Body)	2001	Hybrid body
Netherlands	RJ	Raad voor de Jaarverslaggeving (Council for annual reporting)	1983 1971*	Hybrid body
Norway	NRS	Norsk Regnskapsstiftelse (Norwegian Accounting Foundation)	1989	Private body
Portugal	CNC	Comissâo de Normalizaçâo Contabilística (Accounting standardization commission)	1983	State body
Spain	ICAC	Instituto de Contabilidad y Auditoria de Cuentas (Accounting and Audit Institute)	1988 1965*	State body
Spain	AECA	Asociación Española de Contabilidad (Spanish accounting association)	1979	Private body
Sweden	RR	Redovisningsrådet (Auditing Council)	1989	Private body
Switzerland	FER	Fachkommission für Empfehlungen zur Rechnungslegung (Commission for Accounting Recommendations)	1984	Private body
United Kingdom	ASB	Accounting Standards Board	1990 1970*	Hybrid body

* = Date of foundation of the earliest previous similar body.

Exhibit 4.1 also indicates the body's status. Seven of the seventeen are state bodies which were set up under the authority of a law or decree. The state is ultimately responsible for the standard-setting body in that it:

- sets its objectives;
- defines its powers;
- provides its funds;
- appoints the members of its governing organ.

However there are ten bodies that are not purely state bodies. In Exhibit 4.1, four have been designated hybrid bodies, that is partly state, partly private: they are Italy's OIC, the Netherlands' RJ, the UK's ASB and Germany's DRSC. In the case of both the RJ and the ASB, the state provides some of the finance: the Sociaal-Economische Raad, a Dutch state body, provides two-thirds of the RJ's budget; the British government pays approximately one-third of the costs of the ASB. The British government also nominates the chairman and three deputy chairmen of the Financial Reporting Council, the ASB's supervisory body. However neither the Financial Reporting Council nor the Dutch equivalent, the Foundation for Annual Reporting, are public bodies. Germany's DRSC is a private body, but is officially recognised by the state for the three functions of recommending the accounting principles for consolidated accounts, of advising on changes to laws on accounting and of representing Germany on the IASB. Italy's OIC is formally a private foundation; however the government accountant's office is represented on its governing council, and both the ministry of justice and the ministry of economics send observers to its executive committee.

Six are purely private bodies, which to a certain degree perform public functions. All six (Denmark's RP, Italy's CSPC, Norway's NRS, Spain's AECA, Sweden's RR and Switzerland's FER) were set up largely at the initiative of the national accountancy profession. Both Switzerland's FER and Norway's NRS are the only standard-setting bodies in their respective countries; hence here standard-setting is entirely a private matter. However the Swiss government supports the FER and sends non-voting observers to its meetings. Sweden's Redovisningsrådet was in the past a hybrid body but is now a purely private body. However it is given a limited degree of recognition by the state, since its operations are supervised by a government agency. Both Denmark's RP and Spain's AECA are private bodies that were 'trial-blazers' for standard-setting in these countries, in that, when they were founded, they were the sole body but have since been superseded by state bodies. However they are still influential.

4.2.2   The rules issued by standard-setting bodies

Exhibit 4.2 presents information about the rules issued by the more important standard-setting bodies.[2] These rules are given a wide variety of terms. In

Exhibit 4.2   The standard-setting bodies' rules

Country	Body	Title of the rule	Backed by the law?	Endorsed by the stock exchange?	Authority of the rule
Belgium	CBC/CNC	Avis	No	No	W
Finland	KILA	Instruction	No	No	W
France	CNC	Avis	No	No	MS
Germany	DRSC	Standard	Yes	No	S
Greece	ESL	Opinion	Yes	Yes	MS
Italy	CSPC	Princip 1	No	Yes	W
Netherlands	RJ	Richtlijnen	No	No	MS
Portugal	CNC	Directrez	No	Yes	W
Spain	ICAC	Resolution	Yes (weak)	Yes	MS
Sweden	RR	Recommendation	No	Yes	MS
Switzerland	FER	Empfehlung	No	Yes	MS
UK	ASB	Standard	Yes (weak)	Yes	S

Key: S = strong; MS = moderately strong; W = weak.

fact, the term 'standard' is used only for the rules issued by the UK's ASB and Germany's DRSC,[3] but is used in this book generally to designate the rules issued by standard-setting bodies. In general, the rules issued by standard-setting bodies have the status of recommendations which are not legally binding. However there would appear to be two exceptions to this general rule.

1. *Greece*: Under Law 1819/1988 the auditors of a enterprise's accounts are obliged to check the correct application of the provisions of the Greek accounting plan (imposed by a government decree) and of the opinions of the National Council of Accounting. Hence these opinions are backed by the law.
2. *Spain*: In principle, the president of ICAC has the authority (granted under Royal Decree 1643/1990) to issue rules, in the form of a resolution of ICAC, that are binding on enterprises. However, in 1994, the Spanish superior court of justice ruled that a resolution of ICAC was invalid because, under the Spanish constitution, only Parliament and ministers may issue rules that are binding on persons (see the discussion on this very interesting case in Lande, 1997).
   The Spanish rule seems to apply throughout the EU (except apparently in Greece). Legally binding rules can be issued only by the legislature and by persons (such as ministers) to whom the legislature has specifically delegated this power. However, although the rules issued by standard-setting bodies do not generally have the force of law, they are

nevertheless widely observed by enterprises. The reasons may be analysed as follows:

(a) *Acceptance by the courts*: In all European countries, the law, in addition to laying down certain specific rules, sets out broad general principles that must be respected in the financial statements. Thus, according to the UK's Companies Act, the accounts must give 'a true and fair view'; in the Netherlands, the equivalent phrase is 'give, in accordance with norms that are acceptable in the economic and social climate, an insight...'. There are similar legal provisions in all the other EU countries, based on article 2 of the EU's Fourth Directive. The statute law does not define further what is 'a true and fair view'. The final word on whether an enterprise's accounts comply with this legal requirement lies with the courts of law, where the judges have to decide on the substance to be given to the general principle. Since judges are rarely experts in financial reporting, they will commonly make their judgement on the basis of evidence of what is recommended by persons and organisations that are generally regarded as experts in the field and have a reputation for competence and integrity. In these circumstances it is to be expected that the courts would give weight to the recommendations issued by a standard-setting body, particularly one set up or recognised by the state.

The source of the authority of the standards issued by the UK's ASB is essentially of this nature. Under the UK's Companies Act, the directors of large companies must state whether the accounts have been prepared in accordance with applicable accounting standards, together with details of, and reasons for, any material departures. The ASB has been prescribed as a standard-setting body for this purpose by a decree of the British government (statutory instrument 1990 no.1667). It should be noted that the degree of official recognition of the ASB is rather weak. There is no formal legal obligation placed on the directors of British companies to respect the ASB's standards. They have the right to disregard them, but then they must disclose the non-compliance and give their reasons. However most British companies feel obliged to apply the ASB's standards, given that there is a legal obligation for the accounts to present 'a true and fair view' and given that it seems very likely that the courts of law would accept the ASB's evidence on the meaning of this phrase. In effect the ASB's standards become a source of law. A leading British lawyer has summarised the position in the following terms: '...an accounting standard which the court holds must be complied with to meet the true and fair requirement becomes a source of law in the widest sense of the term' (Arden, 1993). The authority of the standards of the DRSC, the

German standard-setting body, is also remarkably strong. There are three important points that should be made concerning the DRSC's standards:

(a) They apply only to the consolidated accounts of listed companies. They have no impact on the individual accounts, in view of the importance of the latter for tax and dividends.
(b) They may not be contrary to German law (the HGB) or the EU's directives.
(c) They only enter into effect after they have been published by the Ministry of Justice. In effect the ministry has a power of veto over the standards.

However once they have been so published, they are considered to be authoritative interpretations of GoB.[4] Hence in principle they have very considerable authority in respect of the limited set of accounts to which they apply: the consolidated accounts of listed enterprises. Since its foundation, the DRSC has been very active in issuing standards; at the time of writing it has issued some thirty standards.

(b) *Endorsement by the stock exchange*: The stock exchange authorities may insist that the financial statements of listed corporations are prepared in conformity with the rules issued by specific standard-setting bodies and can ensure compliance by threatening to suspend the quotation of the shares of any corporation that does not conform. As Exhibit 4.2 shows, the stock exchange authorities of most countries have endorsed in this way the rules set by the state and hybrid bodies; the principal exception is the Netherlands. This endorsement is probably the single most powerful force that acts to secure the observance of the standards issued by these bodies. Of course this is effective only in respect of listed corporations.

(c) *Convenience*: The accountant who prepares an enterprise's financial statements will first turn to the law for guidance. Where the law is deficient, the accountant will rarely be prepared to develop her own personal rule and is much more likely to follow a rule that has been developed by some other organisation. This has four advantages: it saves intellectual effort (it is not easy to develop a rule that deals in a logical and consistent manner with all aspects of a problem); it avoids the accountant being held personally responsible; it avoids arguments with the auditor; and it increases the chances that the rule is accepted by the courts (the judge is unlikely to be very impressed by a rule supported by only one person).

Exhibit 4.2 includes in the right-most column the author's appreciation of the authority attached to standards, that is the extent to which enterprises respect the rule in drawing up their accounts. The authority is assessed as strong or moderately strong in the case of eight bodies and weak for only three. The general level of authority is assessed as being remarkably high, considering that only in the case of Greece do the rules have the force of law. However, in all countries, the level of compliance with the standards is higher for larger enterprises than for the smaller enterprises, which often disregard them, sometimes out of ignorance and sometimes because they consider them to be irrelevant. This assessment also indicates that the name given to the rule can be misleading. The Greek body's 'opinions' carry far more authority than the Portuguese body's 'directrez' despite the very prescriptive impression given by the latter term.

4.2.3 The composition of the standard-setting bodies

Exhibit 4.3 analyses the composition of the each standard-setting body according to whether the people who make up its decision-making organ (the body the sets the standards) represent:

- the preparers of accounts: enterprises, banks, industrial associations, state corporations and so on;
- the audit profession;
- the users: the shareholders and their advisers (financial analysts), the workers and their representatives (the trade unions);
- the government: ministries, state agencies and so on;
- the stock exchange: the capital market authority, stock brokers and so on;
- independent experts: university professors, lawyers and so on.

The analysis is made on the basis of the group that the person represents, not on his/her qualification or position. For example, where the users appoint qualified accountants to represent them, the persons so appointed are classified in Exhibit 4.3 under the column 'Users' and not under the column 'Auditors'. In some cases the standard-setting body's constitution specifies which groups the members of its decision-making organ are to represent. In other cases, the members of the decision-making body are appointed by a committee on which the different constituencies are represented. In that case the proportions in that body are used. Where neither is the case (as with the UK's ASB and Germany's DRSC), the allocation in Exhibit 4.3 has been done on the basis of the member's main occupation, and, in the case of full time members, of their previous occupation.

The size of the standard-setting decision-making organ varies from 7 persons for Germany's DRSC to 58 persons for France's CNC. The information in Exhibit 4.3 has been presented in the form of percentages in order to ease comprehension.

The last row in Exhibit 4.3 shows that very broadly, on average, the standard-setting bodies are composed of one-third preparers, one-third audit profession, and the remainder split between the other parties. However there are wide

Exhibit 4.3 The composition of the standard-setting bodies

Country	Body	Total members	Preparers (%)	Audit profession (%)	Users (%)	Government (%)	Stock exchange (%)	Individual (%)
Belgium	CBC/CNC	14	21	14	14	50	0	0
Denmark	RR	23	43	9	35	9	0	4
Denmark	RP	8	38	25	38	0	0	0
France	CNC	58	41	17	10	21	2	9
Finland	KILA	12	25	25	0	33	0	17
Germany	DRSC	7	43	43	14	0	0	0
Greece	ESL	23	43	9	0	22	0	26
Italy	CSPC	28	0	82	0	0	4	14
Italy	OIC	15	33	40	13	7	7	0
Netherlands	RJ	13	31	38	31	0	0	0
Norway	NRS	5	20	20	20	0	20	20
Portugal	CNC	38	32	21	0	21	3	24
Spain	ICAC	12	0	50	0	50	0	0
Spain	AECA	13	23	38	8	23	0	8
Sweden	RR	9	44	33	0	0	0	22
Switzerland	FER	23	48	22	22	0	0	9
UK	ASB	9	44	44	11	0	0	0
Average			30	31	13	14	2	10

variation between countries. Thus users are strongly represented in Denmark, the Netherlands, Norway and Switzerland; in fact in the other countries the users make up, on average, only 5 per cent of the board. The most consistently represented group are the preparers; only in Italy's CSPC and Spain's ICAC is their representation less than 20 per cent. In all but two of the seventeen standard-setting bodies listed in Exhibit 4.3, the preparers and the audit profession together make up 50 per cent or more of the decision-making body.

It would seem that, to a greater or lesser extent, the official standard-setting bodies have succumbed to 'regulatory capture', which has been defined as 'the process whereby agencies created in the public interest are subverted to the ends of those supposed to be regulated' (Baldwin and McCrudden, 1987). The group that is most strongly represented are the preparers; the weakest are the users. Where a relatively small group of persons are strongly affected by proposed rules, it may be expected that it will make great efforts to influence the rule-making process with the aim of ensuring that the promulgated rules are to its liking; this is the case with the preparers. However where the group is large and dispersed, and the impact of the rules on each individual group member is weak, then few will make the necessary effort. The preparers, a relatively compact and well-organised group, have succeeded in establishing themselves in a strong position in the rule-making process. On the other hand, the users, dispersed and disorganised, have far less influence.

Over time, in certain European countries, one can discern two tendencies concerning the composition and status of the standard-setting bodies:

1. from being dominated by the accountancy profession to a wider membership, involving other parties such as preparers and users;
2. from purely private bodies to bodies that are given some form of recognition by the state.

For example in the UK, the ASSC, a private body which was dominated by the audit profession, has been superseded by the ASB, a hybrid body on which the auditors are in a minority. Similar developments have occurred in Spain, where the focus of standard-setting has shifted from the AECA (private) to the ICAC (public), in Italy (from the CSPC to the OIC) and in Denmark (from the accountancy profession to the RR).

4.2.4   The 'free riders': Austria and Ireland

There are two European countries that are missing from the list of national standard-setting bodies: Austria and Ireland. They have the common characteristic that their financial reporting is strongly influenced by powerful neighbours: in Austria's case, Germany, and for Ireland, Britain.

1. Austria's financial reporting law, as set out in its commercial code, is virtually identical to Germany's Handelsgesetzbuch. This reflects both

the strong commercial and legal ties between the two countries but also the fact that both incorporate the provisions of the EU directives. The advantages that Austrian accountants derive from this situation have been summarised by an Austrian academic in the following terms: 'As far as company law is concerned, the historical closeness to German commercial law has been advantageous since there is a rich source of jurisdiction and reference works available to deal with numerous problems of interpretation. In a small economic region this resource for problem-solving could only be developed gradually.' (Nowotny, quoted in Merkl, 2004).

2. The position in Ireland is similar. Until 1921, Ireland was part of the UK and governed from London. Thus the British Companies Act applied equally in Ireland. After Ireland gained its independence, it could see little advantage in going its own way in the field of financial reporting, given the close commercial ties between the two countries and the remarkably friendly relationship between the national professional accountancy associations, which each recognised the other's qualification. Hence Ireland tended to adopt the rules developed in Britain, albeit with a certain delay; for example, the Irish Companies Act of 1963 was virtually identical to the British Companies Act of 1948. This habit has continued to the present day. Irish companies are obliged to follow the standards set by the ASB, the British standard-setting body.

4.3   Other bodies

As noted in Section 3.8.5, three other bodies are particularly important in the field of financial reporting:

1. the stock exchanges;
2. professional associations;
3. industrial associations.

4.3.1   The stock exchanges

The authorities that govern the stock exchanges of the European countries all issue rules relating to obligations of listed enterprises. However, in the field of financial reporting, these authorities generally prefer to endorse rules issued by some other body rather than to develop their own detailed rules. Commonly they require that listed corporations draw up their accounts in accordance with the national law and with the standards of the national standard-setting body. This is the case in Denmark, Italy, Greece, Spain, Switzerland and the UK (see Section 4.2.2). For example, the London Stock Exchange requires that the accounts of listed corporations be prepared in accordance with their national law and, in all material respects, with United Kingdom, United States or International accounting standards. In Italy, CONSOB, by resolution 1079 of 1989, requires that listed corporations follow the accounting principles of the CSPC, as long as they do not conflict with the law. On the other hand, the Amsterdam stock exchange has conspicuously declined to require that listed corporations comply with the RJ's guidelines.

In *France*, the Commission des Opérations de Bourse (COB) has had a major impact on the financial reporting of listed corporations, particularly in requiring the preparation of consolidated accounts long before this was a legal requirement. From 1970, it demanded consolidated accounts from corporations that raised new capital, with the effect that, by 1983, over 300 corporations (75 per cent of all listed corporations) were publishing consolidated accounts, although not legally obliged to do so (Pham, 1993). Although the COB has formal powers to issue regulations that are binding on listed corporations, it has made little use of them, preferring to work through the CNC, where great weight is given to its views, and to issue recommendations which, despite their non-binding character, are treated by listed corporations with great respect.

4.3.2 Professional associations

The associations of auditors and accountants influence the regulatory process in two rather different ways:

1. *Membership of official standard-setting bodies*: As shown in Exhibit 4.3, the audit profession *as such* is represented on all standard-setting bodies and, in many, is the single most important group. However, probably of greater significance is that many of the persons that represent other groups, such as the users or preparers, are qualified auditors or accountants; for example, of the 13 members of the Netherlands' RJ, no less than 11 are members of NIVRA, the Dutch professional body.
2. *Issue of recommendations*: It is common for the professional bodies of accountants, such as Germany's Institut der Wirtschaftprüfer (IdW), to issue recommendations to their members. This is also the case in Italy, Sweden and Switzerland. However in the other countries, the professional associations prefer to work through the official standard-setting bodies. This is essentially the case in Belgium, Greece, Ireland, the Netherlands, Portugal and the UK.

The countries of Western Europe differ considerably in the importance of their local accountancy profession and hence in the influences that it exercises over the regulatory process. This subject is dealt with in the Annex to this chapter. The relative importance of the national accountancy profession may be gauged from two pieces of data given in the Annex's Exhibit 4.5: its size (as measured by the number of qualified accountants per million inhabitants) and its seniority (as measured by its foundation date). On the basis of both measures the British profession is the most important in Europe. The British profession is enormous; with 311,000 members it makes up almost two-thirds (63 per cent) of Western Europe's qualified accountants. Only Italy with 81,000 qualified accountants (16 per cent of the European total) comes close to matching Britain. The professional associations of the two other large European countries (France and Germany) were founded much later than those of Britain and Italy, and by comparison are tiny. The number of accountants per million inhabitants is 324 in France and 219 in Germany, compared with 5241 in Britain. This disparity has two effects: the British accountancy profession is far more influential in Britain than the French profession is in France (similarly with the other European countries); and at the European level, the British profession overshadows its Continental counterparts.

4.3.3   Industrial associations

Associations that represent the preparers of accounts are an important element of the regulatory system in most EU countries. As shown in Exhibit 4.3, they are strongly represented on most standard-setting bodies. In addition, in Germany and Italy there is a strong tradition of industrial associations issuing recommendations on accounting matters to their members:

1. *Germany*: The associations of enterprises in particular industrial sectors periodically issue statements on accounting matters. An example is the Chemical Industry Association (Verband der Chemischen Industrie). These statements are quite influential, because they are perceived as being particularly relevant to enterprises in the industry.
2. *Italy*: ASSONIME, the association of Italian enterprises, issues interpretations of legal texts; these are listed in Riccaboni (1999). Olivero (1997) considers that they are influential actors in the standardisation process.

4.4   Individuals

Although in all European countries individuals, such as leading lawyers and university professors, publish their personal interpretations of the laws on financial reporting in the form of books and articles, in only one country are these writings so influential that they may be considered to be an important element of the regulatory process. That country is Germany. Ordelheide has analysed the situation in the following terms: '...the interpretation of German accounting law is a matter of subtle interplay between the bureaucracy, including the courts, and the market. Commentary on the law by experts is largely organised as an information market. The sellers in this market are lawyers, accountants, experts from business and academics. The direct buyers are the publishers of widely read specialist journals and...of very comprehensive commentaries and handbooks on accounting law. The majority of these contributions to the literature...deal with the interpretation of accounting law. First, legal interpretations clarify the meaning of rules that are an explicit part of the law, for example the definition of acquisition cost. In addition, solutions are developed concerning accounting problems that are not explicitly dealt with in the law, such as foreign currency translation or lease accounting. Finally, legal interpretation includes the adaptation of law to newly emerging conditions. The solutions are evolved through juridical interpretation of the principles enunciated in the law. The system of legal interpretation makes the legal system flexible and adaptable. Consistency among the multitude of rules is assured by the need for the interpretations to be compatible with the law' (Ordelheide, 1995, p. 1561).

It is no accident that the 'market for interpretations' developed in a country that, until recently, has no official standard-setting body. It is clear that, in Germany, the three tasks of standards – to interpret the law, to expand the law and to supplement the law – were fulfilled largely through the writings of private individuals, supplemented by the IdW's recommendations.

4.5 The relative importance of laws, standards and other rules

The relative importance of laws, standards and other rules may be assessed as follows:

1. *Laws*: There is no dispute that, as shown in the hierarchy presented in the previous chapter, law has the greatest authority. However the first laws to deal with financial reporting were generally very brief, setting out an obligation for enterprises to prepare accounts with no indication as to their form and content. From this minimal position, the law has gradually become increasingly prescriptive and detailed. More and more obligations have been imposed by the law on enterprises, covering the following matters:

   (a) Which financial statements have to be prepared. In many countries initially the sole legal requirement was to prepare a balance sheet. The obligation to prepare a profit and loss account came later. And recently in certain countries, the law has added further statements to the list, for example in Germany the cash flow statement.
   (b) The contents of these statements. Initially the law was silent on this matter, but gradually the items that had to be included were defined in detail, culminating in the introduction into the law of the detailed specification of the formats to be used for the balance sheet and the profit and loss account.
   (c) The accounting principles to be followed for the preparation of the financial statements, including not only the general principle (such as 'true and fair view' in Britain and 'good accounting practice' in Scandinavia) but also detailed rules of asset valuation and revenue recognition.

(d) The requirement to have the financial statements audited. In many countries this obligation dates from the first company laws, but without any detail on such matters as the auditor's qualifications, his powers, the points to be covered by the audit and the audit report. Gradually over time, the law in most countries has been extended to cover these matters.

(e) The extent to which the financial statements have to be made available to persons outside the enterprise. Whereas initially the enterprise was required to issue its financial statements only to persons connected with the enterprise (such as shareholders, directors and, in certain countries, creditors), now it is a general obligation of all except the smallest enterprises to make their accounts available for all.

Exhibit 4.4 illustrates how the law was extended to cover more and more matters in one European country: Britain. The burst of legislative activity in the 1980s can be attributed to the need to implement the EU's directives. All the European countries that are covered in this chapter (except Switzerland) were subject to the same obligation, resulting in a very substantial increase in the quantity and detail of financial reporting law throughout the Continent.

2. *Standards*: The same explosion in quantity that has been observed in financial reporting law, also occurred with standards, with the important qualification that the standard-setting process started much later. This is very clear from Exhibit 4.1 which shows the date of the foundation of each country's first standard-setting body. To take the example of Britain,

Exhibit 4.4   The relentless growth of British Company Law

Date of Companies Act	Principal additional requirements
1900	Balance sheet to be presented to shareholders
	Balance sheet to be audited by an auditor
1907	Public companies to file balance sheets with the Companies Registry
1928	Limited specification of the content of the balance sheet
	Profit and loss account to be presented to shareholders
1947	Consolidated balance sheet and profit and loss account (limited specification of contents)
	Accounts must give 'a true and fair view'
	Auditor must be a qualified professional
1967	All companies to file accounts with the Companies Registry, where they could be examined by any person
1981	Individual accounts: prescribed formats and valuation rules, as specified in the EU's Fourth Directive
1989	Consolidated accounts: prescribed formats and valuation rules, as specified in the EU's Seventh Directive.

before 1970 there were no standards; currently the poor British accountant is faced with over thirty standards, not counting lesser rules, such as the numerous abstracts of the Urgent Issues Task Force, which provide authoritative interpretations of these standards. The same inflation has occurred with the amount of detail in individual standards. The first British standard issued in 1971 had only four pages. One of the latest ASB standards, FRS 19 on deferred tax, has over fifty pages. Currently the ASB's standards take up over a thousand pages. This mass of detailed prescriptive rules has had a profound influence on the nature of the accountant's craft. Previously she used her skill and judgement in applying general principles to the specific problem of the preparation of the enterprise's accounts. Now it is more a question of applying the rules; the accountant's skill is knowing where to find the appropriate rule in the mass of standards. Other European countries have suffered very much the same fate as Britain. For example, Germany, which before 1998 had not a single standard, now has thirty. Since its foundation in 1998, the DRSC, the German standard-setting body has worked hard to bring Germany up to date in this field.

3. *Other rules*: As laws and standards have increased in importance, the rules of other bodies have tended to become less significant. Basically the function of these other rules is to fill in gaps in the rules of bodies higher up the hierarchy. However, as the detail of laws and standards has expanded, there are fewer gaps. For example, before the recent explosion in the output of standard-setting bodies, the recommendations of the professional accountancy bodies were the principal source of guidance for the accountant who needed help with the application of general principles. Now these recommendations have lost much of their relevance and, in many countries, the professional bodies have largely withdrawn from this activity. Similarly, in the past, the stock exchange was a major source of financial reporting rules. Now they tend to leave this task to the standard-setting bodies, by insisting that listed companies should follow their standards. However there are still a few stock exchange rules that cover points not covered in the law or standards; for example, the London Stock Exchange requires listed companies to provide a summary of the last ten years' profits, whereas the requirement in the law is for only two years.

4.6 The historical development of financial reporting

In very broad and general terms the development of financial reporting in the European countries may be summarised as follows:

1. In the beginning the state through the first company laws set a very general framework and left it to businessmen to fill in the details. Somewhat later, the laws were extended to require that the accounts be audited and the auditing profession was developed to fulfil this task.

2. Gradually, over time, the auditing profession grew in numbers, in status and in competence. It built up a fund of knowledge and experience of what it considered to be good professional practice concerning the form and content of financial statements. The general public and the state began to recognise the auditing profession as the experts in financial reporting matters.

3. The auditing profession began to codify best professional practice in the form of standards.

4. Over time, the financial statements gained in economic and social importance, notably in fulfilling needs other than simply the computation of taxable income and distributable profit. Gradually the investment function of accounts (that is the provision of information to suppliers of finance, see Chapter 2) became the most important function of financial statements, at least in the case of the larger enterprises.

5. As more and more elements in society and in the economy began to be affected by and therefore interested in the financial statements, the auditing profession's monopoly over setting the detailed rules of financial reporting was called into question. It was considered inappropriate that a private body should be the sole judge on matters that affected the well-being of large sections of society.

6. The confrontation between the auditing profession and other groups with an interest in financial reporting provoked two reactions:

   (a) The state increased the amount of detail concerning the form and content of financial statements that was set down in the law. There has been a remarkable shift from accounting practice to specific legal provisions as the basis for the detail of financial reporting.

   (b) The auditing profession was compelled to share the function of etting the standards of financial reporting with other groups in society.

   Both of these moves represented a relative loss of the auditing profession's power to control the form and content of financial statements. The state and the other groups that had an interest in financial reporting decided that 'accounting is too important to be left to the accountants'.

4.7   Concluding remarks: the diversity of national systems

The subject matter of this chapter has been the regulatory system at the level of the individual country. The national system is important because financial reporting in Europe is regulated at the national level. European enterprises are required to follow the rules of the country under whose jurisdiction they fall – in the case of groups, this is the country in which the parent enterprise is registered. Since each country has its own unique system, the result is considerable diversity in the financial reporting of European enterprises. Diversity, not only in accounting but in other fields, such as culture, is one of the most attractive features of Europe. However it also has its drawbacks. The following chapters analyse the disadvantages of diversity and examine the activities of two organisations that seek to overcome them: the European Union and the International Accounting Standards Board.

Annex: The accountancy profession of Western Europe

Exhibit 4.5 presents certain data relating to the accountancy profession of the seventeen West European countries covered in this chapter, notably:

Exhibit 4.5   The accountancy profession of Western Europe

Country	Date of foundation (note 1)	Number of qualified accountants (note 2)	Accountants per million inhabitants	Proportion in practice (note 3) (%)
Austria	1932	6,176	762	100
Belgium	1953	3,957	388	58
Denmark	1912	4,944	933	87
Finland	1925	1,785	343	100
France	1935	19,200	324	83
Germany	1932	17,970	219	100
Greece	1955	1,244	117	95
Ireland	1888	16,094	4,235	36
Italy	1585	81,000	1,409	87
Luxembourg	1984	267	668	100
Netherlands	1895	13,000	818	40
Norway	1930	2,973	661	85
Portugal	1930	764	76	90
Spain	1942	5,795	145	53
Sweden	1923	4,637	418	100
Switzerland	1925	3,000	417	100
United Kingdom	1853	311,301	5,241	27
Total		493,150		
Average of the seventeen countries				
: mean	1926	29,000	1,010	78
: median	1925	5,795	418	90

Notes: 1. Date of foundation of first association of accountants. 2. Members of accountancy associations affiliated with the International Federation of Accountants (IFAC). 3. Proportion of qualified accountants who are in professional practice (as opposed to retired or in employment in industry, commerce, administration or teaching).

1. *The date of foundation of the first association of accountants*: The first association of accountants was the Collegio dei Rasonatii which was founded in Venice in 1588. However the Collegio ceased to exist with the dissolution of the Venetian Republic in 1797. Hence the Scots claim that their body, the Institute of Chartered Accountants of Scotland, which traces its origin to the Society of Accountants of Edinburgh (founded in 1853) is the oldest body that is still in existence. Other associations that can trace their origins to the nineteenth century are those of Ireland and the Netherlands. They were followed, in the first three decades of the twentieth century by the Scandinavian countries and Switzerland. The two largest West European countries were comparatively late in organising their professions: Germany in 1932 and France in 1935. The last countries to act were Belgium (1953), Greece (1955) and Luxembourg (1984).

2. *The number of qualified accountants*: Exhibit 4.5 gives the number of members of associations that are affiliated to the International Federation of Accountants (IFAC). There is no generally agreed definition of the term 'qualified accountant' but that used here has the advantage of being based on the body that is generally recognised as representing the accountancy profession at the international level.

3. *Accountants per million inhabitants*: This statistic enables the reader to assess the relative importance of the accountancy profession in each country. For example, in Austria there are 6176 qualified accountants in a population of 8.1 million, giving 762 accountants per million inhabitants. Austria is below the average of the seventeen countries (1010) but above the median (418). The reason for this marked difference between the mean and the median is that the distribution is highly skewed with two countries (the UK and Ireland) having very many more accountants per head than the average. The UK has nearly eight times more accountants per head than the median European country. In fact, in respect of France and Germany, the UK has, respectively, 16 and 23 times the number of accountants per head, a remarkable indication on how much more important the accountancy profession is in the UK compared with these countries.

4. *The proportion of accountants in professional practice*: One explanation for the great disparity between countries in the relative size of the accountancy profession is given by the statistic in the rightmost column of Exhibit 4.5: the proportion of qualified accountants in practice (as opposed to being employed in industry, commerce, administration or teaching). In Austria the proportion is 100 per cent; all qualified accountants are engaged in professional practice. However this is not the case with other countries; the European mean is 78 per cent and the median 90 per cent. The proportion in the UK (27 per cent) is far lower than the European average. Hence one reason for the far larger number of qualified accountants in Britain is that only a small proportion of them are engaged in audit,

tax advice and other professional activities, compared with their Continental counterparts.

Notes

1. This list of advantages is taken from an analysis made by the Belgian accountancy profession that is quoted in Lefebvre and Flower (1994).
2. Certain standard-setting bodies (Denmark's RR and RP, Italy's OIC, Norway's NSR and Spain's AECA) are not included in Exhibit 4.2 as experience of their activities is so limited.
3. It is a remarkable indication of the pervasive influence of the English language in financial reporting, that, when the DRSC was founded in March 1998, it included the word 'standard' in its title, even though, up to that time, the German word 'standard' was never used in the accounting sense.
4. GoB means (Grundsätze ordnungsmässiger Büchfuhrung or principles of orderly book-keeping). All German enterprises are obliged by law to follow them.

References

Arden, M. (1993). 'ASB Foreword to accounting standards'. *Accountancy* **117**(June).

Baldwin, R. and McCrudden, C. (1987). *Regulation and Public Law*. London, Weidenfeld & Nicholson.

Buijink, W. (1999). 'Netherlands'. *Accounting Regulation in Europe*. S. McLeay. Basingstoke, Macmillan.

Christiansen, M. and Elling, J. (1993). *European Financial Reporting: Denmark*. London, Routledge.

Ebbers, G. (1997). 'Fixed asset revaluation in Europe: interaction between theory, practice and fiscal policies'. *Comparative Studies in Accounting Regulation in Europe*. J. Flower and C. Lefebvre. Leuven, Acco.

Jorissen, A. and Block, H. (1995). 'Belgium – Individual Accounts'. *Transnational Accounting*. D. Ordelheide. Basingstoke, Macmillan.

Lande, E. (1997). 'A comparative study of the normalization process in France and Spain'. *Comparative Studies in Accounting Regulation in Europe*. J. Flower and C. Lefebvre. Leuven, Acco.

Lande, E. and Scheid, J.-C. (1999). 'France'. *Accounting Regulation in Europe*. S. McLeay. Basingstoke, Macmillan.

Lefebvre, C. and Flower, J. (1994). *European Financial Reporting: Belgium*. London, Routledge.

Majala, R. (2004). 'Finland'. *Accounting Regulation in the European Union*. S. McLeay. Basingstoke, Palgrave Macmillan.

McLeay, S. ed. (1999). *Accounting Regulation in Europe*. Basingstoke, Macmillan.

McLeay, S. ed. (2004). *Accounting Regulation in the European Union*. Palgrave Macmillan (forthcoming).

Merkl, D. (2004). 'Lifting the bell jar: the end of corporatist accounting regulation'. *Accounting Regulation in the European Union*. S. McLeay. Basingstoke, Palgrave Macmillan.

Nobes, C. and Parker, R. (2002). *Comparative International Accounting*. Hemel Hempstead, Prentice-Hall Europe.

Olivero, B. (1997). 'The accounting standardisation process in Italy: a French view'. *Comparative Studies in Accounting Regulation in Europe*. J. Flower and C. Lefebvre. Leuven, Acco.

Ordelheide, D. (1995). 'Germany – group accounts'. *Transnational Accounting*. D. Ordelheide. Basingstoke, Macmillan.

Pham, D. (1993). 'Group accounting in France'. *International Group Accounting: Issues in European Harmonization*. S. Gray, A. Coenenberg and P. Gordon. London, Routledge.

Quinn, S. and Sørensen, O. (1997). 'The regulation of financial reporting in Denmark and the Republic of Ireland: a comparative study'. *Comparative Studies in Accounting Regulation in Europe*. J. Flower and C. Lefebvre. Leuven, Acco.

Riccaboni, A. (1999). 'Italy'. *Accounting Regulation in Europe*. S. McLeay. Basingstoke, Macmillan.

Standish, P. (1990). 'Origins of the plan comptable général: a study in cultural intrusion and reaction'. *Accounting and Business Research* **20**(4): 337–51.

Zambon, S. (1998). 'Accounting in Italy'. *International Accounting*. P. Walton, A. Haller and B. Raffournier. London, International Thompson Business Press.

5

The European Union and Harmonisation

The previous chapter demonstrated the great diversity in the financial reporting of enterprises from the different European countries. This variety greatly adds to the interest of the study of European financial reporting, but it also has considerable drawbacks. This chapter analyses these disadvantages and describes the activities of one body that has sought to reduce the diversity: the European Union.

5.1   The European Union

The European Union (EU) is an organisation that embraces virtually all the countries of Western Europe; at present there are fifteen member states, ranging from the largest country of Western Europe, Germany with 82 million inhabitants, to tiny Luxembourg with only 400,000. In fact it is easier to list the European countries, that are not members of the EU. They are the countries of Eastern Europe (Poland, the Czech Republic, Hungary, the successor republics of the former Yugoslavia, Albania and all the countries to the east, such as Russia and Ukraine) plus two 'hold-outs' in Western Europe: Switzerland and Norway. However it should be noted that many of the countries of Eastern Europe are scheduled to join the EU in 2004[1] and it seems doubtful that Switzerland and Norway will remain outsiders indefinitely.

The EU has been described as a United States of Europe in the making. To some commentators this is an exaggeration and certainly the EU's present powers are in no way comparable to those of the federal government of the USA. However the governments of the EU member states have transferred to the EU significant authority in certain fields, notably in the economic sphere. Essentially in these areas, the national governments are obliged, under the terms of the treaty that they signed on joining the EU, to obey that body's laws. One of the areas so covered is financial reporting.

5.2   The EU's interest in financial reporting

For more than thirty years the EU has been very active in the field of financial reporting. Its aim has been to 'harmonise' the accounts of enterprises, that is, to reduce the differences between the member states in this area so that any remaining differences do not constitute an impediment to the EU's efficient operation. There are three reasons why the EU aims for harmonisation; they relate to the common market, to the protection of shareholders and to competition.

5.2.1   The common market

One of the EU's principal functions is the creation and maintenance of a common market among the member states. A common market is an area where there are no barriers to the free flow of goods, services, labour, capital and other elements that constitute the input and output of economic activity. There are two reasons why the European countries sought to create a common market when they founded the EU in 1957: an economic reason and a political reason.

1. The economic reason was to promote the living standards of their citizens by ensuring that they could enjoy goods and services produced in the most efficient way, that is in the country which had the best production facilities, whilst making use the cheapest factors of production (perhaps imported from other countries) and benefiting from the economies of scale that would flow from a market embracing many countries.
2. The political reason was to bring about the integration of the economies of the separate European countries, with the consequence that they would no longer have the capability of waging war against each other. This was the explicit objective of the EU's forerunner, the European Coal and Steel Community founded in 1952, which brought together under a single administration the coal and steel industries of, among others, the arch enemies, France and Germany, so that henceforth neither had a self-sufficient independent armaments industry.

The accounts of enterprises play an important role in the proper functioning of a common market. Capital is an essential input factor. To achieve the most efficient use of capital, an enterprise should be able to raise its capital in any member state (for example where the capital is cheapest) and put it to work in any other member state (for example where the production opportunities offer the greatest profit). However, if the rules of the various member states on the form and content of accounts are very different, these will act as a severe restraint on the efficient operation of the common capital market. For example, a French investor will be reluctant to buy the shares of a German AG if she finds its accounts strange and mystifying; similarly a German AG will be reluctant to raise capital in France if it has to spend resources on explaining and adapting its accounts for French investors. Hence, for the efficient operation of the capital market, the rules of financial reporting should not differ too much from country to country.

However, the effect of a member state's financial reporting rules is not limited to the capital market. The ultimate aim of the EU is to provide a common environment for business throughout Europe. An enterprise that is based in one member state should not experience major difficulties in carrying on business in another member state either through a branch or through a subsidiary company. The financial reporting requirements of the various member states are a major feature of the business environment and can add considerably to the costs of operating in another member state, particularly if these requirements differ significantly from those of the enterprise's home country. If the requirements of the two member states are inconsistent, or, even worse, contradictory, their effects can be most harmful.

5.2.2   The protection of shareholders

The separation of ownership from control in corporations renders their shareholders particularly vulnerable, since in the event of financial failure the shareholders' claims are limited to the assets of the corporation; they have no claim against the personal wealth of the corporation's promoters or managers. For this reason, most countries have enacted laws that are designed to protect the interests of shareholders, notably in relation to the accounts that corporations must render annually to their shareholders. Foreign shareholders are more vulnerable than domestic shareholders. With the creation of the EU, it was to be expected that the number of foreign share-holders would increase. Hence when the EU was founded, special attention was given to the need to protect shareholders. Under the terms of article 54.3(g) of the Treaty of Rome, which set up the EEC in 1957, the EU is obliged 'to coordinate the safeguards which, for the protection of the interests of members and others are required by member states of companies[2] with a view to making them equivalent throughout the Community'. The term 'safeguards' in this article is interpreted to include the preparation and publication of financial statements. This is the sole reference to financial reporting in the treaty and the term is not even mentioned!

5.2.3   Competition: 'the level playing field'

In order for the common market to operate efficiently, it is necessary that the allocation of resources that results from the interaction of market forces should not be distorted by government action, for example, by governments offering subsidies and other benefits to national enterprises. Otherwise one member state would be able to secure for its enterprises a competitive advantage over their foreign rivals. The metaphor of the 'level playing field' is often used to describe the desirable state of the environment in which enterprises should compete with each other within the EU.

The requirement to publish accounts is one of the most important of the obligations imposed by governments on enterprises. In general, enterprises are reluctant to reveal much about their affairs in their published accounts, for fear of aiding their competitors. Hence, if enterprises resident in one member state were to be permitted to get away with publishing uninformative accounts, they would have an unfair advantage over enterprises in other member states. Since, in a common market, there should be no restrictions on where enterprises may establish themselves, there would be a tendency for enterprises to set themselves up in the member state that offered the most favourable financial reporting regime, that is, the regime that did not require the publication of much significant information. Since, in general, governments are in favour of enterprises establishing themselves on their territory (they provide employment and pay taxes), they would be reluctant to see enterprises enticed away by incentives offered by other countries. The result would be a form of auction in which governments vied with each other in offering the most favourable financial reporting regime for enterprises; 'a race to the bottom' as governments competed with each other to weaken their laws. That such a scenario is not just a theoretical possibility is demonstrated by the experience of the USA a hundred years ago. Company law being a state and not a federal matter, certain states sought to attract corporations to their territory by enacting very favourable (that is non-restrictive) laws on company accounts. It is generally agreed that this competition was won by the tiny state of Delaware, which explains why, to this day, there are more corporations registered there than in any other state, including major companies, such as Du Pont. In fact, the financial reporting of American corporations only began to improve, when the federal government intervened and set up the Securities and Exchange Commission which imposed common standards on all large American corporations, irrespective of the state in which they were resident.[3]

In fact, the original EU member states included one country, Luxembourg, which seemed very similar to Delaware in that it had made its business to attract enterprises to locate themselves on its territory by offering a very liberal financial reporting regime. In this situation, the regulation of financial reporting could not be left entirely to the member states, for in that case there would be a real danger of a competitive collapse of the whole system.

5.2.4   Harmonisation before relevance

In relation to financial reporting, the EU's aim is 'harmonisation', which may be defined as the removal of differences that hinder the achievement of its aims in the three areas dealt with above. Harmonisation is not the same as uniformity, since it is not necessary to remove those differences that have no effect or only a limited impact in these areas. Hence harmonisation may be defined as partial but pertinent uniformity. In pursuing this aim, the EU places more emphasis on harmonisation than on relevance. The effective harmonisation of accounts would deal completely with the competition concerns referred to in Section 5.2.3; in fact, a 'level playing field' could be achieved simply by insisting that member states impose no obligations relating to financial reporting. Harmonisation would also go a long way towards resolving the problems related to the common capital market, for, if the accounts of enterprises in all countries were basically similar, both enterprises and shareholders would be less inhibited in investing in other member states. The EU is not uninterested in the quality of financial reporting, for it is concerned to improve both the efficiency of the European capital market and the degree of protection enjoyed by shareholders. However its primary interest is in achieving an acceptable degree of harmonisation.

5.3 The EU's harmonisation programme

The EU sought to achieve the harmonisation of the accounts of enterprises by enacting directives. A directive is a special type of EU law. It is enacted by the EU's legislative organs: the Council of Ministers (which consists of representatives of the governments of the fifteen member states) and the European Parliament (whose members are elected by the citizens of the member states). A directive is addressed to the governments of the member states and it requires them to modify their national laws so as to bring into effect on their territory the directive's provisions. The national governments are obliged to comply with the EU's directives under the terms of the treaty that they signed on joining the EU. However, since they are represented on the Council of Ministers (which is the more powerful of the two legislative organs), they have a considerable influence over the contents of directives, particularly as the other member states are often reluctant to override a country's strong objections.

In the field of financial reporting, the fact that the EU has taken action through directives has had the following consequences:

1. The task of incorporating a directive's provisions into the national law is the responsibility of the member states' governments. Leaving this task to national governments has a number of negative effects, including:

   (a) *Delays*: Often many years pass between the enactment of a directive by the EU and its implementation by a member state. These delays were a major problem in the decade following the enactment of the more important financial reporting directives. For example, Italy did not incorporate the provisions of the Fourth Directive (dealt with in Section 5.4) into its national law until 1991, even though this directive was enacted by the EU in 1978. According to the directive's terms the member states were required to do this within two years, that is by 1980, so Italy was ten years late. However, this is past history now that all member states have enacted the necessary national legislation.

(b) *Divergent implementations*: In amending their national laws, member states may differ in their interpretation of particular provisions of a directive with the result that national laws are not harmonised.

(c) *Non-implementation*: A member state may deliberately or through inadvertence fail to implement a particular provision of a directive.

The EU attempts to monitor the implementation of directives by the member states but not with complete success as the EU's powers of enforcement are very limited.

2. Each member state has retained its own national regulatory system, consisting of laws, standards and so on. Each member state's system consists of elements that are unique to that member state and of elements that are similar to those of other member states resulting from the implementation of the EU's directives.

3. Citizens and enterprises are obliged to obey national law. For them, the provisions of an EU directive have no effect until they are incorporated into national law.

Recently the member states agreed to let the EU set the rules relating to the financial reporting of European companies by means of regulations. An EU regulation differs from a directive in that it does not have to be transformed into national law but is directly applicable to citizens and companies in the member states. The most recent EU law on financial reporting, which was enacted in 2002, is in the form of a regulation. It is analysed in Chapter 7. However it only takes effect from 2005. The currently applicable EU law is based exclusively on directives, of which four are of particular importance:

1. The Fourth Directive of 1978, which deals with the individual accounts, and
2. The Seventh Directive of 1983, which deals with the consolidated accounts
3. The Bank Accounts Directive of 1986
4. The Insurance Accounts Directive of 1991.

The following matters are covered in all four directives:

- The definition of the annual accounts
- Prescribed formats
- Valuation rules
- The 'true and fair view' rule
- Options.

In the following sections, these matters are analysed in the context of the Fourth Directive, followed by a very brief reference to the other three directives.

5.4   The Fourth Directive: the accounts of the individual enterprise

The Fourth Directive deals with the accounts of the individual corporation – the 'individual accounts' as they are often termed. It was enacted in 1978, five years before the Seventh Directive which deals with the consolidated accounts. The EU decided to tackle the individual accounts before the consolidated accounts for two reasons:

1. In Europe, the individual accounts are very important as distributions in the form of tax and dividends are based on them.
2. The individual accounts form the basis for the consolidated accounts. Therefore it would not be logical to legislate for the consolidated accounts until after the rules relating to the individual accounts had been fixed.

In fact in dealing first with the individual accounts, the EU was adopting the sequence followed by every major country, with the difference that, in the case of the EU, there was an interval of only five years between the two legislative acts, compared with several decades in most countries.

5.5   The definition of the annual accounts

These are defined in article 2.1 in the following terms:

> 'The annual accounts shall comprise the balance sheet, the profit and loss account and the notes on the accounts. These documents shall constitute a composite whole.'

There are three important points about this definition:

1. There is no requirement to prepare a cash flow statement.
2. The notes form part of the annual accounts.
3. The three elements together form a 'composite whole'.

The last two points are of considerable legal significance. For example, if something is contained in the notes, it is, by definition, contained in 'the annual accounts'.

The greater part of the directive's text is taken up with the definition of the form and content of these accounts. At the time that the Fourth Directive was being negotiated, it was customary for the EU's principal legislative body (the Council of Ministers) to enact important laws by unanimous vote.

Hence the final text had to be acceptable to all member states. This had the consequence that the text represents an unsatisfactory compromise between two fundamentally different approaches to financial reporting: the rule-bound approach of the Continental European countries and the professional approach that prevailed in Britain, which is characterised by the requirement that the accounts give a true and fair view.

The influence of the Continental countries, particularly Germany and France, is most evident in two of the directive's principal provisions concerning the balance sheet and the profit and loss account: (a) the specified formats, (b) the valuation rules.

5.6   Specified formats

Corporations are required to adopt specific formats for their balance sheets and profit and loss accounts. These formats specify not only the titles of the headings and sub-headings to be used but also their sequence. For the reader of the financial statements, this is the directive's provision that is the most visible, for the accounts of EU companies all look alike, more or less, because they all follow the formats that are laid down in the Fourth Directive. There is a very limited degree of choice, notably that two different formats for the profit and loss account are offered, the difference between them being whether revenue is defined as total sales or as total output and whether costs are classified, according to function or according to nature. The alternative formats are shown in Exhibit 5.1.

The choice of profit and loss account formats is a member state option. Each member state may choose the format to be used by its companies. In fact all member states, with the exception of Italy and Greece, have incorporated both formats into their national law, so that companies may choose between them.[4] The differences between the two layouts are:

1. As to revenue, format A presents the total output, which is made up of sales, plus the increase (or less the decrease) in stocks of finished goods and work in progress (WIP), plus output that has been capitalised (for example, in the case of an automobile manufacturer, any vehicles that have been added to its own fleet). Format B simply reports the total sales.

2. As to costs, format A classifies costs by nature: raw materials, staff costs, depreciation and other operating charges. Format B classifies costs by function: cost of sales, distribution costs and administrative expenses. With format B, the various categories of cost (materials, wages, depreciation and so on that are reported separately with format A) are allocated to the three functions (cost of sales, distribution costs and administrative expenses) using some form of internal costing system.

Exhibit 5.1   The alternative formats for the profit and loss account

Format A: Total output Classification of costs by nature	Format B: Total sales Classification of costs by function

Required in Italy
Company option in other EU member states
  except Greece
Headings
Net turnover (sales)
Variation in stocks of finished goods
  and WIP
Work capitalised
Total output
Raw materials and consumables
Staff costs
Valuation adjustments (depreciation) in
  respect of tangible and intangible assets
Other operating charges
	Required in Greece
	Company option in other EU member
	  states except Italy
	Headings
	Net turnover (sales)
	Cost of sales
	
	Gross profit
	Distribution costs
	Administrative expenses

The remaining headings are identical for the two formats; they include interest receivable and payable, income from investments, extraordinary income and charges, and various measures of profit.

The most significant difference between the two formats is that format B presents a figure for gross profit. This is not possible with format A because it does not present a figure for cost of sales. The author has analysed the advantages and disadvantages of the two formats elsewhere (Flower and Ebbers, 2002). He concludes that format A provides the more reliable information and format B the more relevant information.

As already stated, in most EU countries, companies may choose between the two formats. Most small companies in all EU companies choose format A because it saves them the expense of setting up a costing system to allocate costs to functions. Exhibit 5.2 presents information on the format chosen by the largest European companies (that is those included in Exhibit 1.4), except banks and insurance companies, for which special formats are prescribed in their own directives. Note that no Italian companies choose format B as it is forbidden under Italian law. In the Netherlands there is a strong preference for format B; this is also the case with the non-EU countries (Switzerland and Russia), probably related to the strong influence of the capital market on larger enterprises in these countries; financial analysts prefer this format as it enables the application of break-even analysis. In the three largest countries, France, Germany and the UK, there is no clear preference for one format over the other.

The remaining options relating to formats are far less significant. Both the balance sheet and the profit and loss account may be presented either as a double-sided or as a single-sided statement, which is largely cosmetic.

Exhibit 5.2   The formats used for the profit and loss account by the largest European companies (excluding banks and insurance companies)

Country	Format A: Total output	Format B: Total sales
France	11	8
Germany	5	9
UK	3	5
Italy	4	0
Netherlands	0	4
Spain	2	0
Sweden	0	1
Luxembourg	1	0
Switzerland (not EU)	0	4
Russia (not EU)	0	2
Total	26	33

The imposition of prescribed formats reflects the practice in many Continental European countries prior to the enactment of the Fourth Directive. Thus standard formats were set out both in France's PCG and in Germany's HGB.

5.7   Valuation

5.7.1   The EU's rules

The Fourth Directive's principal valuation rules are set out in article 31.1 in the following terms:

(a) the company must be presumed to be carrying on its business as a going concern;

(b) the methods of valuation must be applied consistently from one financial year to another;

(c) valuation must be made on a prudent basis and in particular:

(aa) only profits made at the balance sheet date may be included;

(bb) account must be taken of all foreseeable liabilities and potential losses arising in the course of the financial year...

(cc) account must be taken of all depreciation whether the result of the financial year is a profit or a loss.

(d) account must be taken of income and charges relating to the financial year, irrespective of the date of receipt or payment of such income and charges.

In addition to the going concern principle and the principle of consistency, this article incorporates into EU law the prudence principle (in subparagraph (c)) and the accruals principle (in subparagraph (d)). The accruals principle is expressed in terms that the author finds obscure and ambiguous; the exact meaning of subparagraph (d) depends crucially on the interpretation of the word 'relating'. In the author's opinion, it is self-evident that the income and charges that are reported in the profit and loss account are, by definition, 'related' to the financial year and hence subparagraph (d) is little more than a truism. On the other hand, subparagraph (c) sets out the prudence principle in very clear and unambiguous terms. It defines the principle in detail with reference to its two concomitant principles: the realisation principle (profits may only be reported if they have been realised[5]) and the asymmetry principle (the valuation basis for liabilities should be different from that for assets). Given these differences in the text, it is clear that the Fourth Directive places more emphasis on prudence than on accruals.

The basic tenet of prudence is that great care should be taken to avoid overstating assets and understating liabilities, even at the risk of making the opposite error (understating assets or overstating liabilities). Hence the value of assets may not include unrealised profits but the value of liabilities must include all foreseeable losses, including those that are unrealised. Prudence is deliberately asymmetrical. Accountants should put a greater effort into avoiding overstating assets (and profit) than into avoiding understating these items. The reasons why accountants favour prudence and why it is asymmetrical were analysed in Chapter 2 (Section 2.2). Essentially most accountants perceive that the consequences arising from the overstatement of assets are more serious than those resulting from their understatement.

In application of the prudence principle the Fourth Directive states that fixed assets and current assets should be valued at historical cost (defined as purchase price or production cost). However article 33 gives member states the option of permitting other valuation methods, notably replacement value for tangible fixed assets and inventories, revaluation for fixed assets and indexation to adjust values for inflation for all assets. This provision is one of the clearest manifestations of the compromises built into the Fourth Directive. To the German government this breach of the prudence principle was anathema and it stated publicly that it will never adopt this option.[6] In contrast the British government implemented this option in full. Hence British companies are permitted (but not required) to report their assets at above historical cost, whereas this is absolutely forbidden for German companies.

In 2001, the EU amended the directive to permit companies to report financial instruments at fair value, as required by the IASB's rules. In 2003, this permission was extended to all categories of assets. Both measures were part of the EU's new policy of seeking convergence between its rules and those of the IASB, which is the subject of Chapter 8.

5.7.2 Prudence in Germany

The EU member states differ considerably in the emphasis that they place on prudence. On the one hand, Germany gives great weight to the prudence principle, considering it to be the basis on which the whole structure of financial reporting is built. On the other hand, Britain places more emphasis on the 'true and fair view' rule. The position in Germany is considered in this section, whereas the 'true and fair view' rule is the subject of the following section.

The role that prudence plays in German financial reporting may be illustrated through an examination of the accounts of the Bosch Group, a very large German engineering company, which is number 59 in the top one hundred European enterprises listed in Exhibit 1.4. Bosch's basic approach is set out in the following note to its accounts:

> The realisation and imparity principles were followed. Assets are not reported at above the cost of acquisition or production.

The two principles referred to in the note are aspects of the overall principle of prudence. According to the 'realisation principle', profits may only be taken when 'realised'; according to the 'imparity principle', assets (and profits) are measured differently from liabilities (and losses). German law sets out one application of the imparity principle in requiring that 'all foreseeable risks and losses which have arisen up to the balance sheet date must be taken into account' (HGB, §252(1)4). There is no such requirement for gains.

The combination of these two principles leads to a third principle, the 'principle of lower value': where there exist two possible values for an asset or a liability, the appropriate value is that which leads to the lower profit, that is the lower value for the asset and the higher value for the liability. The justification is that, if the higher value for the asset were used, a profit would be recognised before it had been realised; similarly with a lower value for a liability.

How Bosch applied these principles may be examined with reference to two areas:

1. *Inventory*: Bosch's policy for the valuation of inventory is set out in its notes as follows: 'We valued inventories at the average cost of acquisition or production, taking into account the principle of lower value.' For inventory, the 'principle of lower value' means the lower of cost or market. In fact all European enterprises apply exactly the same rule, which is laid down in both the EU's directives and the IASB's standards. Hence, at least this aspect of the principle of lower value is widely accepted. However Bosch goes a step further with the following rule: 'We provided for risks relating to inventory and sales through write-offs; where the profit margins were unfavourable, further write-offs were made.' The impression is that Bosch went out of its way to find reasons for writing down inventory.

2. *Translation of foreign currency balances*: Bosch's policy is set out as follows: 'Accounts receivable and accounts payable stated in foreign currencies were translated into Euros at the less favourable of the exchange rate at

the date of incurrence and that at the balance sheet date.' The term 'less favourable' means that receivables were translated at the lower of the two rates and payables at the higher. This is a striking application of the 'principle of lower value'. If the exchange rate has gone up since the receivable or payable originated (that is more Euros for the foreign currency), the new rate must be used for payables (since provision must be made for all foreseeable losses and, following the increase, more Euros must be expended to pay off the liability), but the new rate must not be used for receivables as this would be anticipating unrealised profits (in conflict with the realisation principle).

Most enterprises in other European countries follow the rule that is laid down in the IASB's standards and in US GAAP – that foreign currency receivables and payables are translated at the exchange rate ruling at the balance sheet, with any resulting gain or loss on translation being reported in the profit and loss account. The application of this rule by (inter alia) British companies has provoked a discussion as to whether the reporting of any gains in the profit and loss account conflicts with the provision in the EU's directives that only realised profits may be reported in the profit and loss account. The British accountancy profession has issued guidance to its members to the effect that such profits are indeed 'realised' according to the accruals principle. On the other hand, German accountants are quite certain that the application of the prudence principle prohibits the reporting of such gains. The contrasting approaches in Germany and Britain can be attributed to the differing weight given to the prudence and accruals principles in the two countries. For a fuller discussion on this point, see Flower and Ebbers (2002, pp. 586–89) and Ebbers (1997).

Further evidence of Bosch's attachment to prudence is provided by the following extracts from the notes to its accounts:

Liabilities were stated at the amount owed (implying that they are not discounted).

Accounts receivable and other current assets were stated at face values less write-downs for individual risks and general credit risks. Interest-free or low-interest receivables with maturities of more than one year were discounted. We valued marketable securities included in current assets at the lower of acquisition cost or market.

Other applications of the prudence principle in Bosch's accounts (which also reflect the general practice in Germany) are:

1. The prohibition on reporting fixed assets above historical cost. However, if there has been a fall in the asset's recoverable value, this must be provided for.

2. The prohibition of recognising internally generated intangible assets. The only intangible assets reported in Bosch's balance sheet are those resulting from acquisitions, being principally goodwill.
3. The charging of low value fixed assets (acquisition cost less than €500) against income in the year of acquisition.
4. The use of excessively high depreciation rates for fixed assets. Bosch reports that 'in accordance with tax regulations, we deducted an extra €13 million directly from the acquisition cost of tangible fixed assets'. This is a reference to the use of depreciation rates set by the tax authorities, which are generally higher than those justified by economic considerations. German law allows companies to use such rates in their published accounts and most do so for the individual accounts because of the Massgeblichkeitsprinzip. There is no reason to use them in the consolidated accounts, except a desire to be prudent and possibly to avoid the work of extra calculations.

In valuing assets, every conceivable deduction is made; liabilities, on the other hand, are reported at their full value. Basically, to a German accountant, it is a far more serious error to overstate an asset or understate a liability than it is to understate an asset or overstate a liability. The reason is the asymmetric reward function which was analysed in Chapter 2, coupled with the greater emphasis that Germany puts on the distribution function of the accounts compared with the information function.

In its attitude to prudence, Bosch is certainly more conservative than most other large German enterprises, particularly those who make use of the recent legislative changes (dealt with in Chapter 7) to use internationally recognised standards for their consolidated accounts. However Bosch is certainly very typical of the great majority of small and medium-sized enterprises in Germany, who still base their accounts on German GAAP.

5.8   The 'true and fair view' rule

The British approach to financial reporting is reflected principally in the Fourth Directive's provision that the accounts should give 'a true and fair view'. This requirement is set out in article 2. This article is generally considered to be the single most important of the directive's 62 articles. It is quite short and deserves to be closely studied by any serious student of European accounting. For this reason its principal provisions relating to true and fair are given below:

'Article 2.
3. The annual accounts shall give a true and fair view of the company's assets, liabilities, financial position and profit or loss.

4. Where the application of the provisions of this directive would not be sufficient to give a true and fair view within the meaning of paragraph 3, additional information must be given.
5. Where in exceptional cases the application of a provision of this directive in incompatible with the obligation laid down in paragraph 3, that provision must be departed from in order to give a true and fair view within the meaning of paragraph 3...'

Paragraph 3 states that the annual accounts shall give a true and fair view. Paragraphs 4 and 5 seem to make this requirement the single most important provision in the directive. It would seem to be the criterion against which all the other articles should be judged, first as to whether they are inadequate so that additional information has to be given (paragraph 4) and secondly as to whether they are wrong and should therefore be disregarded (paragraph 5). In fact on reading the forthright language of paragraph 5, one might be tempted to believe that the other articles are unimportant and may be ignored; all that is necessary is to present 'a true and fair view'.

According to Van Hulle (1993), the paragraphs relating to 'a true and fair view' were inserted into the directive's text on the initiative of the British representative on the Council. In effect in 1978 'a true and fair view' was a wholly British principle. To the Continental European countries, such as France and Germany, it was literally a foreign concept. In these circumstances, it is appropriate to consider three questions:

1. What is the meaning of 'a true and fair view' to the British?
2. How have the EU member states from Continental Europe interpreted the principle?
3. What impact has the 'true and fair' rule, as set out in the Fourth Directive, had on the actual practice of financial reporting in the EU?

5.8.1 The 'true and fair view' rule in Britain

In Britain there has been, since 1947, a statutory requirement that company accounts should give 'a true and fair view'. However the meaning of the term is not defined in the Companies Act. In 1983 the British accountancy profession asked two leading lawyers, Hoffmann and Arden, to give their opinion on the meaning of the term 'a true and fair view', which it then published (Hoffmann and Arden, 1983). Given the eminence of the two authors (both later became leading judges), this opinion must be regarded as the best statement available on the subject.

The opinion begins by noting that 'true and fair view' is a legal concept. Although the words 'true' and 'fair' have ordinary meanings that are understood by the population in general, when the full term is applied to a set of accounts, it has a special technical meaning. Since it is a legal term, the question of whether a set of accounts gives a true and fair view (as required by the Companies Act) can be authoritatively decided only by a court. Unfortunately there have been hardly any decided cases on the subject and none of any general significance.[7] However Hoffmann and Arden are sure that, in deciding on the matter, the courts would look for guidance to the ordinary practices of professional accountants. They give the reason in a passage that deserves careful study:

> The important reason is inherent in the 'true and fair' concept. Accounts will not be true and fair unless the information that they contain is sufficient in quantity and quality to satisfy the reasonable expectations of the readers to whom they are addressed. On this question accountants can express an informed opinion on what, in current circumstances, it is thought that accounts should reasonably contain. But they can do more than that. The readership of accounts will consist of businessmen, investors, bankers and so forth, as well as professional accountants. But the expectations of readers will have been moulded by the practices of accountants because by and large they will expect to get what they ordinarily get and that in turn will depend on the normal practices of accountants. For these reasons, the courts will treat compliance with accepted accounting principles as prima facie evidence that the accounts are true and fair.

In analysing the above passage, there are three important points to be made;

1. The starting point is the reader of the accounts – what she may reasonably expect as to the quantity and quality of the information contained in the accounts.
2. The readers in question are businessmen, investors and bankers, who may be expected to have some knowledge of accounting practice. They will expect to receive accounts drawn up using the normal practices of accountants, that is accounts that comply with accepted accounting principles.
3. Hence 'a true and fair view' equals compliance with accepted accounting principles.

Later in their opinion, the authors make clear that 'accepted accounting principles' are not simply the whim of the individual accountant but are principles that are widely adopted in practice. In particular they consider that accounting standards issued by appropriate professional bodies would be considered by the courts as providing strong evidence of what constitutes accepted accounting principles. This was confirmed in a later opinion, in which Arden (1993) stated that the standards issued by the UK's Accounting Standards Board should be considered as providing evidence of what constitutes a true and fair view. In a more recent article, which neatly summarises the present position in the UK, Arden stresses a further important point: 'true and fair view' is not a static concept.... 'the views of accountants change. Accordingly it follows that, since the court is seeking a contemporaneous meaning for the requirement, what is necessary to show a true and fair view will be subject to continuous update and change. In this way the true and fair view requirement is, in English law, a dynamic concept' (Arden, 1997).

The rather startling conclusion is that in law 'a true and fair view' is defined not by any reference to the concepts of 'truth' and 'fairness' but by the practice of professional accountants. This point is now widely accepted by academic and legal commentators.

There is an academic school that considers that the notion of 'true and fair' was developed by the British accountancy profession as a means of bolstering its status. A distinguishing feature of a profession is that there should be a body of knowledge, access to which is restricted to members of the profession. Ideally this knowledge should be a 'mystery' to outsiders. Only members of the profession understand it, understanding being passed on from generation to generation through a system of apprenticeship. The 'true and fair view' concept seems to be ideally suited to be a 'mystery' that only the professional accountant can master. This viewpoint was adopted by Hopwood (1990) in explaining how 'true and fair view' came to be included in the Fourth Directive. In Britain the accountancy profession had secured for itself a privileged role in determining the rules that governed financial reporting, a role protected by the statutory requirements relating to 'true and fair view'. However, with Britain's entry into the EU, there was a considerable danger that this cosy arrangement would be upset by the imposition of a more legalistic approach; the first draft of the Fourth Directive set out an essentially German approach to the regulation of accounting which left no role for the accountancy profession. In Hopwood's opinion, expressed in his rather idiosyncratic prose, 'emphasising the need for an experiental, contextually grounded and judgmental approach to accounting which required a form of discretionary self-regulation rather than the standardising concerns of the law and the State, a true and fair view came to stand for a particular position on the possibilities for the regulation of accounting rather than a concern with accounting itself. If British concerns were to prevail, the discretionary powers of the auditor and the accounting profession must also prevail, rather than regulation by the State'.

It is of interest that the British proposal relating to 'a true and fair view' was supported by the accountancy professions of the other EU member states. This is logical as it represented an enhanced role for the professional accountant. However it is rather a mystery that it was eventually accepted by the government representatives in the Council, since governments are not normally disposed to sharing their regulatory powers with other bodies. It is possible that in the 1970s the other member states still displayed a certain feeling of goodwill towards the newcomer or accepted Britain's own assessment that it was peculiarly expert in accounting matters.

In Britain, the 'true and fair view' rule is a major influence on financial reporting, as is evidenced by the following three examples:

1. The British accounting standard SSAP 19 requires that depreciation should not be charged on properties held by a company for investment purposes. This is contrary to article 35.1(a) of the Fourth Directive (and to the British Companies Act) which requires that depreciation be charged on all assets with limited economic lives. This disregard of the law is justified on the grounds of showing 'a true and fair view'.
2. Another standard, SSAP 20, requires that translation gains on unsettled foreign currency loans be taken to income, which, since the gains are unrealised, contravenes article 31.1.c(aa) of the Fourth Directive. Again, the need to show 'a true and fair view' is cited in justification.
3. A third standard, SSAP 9, implies that the LIFO method of stock valuation should not ordinarily be used by companies, because it does not give 'a true and fair view' of the stock's value in the balance sheet. However LIFO is specifically permitted both in the Fourth Directive (article 40) and in the British Companies Act. This is a case where the 'true and fair view' rule is used to restrict the freedom of the preparers of accounts.

In all three cases, one has the strong impression that the standard-setter decided what it wanted to do and then invoked the 'true and fair view override' as a means of getting round the awkward fact that this was contrary to the law, rather than starting out with 'a true and fair view' as the overriding objective. Many British companies have assets covered by SSAP 19 and SSAP 20 and follow these standards in drawing up their accounts. In doing so, they are obliged to invoke the 'true and fair view override' as the justification for not obeying the letter of the law. Hence it is rather common for British companies to refer to the need to disregard the law in order to present 'a true and fair view'. A survey of the 2002 accounts of 337 British companies listed on the London Stock Exchange (which included all the leading companies) revealed that 84 companies (25 per cent of the total) invoked the true and fair override (Company Reporting, 2003). Of these 84 companies, almost half (45 per cent) did so in respect of the non-depreciation of investment properties (SSAP19).

5.8.2   The 'true and fair view' rule in Continental Europe

Although the phrase 'a true and fair view' was incorporated into the directive at Britain's suggestion, this does not have the effect that the phrase's meaning throughout the EU is to be determined by its meaning in Britain. As Karel Van Hulle (1993) points out, with the incorporation of the concept in a directive, it has become part of EU law. The final answer on the meaning of the concept and its implications lies with the European Court of Justice. This has two implications: the first is rather theoretical – that one day the European Court of Justice will decide that the British are mistaken in their interpretation of the term – there is no immediate prospect of that happening. However the second implication has much more immediate relevance – that in deciding what the concept means in other EU countries, the European Court of Justice will refer to law and practice throughout the EU and not exclusively to that in Britain. In the view of Karel Van Hulle (1993) the true and fair view concept adds an element of flexibility to the directive, commenting 'this is highly desirable in an international context because of the socio-economic, cultural and legal differences between member states. It is perfectly possible that annual accounts which are regarded as true and fair in one member state would not be interpreted as such in another member state'. Mrs Justice Arden, the joint author of the Hoffmann and Arden opinion quoted above, comes to much the same conclusion: 'in my view, the true and fair view requirement may develop separately in each member state' (Arden, 1997, p. 679).

The question of the different interpretations of the 'true and fair view concept' at the level of the member state will now be considered in relation to Germany and France: two of the largest member states with contrastingly different accounting traditions.

'True and fair view' in France

In 1983, the French lawmaker implemented article 2.3 of the Fourth Directive as article 9 of the Code de Commerce using the following words: 'Les comptes annuels doivent être réguliers, sincères et donner une image fidèle du patrimoine, de la situation financière et du résultat de l'entreprise' (the annual accounts must be regular, sincere and must give a faithful image of the enterprise's wealth, financial position and results). As Alexander (1993) points out there are three separate obligations:

1. the accounts must be regular;
2. the accounts must be sincere;
3. the accounts must give 'une image fidèle'.

The first two obligations pre-date by over a decade the Fourth Directive, being first imposed by the French Company Law of 1966. The Plan Comptable Général (PCG) gives further guidance on their meaning. Regularity is a very straightforward concept: it is defined in the PCG as 'conformity with the rules and procedures in force'. Accounts are regular if they comply with the rules. However sincerity is not so clear-cut. According to the PCG, it means good faith: 'sincerity is the application, in good faith, of these rules and procedures in relation to the knowledge that those with accounting responsibilities must normally have of the reality and importance of operations, events and situations'. The concept of sincerity was presumably added to that of regularity to cover the situation where the management sought to mislead by interpreting the rules in a strained or perverse fashion. The rules must be applied in good faith. One may add that, in practice, sincerity has often been interpreted as the equivalent of prudence: that a manager will generally be considered to have acted in good faith if she makes prudent valuations, not overvaluing assets or understating risks. In fact, the PCG adds prudence as a further requirement of accounts, defining prudence as 'the reasonable appreciation of facts in order to avoid the risk of transfer, in the future, of present uncertainties capable of damaging the wealth and results of the enterprise'.

When the new requirement of giving 'une image fidèle' was added to the three pre-existing obligations, there was considerable discussion in France as to its precise meaning. Certain commentators saw the new demand as offering an opportunity to effect a fundamental reform of French accounting, freeing it from the dominance of regularity, sincerity and prudence. However this did not happen and, in the decades since the implementation of the Fourth Directive, a consensus has developed in France which gives far less importance to 'une image fidèle'. The present position may be characterised as follows:

1. The requirements of regularity and sincerity are very important. The 'image fidèle' concept only becomes important when there are difficulties in applying the rules, for example, because there is no generally accepted rule, because there are several rules or because the rules are ambiguous or unclear and thus need to be interpreted. The 'image fidèle' concept provides the criterion for choosing between different rules and for interpreting the rules.
2. When, even though the rules have been correctly applied, the accounts do not give 'une image fidèle', then additional information must be given in the notes. This is required by article 9 of the Code de Commerce which implements article 2.4 of the Fourth Directive.

All French commentators are agreed on these two points. The only disagreement is whether there is a possible third point, that, when the strict application of a rule is misleading, then it must be disregarded in order to give 'une image fidèle'. This is, of course, the import of article 2.5 of the Fourth Directive which is incorporated almost word for word in article 9 of the Code de Commerce, which, following the Fourth Directive, limits its application to exceptional cases. Most commentators consider that 'exceptional cases' are so rare as to be effectively non-existent, that is in 100 per cent of cases the rules must be followed; they cannot conceive of a situation where, with full information given in the notes, the accounts as a whole do not give 'une image fidèle'. For these commentators, the notes play a very important role in allowing the individual company to present the facts relating to its particular situation. On the other hand, the balance sheet and the profit and loss account present the information relating to the company in a standard form that permits comparison with other companies. If companies were permitted to disregard the rules relating to the balance sheet and profit and loss account, this would lead to the presentation of non-uniform accounts and to the loss of all the benefits of harmonisation. The information specific to the individual company should be presented in the notes. The position is explained very well by Roberts (1993): 'The annexe[8] is the ideal instrument of liaison between the general standardisation of accounting and the characteristics which are specific to the business. In an accounting system where... a priority has been accorded to uniformity across business for financial reporting, the notes to the accounts offer a possibility of reconciling this priority with the need to provide financial information which is useful to outside parties. By completing and commenting on the balance sheet and profit & loss account, the annexe ensures that "une image fidèle" will be given to these outside parties.'

Other commentators, whilst accepting that, in 99.99 per cent of cases, the rules should be followed, insist that the 'image fidèle' provision does offer a real opportunity for disregarding the rules in the exceptional 0.01 per cent cases. However the argument is rather academic. Alexander (1993) asks the question whether the concept of 'une image fidèle' has brought about an alteration in the accounts of a single French company. Burlaud (1993), a leading French professor, in reply, states that he shares Alexander's pessimism, but adds a most interesting nuance. The 'image fidèle' concept may have little impact at the level of the enterprise but it has a significant impact on the regulator. Through the existence of the 'image fidèle' objective, both in the EU directives and in French law, the regulator is encouraged to set rules that favour substance over form and thus moderate the influence of prudence and taxation in financial reporting. Burlaud concludes that the concept of the 'image fidèle' is above all a guide for standard-setters and rarely one for business. It may well be that French enterprises find no need to disregard the rules in order to present 'une image fidèle', because the rules have already been adapted sufficiently by the regulator. However it must be emphasised that in devising new rules, the French regulator always respects the specific rules of French law. In effect, 'une image fidèle' is used as a criterion for interpreting existing rules and for developing new rules, and not as a justification for disregarding the established rules.

'True and fair view' in Germany

In 1985, the German legislator implemented article 2.3–2.4 of the Fourth Directive as Section 264(2) of the Handelsgesetzbuch, using the following words:

'Der Jahresabschluß... hat unter Beachtung der Grundsätze ordnungsmäßiger Buchführung ein den tatsächlichen Verhältnissen entsprechendes Bild der

Vermögens-, Finanz- und Ertragslage der Kapitalgesellschaft zu vermitteln. Führen besondere Umstände dazu, daß der Jahresabschluß ein den tatsächlichen Verhältnissen entsprechendes Bild im Sinne des Satzes 1 nicht vermittelt, so sind im Anhang zusätzliche Angaben zu machen.'

(The annual accounts shall, in compliance with the principles of orderly book-keeping, convey a picture of the company's wealth, financial position and results that is in accordance with the facts. If special circumstances result in the accounts not conveying a picture of the company's wealth, financial position and results that is in accordance with the facts within the meaning of sentence 1, then additional information should be given in the annex.)

There are four important points to be made about the legal formulation given above:

1. The German phrase which is translated as 'a picture...in accordance with the facts' is quite different from the English phrase 'a true and fair view'.
2. The requirement to convey 'a picture...in accordance with the facts' is subject to the additional requirement that this be in compliance with the principles of orderly book-keeping.
3. When, in special circumstances, the accounts do not convey 'a picture... in accordance with the facts', additional information must be given in the annex. This is essentially the same rule as in France.
4. There is no provision in German law that other rules may be disregarded if that is necessary to convey 'a picture...in accordance with the facts', as provided in article 2.5 of the Fourth Directive. The above excerpt gives the entire German law on 'true and fair view'. In effect, Germany has not implemented article 2.5 of the Fourth Directive.

Point 2 above makes it very clear that the German principles of orderly book-keeping (Grundsätze ordnungsmäßiger Buchführung, often shortened to GoB) have priority and that the requirement to convey 'a picture...in accordance with the facts' may not be used as a justification for disregarding them. These principles are defined elsewhere in the law; in general they are a more rigorous version of the valuation principles set out in article 31 of the Fourth Directive, with a more marked emphasis on prudence. Furthermore, since paragraph 5 of article 2 of the Fourth Directive has not been incorporated into German law, there is no way in which German enterprises may legally disregard the rules in drawing up their accounts. The basic rule is very clear. The accounts must be drawn up according to the rules. If they then do not convey 'a picture...in accordance with the facts', then additional information must be given in the annex. The implication is that the accounts with this additional information would then convey 'a picture in accordance with the facts'. Two points should be made in this connection:

1. German accounting is very much based on the reporting of facts. A balance sheet which reports a plot of land at its purchase price of fifty years ago cannot be faulted as not presenting the facts. Germany prefers the undisputed fact of historical cost to the much more subjective 'fact' of a hypothetical market value or replacement cost.
2. The annex is part of the 'accounts'. The requirement to present 'a picture... in accordance with the facts' relates to the accounts taken as a whole (in both the Fourth Directive and in German law). It is very difficult to claim that accounts in which sufficient additional information is given in the annex do not present 'a picture... in accordance with the facts'.

The predominance of the detailed rules of the law over the general rule to convey 'a picture... in accordance with the facts' is brought out very clearly in the official commentary of the German government on Section 246 of the Handelsgesetzbuch: 'The form and content of financial statements derive in the first instance from the specific rules of the laws and ordinances... The general rule need only be referred to if doubts arise in the interpretation and application of individual rules or if uncertainties in the legal provisions need to be resolved. The general rule does not therefore take precedence over the legal provisions in the sense that it permits the form and contents of financial statements to be determined in deviation of these rules.' (Translation from Brooks and Mertin, 1986.)

There is a broad consensus in Germany on the above analysis of the position with regard to 'true and fair view'. There is controversy only on a rather minor matter: whether the requirement to convey 'a picture... in accordance with the facts' applies only to the annex; or whether it also applies to the balance sheet and the profit and loss account, which would only occur when the rules give insufficient guidance (for example, a choice has to be made between two or more rules or the rules are ambiguous). In fact most German commentators support the 'separation thesis' whereby the requirement to convey 'a picture... in accordance with the facts' applies only to the annex.

In comparing Germany with France, one is struck by two similarities:

1. The continued prevalence of rules that predate the Fourth Directive: for France regularité and sinceré; for Germany the 'Grundsätze ordnungsmäßiger Buchführung'.
2. When the accounts do not present 'une image fidèle/a picture... in accordance with the facts', the practice is to continue to apply the specific rules that determine the form and content of the balance sheet and the profit and loss account, and to provide additional information in the notes (annexe or Anhang). In effect, in both countries, the general rule has no effect on the balance sheet and profit and loss account.

5.8.3   The impact of the 'true and fair view' rule on European financial reporting

The impact of the 'true and fair rule' on financial reporting in the EU member states may be summarised as follows:

1. In Britain, the inclusion of this rule in the Fourth Directive meant that this directive's impact was largely limited to matters of format and presentation. In other areas, British accountants were able to carry on much as before. In fact, the ASB (the British standard-setter) has used the rule to extend, in a very significant fashion, the scope and authority of its standards. Ireland closely follows Britain in this matter.
2. In France and Germany, the rule has had no perceptible impact on the financial reporting practice of companies. It is claimed that it has had an impact on the behaviour of the standard-setters in encouraging them to favour substance over form in framing their rules. With exception of the EU member states considered in (3), the position elsewhere is similar.
3. In three member states, there was, prior to the Fourth Directive's enactment, a very similar general rule. In the Netherlands, accounts were required to give 'een getrouw beeld' ('a faithful picture') which is exactly the phrase used in the Dutch version of the Fourth Directive. In Denmark and Sweden, accounts had to be drawn up in accordance with 'good accounting practice'. Thus in these countries, the concept of 'true and fair view' was not foreign and accountants had no problems in applying it. For example, Christiansen (1995) points out that Danish accountants use the 'percentage of completion' method of accounting for long-term contracts, even though it conflicts with the realisation principle in article 31 of the Fourth Directive on the grounds that it is necessary that the accounts give 'a right-looking picture' (the Danish translation of 'a true and fair view').

5.9   Options

A feature of the Fourth Directive is the large number of 'options'; these are provisions of the directive which offer a choice of rules. Basically these options were inserted in the text, in order to gain the support of the governments of particular member states when the directive was being considered by the Council. There are two types of options:

1. 'Member state options': These are rules where the choice is left to the government of the member state; it can decide whether or not to incorporate a particular rule into its national law.
2. 'Company options': These are rules where the choice is left up to the preparer of the accounts.

Most of the options in the Fourth Directive are 'member state options'. Once the government has decided which option to incorporate into its law, the enterprise has no choice but to obey the law. However in certain cases the government may adopt the option in a way that also offers a choice to the enterprise. Two of the more important options have already been mentioned:

1. The alternative formats for the profit and loss account.
2. The alternative valuation rules for certain categories of assets.

Other significant options are:

1. *Financial holding companies*: Member states may prescribe special formats for financial holding companies, which are defined as companies whose sole object is to acquire and hold shares in other companies without involving themselves in their management. It is obvious that this option was inserted at the demand of Luxembourg, where very many such companies are located, principally because of that country's liberal laws.
2. *Prepayments*: They may be shown either as part of current assets or as a separate item at the foot of the balance sheet. This option was inserted to accommodate the differing practices relating to prepayments in the member states (in Britain they are always reported among the current assets; in Germany they are always shown as a separate item). There is a similar option for deferred income.
3. *Small companies*: Member states may permit small companies to draw up abridged balance sheets and not to publish their profit and loss accounts. Small companies are defined as those which do not exceed two of the three following limits: balance sheet total €3.65 million, turnover €7.3 million, number of employees 50. This is an option that all member states have implemented in response to lobbying by these companies.
4. *Tax-driven values*: Member states may continue to permit corporations to report assets at values determined for tax purposes.

5.10   The Seventh Directive: the consolidated accounts

The principal provisions of the Seventh Directive are:

1. The parent enterprise of a group above a certain size is required to prepare and publish consolidated accounts, consisting of a consolidated balance sheet, a consolidated profit and loss account, and notes, covering the parent enterprise, subsidiaries and associates.
2. The terms 'parent enterprise', 'subsidiary' and 'associate' are precisely defined, subject to a number of options.

3. Both the acquisition method and the merger method of capital consolidation are permitted, the latter as an option.
4. Goodwill is to be capitalised and amortised over five years, with an option for a longer period and another option permitting direct write-off to reserves.
5. Small groups. There is a Member State option in relation to small groups, which may be exempted from the obligation to prepare consolidated accounts. A small group is defined as one that does not exceed two of the following three limits: total assets €14.6 million, turnover €29.2 million and total employees 250.
6. On most other matters, the Fourth Directive's rules apply also to the consolidated accounts, notably formats, valuation methods and the 'true and fair' rule.

5.11   The banks and insurance directives

There are two separate directives:

1. The EU directive of 1986 on the annual accounts and consolidated accounts of banks and other financial institutions.
2. The EU directive of 1991 on the annual accounts and consolidated accounts of insurance undertakings.

The principal function of these directives is to define the formats of the balance sheet and profit and loss account, which are quite different from those set out in the Fourth Directive. There are also significant differences in the valuation rules, particularly for insurance undertakings. However the true and fair view rule applies equally to both types of company.

Banks and insurance companies play a very significant role in the European economy. As shown in Exhibit 1.4, they make up 41 of the 100 top European enterprises. However the accounts of these companies are highly specialised and are not covered in detail in this book, which concentrates on the accounts of industrial, commercial and service enterprises.

5.12   The impact of the EU's directives

There can be no doubt that the four directives have had a considerable impact on financial reporting within the EU. This impact has been most marked in two areas:

1. *Improved quality*: Previously, many member states had very rudimentary financial reporting laws. Hence the reform of their laws occasioned by the need to implement the directives led to a marked improvement in

the quality of financial reporting. This was particularly the case with Italy and Spain and the smaller member states, Belgium, Portugal and Greece.
2. *Consolidated accounts*: In many member states, before the implementation of the Seventh Directive, there was no legal requirement for consolidated accounts. Now they are prepared by larger groups in all EU member states.

However the extent to which the directives have achieved harmonisation is rather limited. In this connection a number of points can be made.

1. *Matters not covered*: The directives fail to deal with many of the more important issues of financial reporting. For example, the following matters are either not covered or dealt with in a very cursory and unsatisfactory manner: foreign currency translation, leasing, pensions, long-term contracts, derivatives, off balance sheet financing and brands.
2. *Non-implementation*: Certain member states have failed to implement particular provisions of the directives. An example is Germany, which has failed to include in its national law that, in exceptional cases, the directive's rules must be disregarded if this is necessary to give a 'true and fair view'. However it is doubtful whether this particular omission has had a negative impact on harmonisation. In fact one may speculate whether in fact the 'true and fair rule' itself is the source of much disharmony, as it introduces a subjective element into the preparation of accounts. It should be noted that in the decade following the enactment of the Fourth and Seventh Directives, non-implementation was a major problem as many member states were very slow in passing the necessary legislation. However, when the last member state (Italy) enacted the necessary law in 1991, this particular problem was finally resolved.
3. *Soft transformations*: This is a term invented by Ordelheide (1990) to describe the implementation of a directive's provisions into national law in such a way that, although the letter of the directive is respected, the intention of the EU legislator is thwarted. A notable example is Germany's action in making it a legal requirement for corporations to publish their accounts but fixing no penalty for non-compliance, with the result that smaller corporations rarely publish their accounts.
4. *Options*: Both the Fourth and Seventh Directives contain a great number of options, that is, provisions that a member state may decide whether or not to implement. When one member state implements an option and another does not, the effect is that the accounts of enterprises in the two countries are no longer harmonised. There are no less than 51 options in the Seventh Directive. Nobes (1990) has estimated that, with all the possible combinations, there are 2,000,000,000,000,000 different ways of preparing the consolidated accounts. Of course this exaggerates the impact of options as only a tiny fraction of the possible combinations are in fact available given the way in which the member states have implemented

the directive. Also many options relate to trivial matters. However some relate to important matters. The more significant options (those that have the greatest impact on reported income and values of assets and liabilities) are:

- *Asset valuation*: The member states have the choice of no less than four methods – historical cost, replacement cost, inflation adjustment and revaluation.
- *Tax-driven asset values*: In principle these are forbidden but member states may opt to retain them.
- *Inventory*: Enterprises are permitted a wide range of valuation methods – weighted average, LIFO, FIFO or 'some similar method'.
- *Provisions*: Member states may permit the setting up of provisions for charges that are not a liability of the enterprise.
- *Definition of a subsidiary*: Member states have the option to define a subsidiary according to the criterion of de facto control.
- *Goodwill*: Member states may permit goodwill to be amortised over a period longer than five years or to be written off directly against reserves.
- *Capital consolidation*: The merger method ('pooling of interest') is a member state option.

5. *Skin-deep harmonisation*: The directives are far more detailed and prescriptive on the form of accounts than on the principles to be followed in their preparation. Standard formats of the balance sheet and the profit and loss account are laid down in the Fourth Directive. However the principles to be followed in establishing the figures to be reported in these formats are either expressed in vague terms or are left as options. The result is 'skin-deep harmonisation': the accounts are harmonised as to their form but not as to the information that they convey.

Exhibit 5.3 presents the relationship between the EU's financial reporting rules and those of the member states in the form of a Venn diagram. Each circle represents the set of rules of a particular body. There are two circles for the EU: the outer one represents the totality of the rules of the EU's directives (both the mandatory provisions and the options); the inner one the set of the mandatory provisions. In addition there are circles that represent the rules of two hypothetical member states. The diagram shows the various logical possibilities; it is not intended to give an indication of the relative number of rules in each set. In fact theoretically some of the indicated sets should be empty. Thus area A+B represents the EU's mandatory rules that have not been incorporated into the national rules of member state II, and area H+J, the rules of member state I that are in conflict with the EU's rules. In both cases there is a breach of EU law. In reality, rules in areas A, B, C (non-implementation of mandatory EU rules) and H, J, K (conflicts with EU

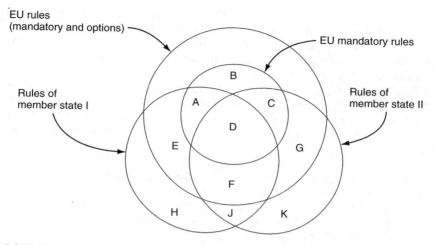

EU rules
(mandatory and options)

EU mandatory rules

Rules of
member state I

Rules of
member state II

Exhibit 5.3   The relationship between the EU's rules and the member states' rules

rules) are comparatively rare but they do exist. What are most important are the areas E and G: EU options implemented differently by different member states. Ideally the areas D and F (identical rules in the two member states) should cover most of the rules in both member states, which would indicate a high degree of harmonisation. However in reality the areas E and G cover a significant proportion of member states' rules.

The Directives are a mixture of prescription and flexibility. The element of prescription is provided principally by the rules that are imposed for the format of the financial statements. The element of flexibility is provided by the provisions relating to 'true and fair view'. The advantage of prescription is that it is the surest way to achieve the EU's objective of harmonised accounts. The disadvantage of prescription is that the imposed rules are not necessarily appropriate for all enterprises and their imposition in any particular case may lead to the financial statements that are seriously misleading. In principle, this disadvantage of prescribed rules should be countered by the application of the provisions relating to 'true and fair view'. In theory the application of the prescribed rules in most cases, with resort to the 'true and fair' provisions in exceptional cases, should ensure the preparation of financial statements that are harmonised (as far as feasible) without being misleading.

However, as the analysis in this chapter has demonstrated, this happy balance has not been achieved. The principal reason for this is the large number of options that the Fourth Directive offers to the member states. In no sense does the Fourth Directive lay down a single set of rules to be followed by all enterprises. The principal reasons why the accounts of companies in different EU member states (and often within a member state) are not harmonised is not that individual companies have resorted to the 'true and fair view' override, but because companies are permitted to use dissimilar methods under the national laws, which incorporate the Fourth Directive's options and because the Fourth Directive does not cover a number of important matters. In fact the very limited use made of the 'true and fair view' provisions by individual companies is a cause for regret, as it implies that full use is not being made of the opportunities that the Directive offers to present the most meaningful accounts. On the other hand, the systematic use of the 'true and fair view' provisions by the UK's ASB to override the specific rules of the Fourth Directive (and of British law) must be condemned as an abuse which seriously damages the comparability of accounts between the UK and the rest of the EU.

In May 2003, the EU amended the directives in order to permit companies to draw up their accounts according to the IASB's rules. This development is covered later in Chapter 7. At the time of writing, the EU member states had not begun to implement these amendments so that as yet they have had no impact on the financial reporting of European enterprises.

5.13   The EU's limitations as a rule-maker

It is apparent from the foregoing analysis that the EU is *not* a European super state, the equivalent in Europe of the United States of America. The EU member states still retain their national identities and most of the powers of government. Only in limited areas have they surrendered powers to the EU institutions.

This is clearly the case with financial reporting. The various countries have all retained their national accounting systems. The impact of the EU's efforts at harmonisation through its directives has been very limited. In fact, in financial reporting, the differences within the EU are greater than the differences between certain EU member states and the rest of the world.

Notes

1. Eight East European countries are scheduled to join the EU in May 2004 (Poland, Hungary, the Czech Republic, Slovakia, Slovenia, Estonia, Latvia and Lithuania) along with two Mediterranean island states, Cyprus and Malta.
2. The term 'company' used in the Treaty of Rome and subsequently in all EU acts covers essentially the same field as the author's preferred term 'corporation'.
3. There is a respectable academic school that claims that the 'race to the bottom' would not happen. Thus Sunder (2002) writes:

> While the managers of corporations may have personal incentives to chose incorporation in states that favour their own interests at the cost of others, the shareholders are hardly constrained to buy shares of such firms. If the legal

regime of a state favours one class of agents over another, a competitive system allows the latter group to choose and value the companies in another state. This competition directs the investment capital towards the latter jurisdiction, lowering the cost of capital for companies who choose to incorporate there. Such reaction of the shareholders to incorporation choices forces the managers to choose, in their own interest, incorporation in lower cost of capital jurisdictions.

This argument is very similar to that used by Benston against government regulation of financial reporting (see Section 3.2 of Chapter 3). Both Sunder and Benston argue that market forces will compel managers to do something against their personal interests. The arguments are logical but the author doubts whether the real world is as they describe. In particular he is very sceptical of Sunder's claim that the fact that more corporations (over 300,000) are registered in Delaware than in any other state of the USA is an indication of the high quality of its corporation law.

4. In Belgium and France, companies are obliged to use format A for the individual accounts but are allowed a choice for the consolidated accounts. One reason for this rule is that the national income accounts (which reports magnitudes such as total wages) are based on the data in the individual accounts.
5. In relation to the realisation principle, the English version of the Fourth Directive is unclear as it refers to 'profits made' not to 'profits realised'. The French and German versions are much clearer as they refer to 'bénéfices réalisés' and 'realisierten Gewinne'. The British legislature in incorporating the Fourth Directive into the British Companies Act used the phrase 'profits realised'.
6. The minutes of the Council meeting that adopted the Fourth Directive includes the following declaration: 'The German delegation states that, for reasons of monetary and economic policy, the Federal Government cannot accept valuation methods designed to take into account inflation as authorized by the Fourth Directive article 33...It will therefore not permit such valuation methods in the Federal Republic of Germany.' (Quoted in Van Hulle [2001], p. 840.)
7. The most important case was decided by a low level court and did not establish any precedents that are binding on other courts; see Ashton (1986).
8. The annexe is the French term for the notes.

References

Alexander, D. (1993). 'A European true and fair view?'. *European Accounting Review* 2(1), May 1993.

Arden, M. (1993). 'ASB Foreword to accounting standards'. *Accountancy* **117** (June): 120.

Arden, M. (1997). 'True and fair view: a European perspective'. *European Accounting Review* **6**(4).

Ashton, R. K. (1986). 'The Argyll Foods case: a legal analysis'. *Accounting and Business Research* (65).

Brooks, J. and Mertin, D. (1986). *New German accounting legislation* Düsseldorf, IDW-Verlag.

Burlaud, A. (1993). 'Commentaires sur l'article de David Alexander'. *European Accounting Review* 2(1), May 1993.

Christiansen, M. 'Denmark – individual accounts' in Ordelheide (1995).

Company Reporting (2003). True and fair override, Company Reporting, February.

Ebbers, G. (1997). 'Foreign currency reporting in Europe'. *Comparative Studies in Accounting Regulation in Europe*. J. Flower and C. Lefebvre. Leuven, Acco.

Flower, J. and Ebbers, G. (2002). *Global Financial Reporting*. Basingstoke, Palgrave.

Hoffmann, L. and Arden, M. (1983). 'Counsel's opinion on true and fair'. *Accountancy*, November.

Hopwood, A. (1990). 'Ambiguity, knowledge and territorial claims: some observations on the doctrine of substance over form'. *British Accounting Review*, March.

Nobes, C. (1990). 'EC Group Accounting – two zillion ways to do it'. *Accountancy* **106** (December).

Ordelheide, D. (1990). 'Soft transformations of accounting rules of the fourth directive in Germany'. *Les Cahiers Internationaux de la Comptabilité*, Editions Comptables Malesherbes, Paris, Cahier no. 3.

Ordelheide, D. (1995). *Transnational Accounting*. Basingstoke, Macmillan.

Roberts, A. (1993). 'Reflections of a true and fair view in France'. *University of Reading*, Discussion paper no. 36

Sunder, S. (2002). 'Regulatory competition among accounting standards'. *Journal of Accounting and Public Policy* **21**(3): 219–34.

Van Hulle, K. (1993). 'Truth and untruth about true and fair'. *European Accounting Review* **2**(1), May 1993.

Van Hulle, K. (2001). 'European Union – individual accounts'. *Transnational Accounting*. D. Ordelheide. Basingstoke, Palgrave Publishers. **1**.

6
The IASB and Globalisation

The subject of this chapter is the International Accounting Standards Board (IASB). In recent years the IASB has become a very important actor in European financial reporting. How this came about and the role that the IASB now plays in Europe is explained in the next chapter. The present chapter sets the scene for the succeeding chapter by presenting a detailed analysis of the IASB, covering its objectives, organisation, operations and achievements.

6.1 The multinational enterprises and globalisation

The IASB's principal function is to issue international accounting standards – standards to be used by enterprises throughout the world, particularly by the largest enterprises which have operations in many countries, that is the multinational enterprises, which are hereafter identified by their initials: MNEs. But before considering the IASB in detail, this chapter discusses why its standards should be considered necessary or desirable. This involves an analysis of the problems faced by the MNEs.

6.1.1 The problems facing the multinational enterprises

In recent years, with the ever-growing globalisation of the world's economy, the importance of the MNEs has increased considerably. As was demonstrated in Chapter 1, there are many European enterprises in this category. In fact, European enterprises make up over half of the world's top one hundred MNEs.[1]

The diversity of national accounting systems that has been analysed in previous chapters causes problems for MNEs in two areas:

1. Internal management
2. External financing.

Internal management

The typical structure of a MNE is a group that consists of a parent corporation (based in a particular country), which controls a large number of subsidiary enterprises (based in countries scattered around the globe). To assure effective management of the group, it is essential that all the corporations in the group use the same principles in drawing up their accounts. The management of an American parent corporation would find it very difficult to assess the true performance of its European subsidiaries if, for example, its German subsidiary stated its assets at historical cost and its British subsidiary reported them at market value. Hence most MNEs have developed standardised accounting principles for all the group enterprises, irrespective of the country in which they are based. The foreign subsidiaries are required to submit reports to the parent enterprise using the group's standardised accounting principles. However the foreign subsidiary is also obliged to draw up a set of financial statements according to the law of the country in which it is located. The need to prepare two sets of accounting reports based on different principles (one for the parent enterprise and another for the local regulatory authority) creates two rather different problems for the group management:

1. *Consistency*: The two reports may give quite different messages (for example, that to the parent indicates a loss, and that according to local law a profit) which can lead to confusion and uncertainty over measuring the performance of the foreign subsidiary. The group management may insist that performance be measured according to its standardised principles. However this does not prevent the local management feeling that it is being treated unfairly in that its performance is being measured according to principles that are not accepted locally.
2. *Cost*: It is costly to maintain the accounting systems that are required for the preparation of two different financial statements.

Clearly there would be great improvements in consistency and economy if both the internal management accounts and the external financial statements of all enterprises in the group could be based on the same set of accounting principles.

External financing

With the expansion of their activities, the MNEs came to require additional capital. As their capital needs came to exceed the capacity of the capital market in their home country, they turned to other countries. More and more MNEs sought a listing on a stock exchange outside their home country. The motives were not exclusively financial; as Biddle and Saudagram (1991) have pointed out there are benefits in other areas, such as marketing (publicity for the enterprise's products in the foreign country) and politics (improving relations with the foreign government by demonstrating a commitment to the country). Above all, listing on a foreign stock exchange (or better still several such exchanges) can be a signalling mechanism that the enterprise considers that it is no longer limited to its national base but is truly a 'global player'. It is logical that a 'global player' should seek its capital on the global capital market.

However when the MNEs sought a listing on certain stock exchanges they discovered that their accounts were not acceptable to the regulatory authorities of the foreign country. In order to obtain a listing, they were obliged to prepare two sets of accounts, one in conformity with their national law and one to satisfy the foreign stock exchange. This was clearly thoroughly unsatisfactory. Not only was it costly but the provision of two sets of accounts, presenting different figures for key items such as profit, was confusing to investors and to the public at large.

6.1.2 The case of Daimler Benz

These problems are well illustrated by the recent experience of Daimler Benz, the German corporation which through a subsequent merger now goes under the name DaimlerChrysler. Daimler Benz is clearly a global player. Some years ago it evidently decided to convert itself from a basically German enterprise into a worldwide corporation. A major element in this new strategy was for its shares to be listed on the major stock exchanges of the world. The shares had been listed for decades on the Frankfurt stock exchange. But, for a world-wide corporation, this was too limited; it needed access to the international capital market. Hence by 1991, it had sought and been granted listings on five major non-German stock exchanges: Zurich, Tokyo, London, Vienna and Paris. However, in order for Daimler Benz to be truly a worldwide corporation, it was essential that its shares should be listed on Wall Street. The New York Stock Exchange is, by far, the world's largest. In 1999, its market capitalisation at $16,604 trillion exceeded that of the next ten largest non-American stock exchanges combined.

Radebaugh and Gebhardt (1995) have analysed the factors that led Daimler Benz to seek a listing on Wall Street as follows:

1. *Increased marketability of Daimler Benz shares*: The extent to which Daimler Benz was dependent on the German stock exchanges to provide a market for its shares is demonstrated by two statistics for the year 1992: 90 per cent of all purchases and sales of Daimler Benz shares took place on German stock exchanges, and over 11 per cent of trades on the German stock exchanges were of Daimler Benz shares. Clearly there was a need to develop new markets so as to improve the marketability of Daimler Benz shares.
2. *Reduced dependence on German bank finance*: Daimler Benz, like many German enterprises, was heavily dependent on German banks for finance. With the increase in German interest rates caused by the enormous growth

in government expenditure following German reunification, the burden of interest costs increased significantly. There were clear economies to be gained by increased equity financing, but this could not easily be achieved on the German capital market.

3. *Convenience for American shareholders*: Although in 1992 over half of Daimler Benz's shares were held by just three shareholders, the remainder were widely held, and, of these shareholders, over half were resident outside Germany. Clearly Daimler Benz would be a more attractive investment for Americans if its shares were listed on Wall Street.

4. *Investment in America*: The USA was an important market for Daimler Benz products and the enterprise had decided to increase its physical investment there in order to serve that market.

However, when Daimler Benz applied for a listing on Wall Street, it found that its financial statements, which were drawn up in accordance with German law, were not acceptable to the Securities and Exchange Commission, the American regulatory authority. In order to be listed, Daimler Benz had to prepare a reconciliation statement, which presented figures for profit and equity according to US GAAP. Not only was this costly but, more seriously, it revealed remarkable differences between the figures for profit and equity under the two sets of accounting rules, as is shown in Exhibit 6.1. The different rules applicable in Germany and the USA resulted in different figures reported in respect of a large number of items of which the more important are listed separately in the exhibit. The largest single item concerns provisions and the related taxation. Provisions that Daimler Benz had made in previous

Exhibit 6.1   Daimler Benz reconciliation statement

	Net income DM (millions) 1993	Equity DM (millions) 31 December 1993
According to German accounting rules	602	17,584
Adjustments		
Provisions, reserves and valuation differences	(4,262)	5,770
Long-term contracts	78	207
Goodwill	(287)	2,284
Pensions	(624)	(1,821)
Foreign currency translation	(40)	85
Financial instruments	(225)	381
Other valuation differences	292	(698)
Deferred taxes	2,627	2,489
Total adjustments	(2,441)	8,697
According to US GAAP	(1,839)	26,281

Source: Form 20-F submitted to the SEC.

years were not recognised under US GAAP. The elimination of these provisions in the US GAAP balance sheet led to a large increase in equity. However in 1993, Daimler Benz had made a transfer from these past provisions to its income statement. As the original provision was not recognised under US GAAP, so the transfer to income in 1993 was not recognised. The elimination of the credit from the income statement led to a large fall in reported net income under US GAAP. Hence for 1993 Daimler Benz reported a net profit of DM 602 million under German accounting rules and a net loss of DM 1839 million under US GAAP. On the other hand, its equity at 31 December 1993 was reported at DM 17,584 million under the German rules and DM 26,281 million under US GAAP. Investors were undoubtedly puzzled by these disclosures and no doubt asked themselves the question as to which set of accounting rules represented the correct figure. They probably concluded that neither figure was to be trusted.

The problems of Daimler Benz and similar MNEs would have been greatly eased if there had been available a single set of financial reporting rules that was accepted by all the regulatory authorities, that is those both of the home country (Germany in the case of Daimler Benz) and of the foreign country (the SEC). The IASB's principal mission is to create such a set.

6.2 The IASB's predecessor: the IASC

The IASB was formally set up in April 2001, when it took over from its predecessor body, the International Accounting Standards Committee (IASC) which was dissolved. The similarity in names between the two bodies is a cause of much confusion. The difference is a single letter: B for 'Board' in the IASB versus C for 'Committee' in the IASC. Since the IASB is, in many important respects, a continuation of the IASC, some knowledge of the IASC is necessary in order to understand fully the IASB's present position and activities.

6.2.1 The IASC's formation

The IASC was founded in 1973 at the initiative of Henry Benson, a British chartered accountant, who was at that time head of Coopers Brothers, the accountancy firm which through subsequent mergers became Pricewater-houseCoopers. The original members of the IASC were representatives of the accountancy profession of the following nine industrialised countries: Australia, Canada, France, Germany, Japan, Mexico, Netherlands, the United Kingdom and the USA.

6.2.2 The IASC's objectives

The objectives of the IASC, as set out in its constitution, were:

1. to formulate and publish in the public interest accounting standards to be observed in the presentation of financial statements and to promote their worldwide acceptance and observance; and

2. to work generally for the improvement and harmonisation of regulations, accounting standards and procedures relating to the presentation of financial statements.

In effect the IASC's formation represented the response of the professional accountancy bodies of the major western industrialised countries to the problems of the MNEs mentioned above.

6.2.3   The IASC's characteristics

However, right from its formation, the IASC was characterised by two important features which had a major influence on its operations and effectiveness:

1. The IASC was a private body set up by the professional accountancy bodies of a number of countries. It was not a government body; it had no official status.
2. Hence the International Accounting Standards (IASs) issued by the IASC had no official status, except in so far as they were endorsed by other bodies. The IASC had no means of enforcing compliance with its standards; it had no authority to impose its standards on enterprises or even on accountants and auditors, who were all primarily obliged to follow national laws and standards. The IASC was quite frank about its limitations, admitting 'neither the IASC nor the accountancy profession has the power... to require compliance with international accounting standards'.[2]

It would not be an exaggeration to describe the history of the IASC over the quarter century of its existence as a continued struggle to mitigate and overcome the disadvantages that stem from these two characteristics.

However despite these drawbacks, over these years, the IASC succeeded in issuing over forty IASs, a very substantial output.

6.2.4   The need for reform

In the late 1990s it became increasingly clear that there was a need for a fundamental reform of the IASC if it were to achieve its objective of issuing high quality standards which would be accepted and applied by the MNEs. The following were considered to be the IASC's principal weaknesses.

Domination by the accountancy profession

Initially the IASC considered that the creation of standards was a purely technical matter which concerned only the experts in the field, that is the accountancy profession. Hence, at first, the IASC Board (which was the body that decided on standards) was made up exclusively of representatives of the national accountancy associations. However, gradually over time, the IASC came to appreciate the need to broaden its organisation so as to increase the acceptability of its standards. In later years, the IASC Board was expanded to include:

1. Certain preparers and users. Organisations that represented the financial analysts, the financial executives and the Swiss Holding Companies were co-opted onto the board.
2. Observers from the users (IOSCO[3]) and other standard-setters (the European Commission and the FASB).

However even at the end the IASC Board was still dominated by the accountancy profession – the members nominated by the national professional accountancy associations were in a clear majority with 13 votes against 3 votes for the co-opted organisations, and the observers had no votes.

Inadequate and incomplete compliance with standards

A major problem was compliance by the MNEs with the IASC's standards. Even when a company claimed that its accounts complied with these standards, it would often be discovered on closer examination that it had failed to apply correctly all the standards, frequently omitting those which were not to its liking. The IASC had no means of enforcing compliance with its standards or of disciplining companies that transgressed.

Poor cooperation with national standard-setters

It became abundantly clear that, for the IASC's standards to gain widespread acceptance, they needed to be endorsed by the standard-setting bodies and regulatory authorities of the more important countries. This implied that these bodies should be closely involved in the development of the IASs. However governmental bodies had great difficulties in working with the IASC, because of its lack of official status. In later years a pragmatic solution was found whereby certain of these bodies sat on the IASC Board as observers (for example, the European Commission, the FASB and the SEC – through IOSCO) or were represented in national delegations (Sir David Tweedie, the chairman of the ASB, was a member of the UK delegation). However this was obviously a stopgap measure and it was clearly desirable that the participation of national standard-setting and regulatory authorities in the IASC's activities be placed on a more permanent and formal basis.

Inefficient decision-making

Over time the IASC, in an attempt to improve the acceptability of its standards, gradually increased the size of the Board. It added members from the developing countries; it co-opted organisations that represented the preparers and the users; it invited influential bodies to attend Board meetings as observers. However the increase in the size of the Board created its own problems. In the end, in 2000, the Board had sixteen members, each of whom was entitled to be represented by three persons at Board meetings. When observers and IASC staff were added, the total number of persons attending Board meetings regularly exceeded 70. This was far too many for efficient decision-making by a body which under its constitution should consider and approve every IAS, exposure draft and interpretation issued in the name of the IASC. In effect there was a conflict between the need to have a wide representation of interests on the Board and efficient decision-making.

Lack of resources

Throughout its existence the IASC was run in a very amateurish fashion. The members of the Board (the body that decided on the standards) were all part-timers who came together for meetings of three or four days some four times a year. Their main occupations were as partners in accountancy firms, finance directors, university professors and so on, and they were able to give only sporadic attention to the IASC's affairs. They were assisted by a small secretariat which was not organised on a permanent basis. The only permanent official was the Secretary General; all the rest were seconded on short-term assignments from other bodies, principally audit firms. This was thoroughly unsatisfactory as it reinforced the impression that the IASC was dominated by the auditors. In effect the IASC suffered from a chronic lack of resources. Even at the end of its existence its annual expenditure never exceeded €3 million, compared with more than twice as much for the USA's FASB.

6.3   Proposals for change

In 1997, the IASC set up a working party to consider its future structure in the light of the problems outlined in the previous section. In 1998, the working party issued a report 'Shaping IASC for the future' (IASC, 1998) which presented a comprehensive analysis of the problems confronting the organisation and suggested ways in which it might be reformed. This report is a most useful source of information on the IASC's structure and its perceived weaknesses. One year later, in November 1999, the working party issued its definitive recommendations for the reform of the IASC (IASC, 1999). Early in 2000 the IASC adopted a revised constitution, based on the working party's recommendations, which came into effect in April 2001, when the IASB replaced the IASC.

6.4   The International Accounting Standards Board (IASB)

6.4.1   Objectives

The objectives of the IASB are stated in its constitution to be:

(a) to develop, in the public interest, a single set of high quality, understandable and enforceable global accounting standards that require high quality, transparent and comparable information in financial statements and other financial reporting to help participants in the world's capital markets and other users make economic decisions;

(b) to promote the use and rigorous application of these standards;

(c) to bring about convergence of national accounting standards and International Accounting Standards to high quality solutions [*sic*].

The differences between these objectives and those of the IASC (see Section 6.2.2) may be summarised as follows:

1. There is a greater emphasis on enforceability. Thus in paragraph (a) it is stated that, in addition to being 'of high quality' and 'understandable', the IASB's standards should be 'enforceable'. Furthermore, in paragraph (b), the IASB sets itself the objective of promoting the 'rigorous application' of its standards. Undoubtedly these points were included in response to the criticism that compliance with its standards had been unsatisfactory (see Section 6.2.4). The SEC had been particularly critical in its comments on the proposed reforms (SEC, 2000).

2. There is specific reference (in paragraph (a)) to the world's capital markets and to users making economic decisions. It is made clear (as was not the case with the IASC) that the IASB adopts the Anglo-Saxon approach to financial reporting (information for decision-making) and not the Continental European approach (protection of creditors and basis for assessment of taxes).

3. There is a specific reference to national standards.

4. There are three references to 'high quality'. To a certain extent this is 'puff' as one would hardly expect that the IASB would set as its objective the development of 'low quality' standards.

6.4.2 Structure

The IASB's structure under its new constitution is set out in Exhibit 6.2. Formally it is a not-for-profit corporation, incorporated in the state of Delaware, USA. The author finds it ironic that the IASB chose to adopt the legal form of a Delaware corporation, in view of that state's reputation for a lax financial reporting regime, at least in the past.[4] The body's formal title is 'The International Accounting Standards Committee Foundation', which is very confusing as it refers to 'Committee' and not 'Board'. To avoid confusing the reader, in this book , the body is always referred to as the International Accounting Standards Board (IASB). It consists of the following bodies.

The trustees

The trustees' function is to secure the independence of the standard-setting body, by isolating it from outside pressures. The trustees appoint the members

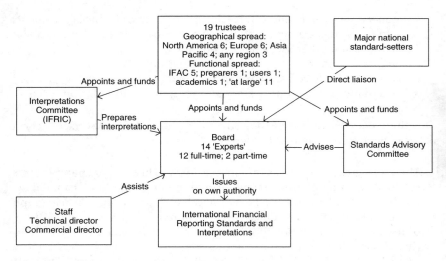

Exhibit 6.2   The IASB's structure

of the standard-setting body and raise the funds necessary for its operations. They also have an overall responsibility for ensuring that the whole organisation operates efficiently. However they are excluded from all technical matters relating to accounting standards.

In May 2000 the first board of 19 trustees was appointed. The chairman was Paul Volcker, an American citizen and former chairman of the US Federal Reserve Board. The great majority of the trustees came from North America (six from the USA and one from Canada) and Western Europe (seven); there were two trustees from Japan and one from Australia. The remaining two trustees were from Brazil and Hong Kong.

The Board

The Board is the body that issues international accounting standards and interpretations. It does this on its own authority; the trustees have no right to interfere. The Board consists of fourteen persons appointed by the trustees, twelve full-time and two part-time. They are selected for their technical knowledge, skills and experience in financial reporting and international business. The Board members are considered to be independent 'experts'; they do not represent any particular constituency, whether geographical or functional. In selecting the Board members, the trustees follow criteria set out in the Constitution:

- The Board should not be dominated by any constituency or geographic interest.
- At least five members should have a background as practising auditors.

- At least three should have a background as preparers.
- At least three should have a background as users.
- At least one member should have an academic background.

Seven of the full-time members are designated as having formal liaison responsibility with respect to one or more national standard-setters (those of the USA, UK, Japan, Australia, Canada, France and Germany). One of the full-time members is designated by the trustees as the chairman and chief executive of the IASB, that is he combines the functions that under the former regime were performed by the Board Chairman and the Secretary General. In June 2000 the trustees appointed Sir David Tweedie, the former chairman of Britain's ASB, as the first chairman of the new IASB.

International Financial Reporting Interpretations Committee (IFRIC)

This consists of twelve members chosen by the trustees. The IFRIC's function is to review on a timely basis accounting issues that are likely to receive divergent or unacceptable treatment in the absence of authoritative guidance. The basic problem is that, where the IASB's standards are ambiguous, imprecise or lacking detail, enterprises may interpret them in a way that the IASB considers to be incorrect and contrary to the standard's objectives. This may arise in two rather different situations:

1. Where different enterprises apply different interpretations to the provisions of an IASB standard. This often occurs when the standard fails to specify clear rules on how to account for a particular transaction or event, possibly because at the time that the standard was issued these were not significant.
2. Where an enterprise deliberately applies a strained or perverse interpretation to a standard's provision as a justification for not reporting in accordance with its spirit.

The solution is for the IASB to issue interpretations of its standards. The IFRIC prepares these interpretations which have to be approved by the Board before they are issued.

Standards Advisory Committee (SAC)

The SAC consists of about fifty members appointed by the trustees. The members represent a wide range of constituencies: there are members from Asia (including China and India), from East Europe (Russia and Estonia), Africa and Latin America, but the majority come from the EU, USA, Japan and Australia. According to the IASB's constitution, the SAC's function is to provide a forum for participation in the IASB's activities by parties with an interest in financial reporting. It should advise the IASB on agenda decisions and give its opinions on proposed standards. In effect the SAC is the IASB's official liaison body with certain important opinion makers, notably:

- National standard-setters: as already mentioned, the seven most important national standard-setters have a direct connection with the IASB through a specified board member; the other less privileged national standard-setters (such as China and Korea) have to be content with membership of the SAC.
- The accountancy profession: no less than fourteen of the fifty members are professional accountants.
- International organisations, such as the World Bank, the IOSCO and the European Commission.

Staff

The working party's report envisaged that the Board would be supported by a high quality technical staff, whose members would be employed on a permanent basis by the IASB. At present the IASB has a staff of about forty, more than twice the number of its predecessor. There has been an enormous increase in resources – the IASB's revenue in its first year (2001) was over £14 million, compared with the IASC's £2 million in its last year (2000).

6.4.3   The composition of the IASB's board

Exhibit 6.3 sets out the names of the members of the initial Board, together with a limited amount of information about each of them.

The first piece of information is their previous position, before joining the IASB. Five were standard-setters, being full-time members of their national standard-setting body. Four were executives in major multinational enterprises, with responsibility for the accounting function. Three were partners in audit firms and two were professors. All had to resign from their previous jobs, except for Mary Barth and Robert Herz,[5] who were appointed as part-time members of the Board and, as such, were permitted to continue their outside activities. The author has made an analysis of the background of the members of the initial Board, taking into account not only their position immediately before joining the Board but also positions occupied in the previous twenty years, with the aim as classifying them as standard-setter, auditor, preparer, user or academic. Only the last twenty years have been taken into account and more weight has been given to the more recent years, on the grounds that the more remote career experience is less relevant. Certain of the new members present no problems in classification; thus Harry Schmid, who spent his whole career as an accountant with Nestlé, the Swiss multi-national, is classified wholly as a preparer. His work as a member of the Swiss standard-setting body is disregarded as it was part-time. However, other members have had much more varied careers. For example, during the past twenty years,

Exhibit 6.3 The composition of the IASB's initial board

	Previous position	Nationality	Qualified accountant	Connection with	
				National standard-setter	Old IASC
Sir David Tweedie	Chair ASB (UK)	UK	Yes	Chairman of ASB	Board member
Tom Jones	CFO of Citicorp	UK	Yes	on FASB's EITF	Board member
Mary Barth*	Professor	USA	Yes	on FASB's Advisory Council	
Hans-Georg Bruns	Chief accountant, Daimler Benz	German	No	on DRSC's working party	
Anthony Cope	Board member FASB	UK	No	Member of FASB	Observer
Robert Garnett	Vice-President, Anglo-American PLC	UK**	Yes	on South Africa's APB	
Gilbert Gélard	Partner KPMG, France	French	Yes	Member of CNC	Board member
Robert Herz*	Partner Deloitte & Touche	USA	Yes	on FASB's EITF	
James Leisenring	Board member FASB	USA	Yes	Member of FASB	Board member
Warren McGregor	Director, AARF	Australian	Yes	on staff of AARF	Board member
Tricia O'Malley	Chair ASB (Canada)	Canadian	Yes	Chair of CICA's ASB	
Harry Schmid	Chief accountant, Nestlé	Swiss	No	Member of Swiss FER	Board member
Geoff Whittington	Professor	UK	Yes	Member of ASB	
Tatsumi Yamada	Partner PwC	Japanese	Yes	Member of BADC	Board member

* Part-time member.

** Robert Garnett is also a South African citizen.

Robert Garnett has been a partner with Arthur Andersen (auditor), investment manager with a venture capital group (user) and Executive Vice President of Anglo-American PLC (preparer). Taking account of the length of time that he spent in each capacity and giving more weight to the more recent past, the author assesses Robert Garnett as being 15 per cent auditor, 50 per cent preparer and 35 per cent user. The full results for all fourteen members are presented in Exhibit 6.4. The overall position is shown in the last line of this table. The weightings of the various groups are: standard-setters 25 per cent; auditors 31 per cent; preparers 26 per cent; users 5 per cent and academics 13 per cent. These weightings reflect more or less the criteria that trustees were obliged to take into account in the selection process (see Section 6.4.2 (b) above) with the important exception that the users are under-represented.[6]

The second piece of information concerns nationality. Five members are British citizens. This is a remarkably high number, given that, in economic terms (size of GDP), Britain ranks behind the USA, Japan and Germany. However the high figure for British citizens is rather misleading, as Robert Garnett is also a citizen of South Africa, where he spends half his time, and both Anthony Cope and Tom Jones have been resident in the USA for at least the last twenty years. The more reliable figure is that ten of the fourteen members are from the 'Anglo-Saxon' countries: UK, USA, Canada, Australia and (in its approach to financial reporting) South Africa.

The third piece of information concerns the qualifications of the new members. No less than eleven are qualified accountants, being members of their national professional body. Of the three who are not qualified accountants,

Exhibit 6.4   The background of the members of the IASB's board

	Standard-setter (%)	Auditor (%)	Preparer (%)	User (%)	Academic (%)
Sir David Tweedie	70	30			
Tom Jones	10		90		
Mary Barth		20			80
Hans-Georg Bruns			100		
Anthony Cope	60			40	
Robert Garnett		15	50	35	
Gilbert Gélard		80	20		
Robert Herz		100			
James Leisenring	100				
Warren McGregor	100				
Tricia O'Malley	10	90			
Harry Schmid			100		
Geoff Whittington					100
Tatsumi Yamada		100			
Overall	25	31	26	5	13

two, Hans-Georg Bruns and Harry Schmid, are company accountants from countries where the professional accountancy bodies represent only auditors. In effect, the only non-accountant on the new board is Anthony Cope, who is a chartered financial analyst.

Another aspect of the technical expertise of the new members is their experience of standard-setting. It is quite remarkable that all fourteen members are closely connected with their national standard-setting body. Eight were full members of their national standard-setting body: two each from the UK's ASB and the USA's FASB, with one each from the standard-setting bodies of France, Germany, Switzerland and Japan. The others were either staff members (Warren McGregor) or have served on committees or task forces. The four former members of the ASB and FASB will probably form a cohesive and therefore effective block.

Half of the new board sat on the IASC Board, either as full members or as observers. In fact Tom Jones was the IASC's last chairman. This proportion strikes a good balance between assuring continuity and bringing in new blood.

6.5   The IASB's operations

At its first meeting, the IASB adopted all the existing International Accounting Standards of its predecessor so that these have the status of its own standards. The IASB has adopted a very ambitious programme which consists of both amendments to the IASs and the issue of new standards, which are to be given the title International Financial Reporting Standards (IFRS). It is concentrating on contentious issues, such as financial instruments (with a proposal to amend the IASC's standards on this subject), business combinations and stock options (for which an IFRS was issued in early 2004). It issued its first International Financial Reporting Standard, IFRS 1 'First-time adoption of IFRS' in June 2003. This standard was highly topical, given the requirement for European listed companies to adopt the IASB's standards from 1 January 2005. The standard's rules are reasonable and logical, including common-sense solutions for many of the problems faced by companies switching over to the IASB's standards, for example there is no requirement for the IASB's rules to be applied retrospectively to past acquisitions. The standard's most important provision is that the comparative figures in the accounts relating to the previous financial year must also be based on the IASB's standards. This implies that European companies must already start recording transactions according to the IASB's standards in January 2004.

In developing a standard, the IASB adopts a complex procedure, known as 'due process', that consists of the following steps:

(a) Putting an item on the agenda. The Board has complete discretion in deciding whether to initiate a project which would have as its aim the issue of a standard on a particular subject. It claims[7] that it consults widely before setting its agenda, particularly with the Standards Advisory Committee, national standard-setters and security regulators.

(b) Setting up an advisory group. The IASC invariably sets up a steering committee to prepare the text of a proposed standard. The IASB's constitution states that it will 'normally' set up such a body.

(c) Research and informal consultation. The IASB may outsource research to third parties, such as national standard-setters. Before publishing any proposals it will consult with 'insiders' such as national standard-setters (through the Board member responsible for liaison) and the Standards Advisory Committee. As part of this process, the IASC invariably published a draft statement of principles, inviting comments from the public. The IASB's constitution states that it will 'normally' publish such a statement.

(d) The IASB, after having reviewed the comments received, prepares an exposure draft, which sets out the proposed text of the standard. The text is considered by the Board. With the IASC, it was very common for the discussion at Board level to be very lively, with votes being taken on contentious issues. For the exposure draft to be issued, eight of the fourteen members must vote in favour. The exposure draft is then published with a general invitation to submit comments.

(e) The IASB considers the comments received and prepares the text of the proposed standard. The discussion at Board level is similar to that for the exposure draft, with the same majority (eight votes in favour) for the issue of a standard.

The following general points may be made concerning this procedure:

1. Many steps consist of the IASB issuing a document, inviting comments, reviewing the comments received and then revising the document.

2. Except in the early stages of a project, there is considerable openness. This is achieved through the publication of various documents and by opening the meetings of the Board to the public.

3. The aim of 'due process' is to ensure that all persons who may be affected by the proposed standard have an opportunity of presenting their viewpoint and of influencing the final decision. Although the IASB cannot accept that any powerful party (such as the preparers or the audit profession) should have a veto over its proposed standards, it certainly needs to be forewarned of any major objections of these parties which would lessen the standard's acceptability. By giving them the opportunity of voicing their objections, the IASB increases the chances of finding a compromise that is acceptable to all parties and, at the very least, can claim that it has acted reasonably. A secondary aim of 'due process' is to discover and correct any technical problems, such as points not covered and inconsistencies in the draft.

4. Although at the time of writing, it is too early to make an informed judgement on the way in which the IASB carries out its 'due process', the author has the impression that it places more weight on consultation with national standard-setters than with the wider public. It is noteworthy that, in the early stages of a project, when outsiders have the greatest chance of influencing the standard-setter's thinking, the IASB has tended to restrict its consultations to 'insiders' – that is the SAC and those national standard-setters with whom it has direct links. The old IASC invariably issued a draft statement of principles during this stage. The IASB has not done so for any project, despite being required by its constitution to do so 'normally'.[8] Many preparers have criticised the IASB for failing to take account of their views. On this point, see Section 8.3.3 of Chapter 8.

5. The majority required for the issue both of an exposure draft and of a standard is surprisingly low (8 votes out of 14, being 57 per cent). With the IASC, the required majorities were considerably larger: 66 per cent for an exposure draft and 75 per cent for a standard. The lower majority with the IASB certainly increases the likelihood of that body issuing rigorous standards but also raises the danger that the views of minorities will be over-ridden, with negative effects on the standard's acceptability.

6.6   Comments on the IASB's structure

Although it is too early to pass a definitive judgement on the effectiveness of the IASB's structure, it is possible to make some general remarks:

Independence from the accountancy profession

The IASC was much criticised as being dominated by the accountancy profession. The trustees were introduced into the new structure specifically to demonstrate that the Board (the standard-setting body) was independent of the accountancy profession. However this raises the question as to how the trustees are appointed. The IASC took great care to ensure that the first trustees of the IASB were appointed in such a way that no one could doubt their independence. It entrusted the task of selecting the first trustees to a high-powered Nominations Committee of seven persons of whom only one was a professional accountant. Of the rest, four were heads of national regulatory authorities (of the USA, Britain, France and Hong Kong), one was the deputy head of the German standards board and one was the head of the World Bank. Certainly this committee was not dominated by accountants; however, equally clearly it was dominated by the developed countries and by persons connected with the capital market.

In selecting trustees the Nominating Committee followed certain guidelines as to the geographical spread and the functional spread. Thus five of the nineteen trustees were to be appointed in consultation with IFAC (the professional accountants). However these trustees would be in a clear minority in the total of nineteen. In fact the largest elements are the eleven 'at large' trustees who are selected to represent the public interest. However, although professional accountants make up a minority of the trustees, this is not the case with the Board. As shown in Exhibit 6.3, qualified accountants are in a clear majority on the Board, providing no less than eleven of the fourteen members. At the level of the body that actually sets the standards, the accountants have succeeded in maintaining their dominance.

Dominance of the developed countries and of the Anglo-Saxons

A further criticism of the IASC was that it was dominated by the developed countries. It is clear that this will be the case with the IASB to an even greater extent. This is even more true with respect to the dominance of the Anglo-Saxons which was such a marked feature of the IASC. The two most influential positions in the new structure are occupied by Anglo-Saxons: the chairman of the trustees is the American, Paul Volcker and the chairman of the Board is the Scot, Sir David Tweedie.

With ten of the fourteen members, the 'Anglo-Saxons' will clearly dominate the new Board. In fact given that, under the IASB's constitution, the votes of only eight of the fourteen members are required for the approval of a standard, the 'Anglo-Saxon' members are in a position to secure the passage of any measure on which they are agreed, ignoring the objections of the other members. The *Financial Times* (2001) commented that the composition of the new board would inevitably provoke controversy. There are two anomalies:

1. The relative neglect of Japan and the countries of Continental Europe. Although their combined GDP well exceeds that of the 'Anglo-Saxon' countries, they have only four members. The author particularly regrets that there are no members from the Netherlands or from the Scandinavian countries. The trustees (who selected the new members) seem to have taken no heed of the high standing of the Dutch accountancy profession or of the long experience of Scandinavian multinational companies in applying the IASs.[9]

2. The complete neglect of the less developed countries. The whole of Latin America, Asia (apart from Japan) and Africa (apart from South Africa) are completely unrepresented. The ACCA, the British professional body with the greatest interest in the developing countries, has criticised the new board as having insufficient experience of the developing world, its technical director commenting: 'most of the appointments reinforce the perspective of the larger companies from developed economies ... the new membership does not go far enough in redressing the perception of exclusion, particularly for developing and transitional economies'.[10] The author was not surprised at the exclusion of the developing countries. In its last years, the IASC spent virtually all its energies in developing standards appropriate for the global capital market. Previously the

IASC had considered that one of its prime functions was to develop standards that were appropriate for all countries and ensured that at least three developing countries were represented on the Board. The change in approach was signalled when the IASB adopted a constitution that included the objective 'to help participants in the world's capital markets' and has been confirmed with not a single person from a developing country on the new board.

Cooperation with national standard-setters

The new structure makes explicit provision for the national standard-setters. Seven members of the Board have special responsibility for liaison with one or more national standard-setters. In most cases they are former members of the national body, but not current members as they are full-time members of the IASB. These Board members are expected to attend meetings of the national body and there seems to be little doubt that they will act as the IASB's advocate within the national body and the national body's advocate within the IASB. There seems to be no concern on anyone's part that this close relationship would compromise the IASB's independence. Since there are only seven such liaison members, only the standard-setting bodies of certain privileged countries will benefit from this special relationship, notably USA, UK, France, Germany, Japan, Canada and Australia. The smaller countries are excluded. With the IASB, it would seem, to adapt the words of George Orwell, that 'all national standard setters are equal but some are more equal than others'.

The neglect of users

As shown in Exhibit 6.4, the users of financial statements are very poorly represented on the IASB. Only two members have any significant background as users; they are Anthony Cope, who before joining the FASB in 1993 worked for thirty years as a security analyst, and Robert Garnett, who is a member of the Investment Analysts Society of Southern Africa and who, in the course of a very varied career, worked for some ten years for a venture capital group and a merchant bank. However, in neglecting the users, the IASC is following the practice of standard-setting bodies throughout the world. Only one of the FASB's seven members has a background as a user, and, on the standard-setting bodies of the European countries, users make up only 13 per cent of the members.[11] Truly the users are the 'Cinderella' of the standard-setting process. According to the IASB's constitution there should be a minimum of three Board members with a background as users of financial statements. Thus, in appointing only two users, the trustees were not only neglecting an important constituency but were also disregarding their own constitution. Paul Volcker has claimed that Geoff Whittington may be considered to be a user, because of his experience with the UK's Monopolies Commission, of which he was a member from 1987 to 1996. However this was only a part-time appointment; Geoff Whittington's principal activity throughout his career has been as an academic, as Professor of Accounting, first at the University of Bristol and latterly at the University of Cambridge. Whatever 'spin' the trustees seek to place on their appointments, they cannot hide the fact that, on the new board, there is only one person, Anthony Cope, whose principal career experience was as a user.

The rise of the professional standard-setters

The members of the new Board, whose previous full-time position was as standard-setters may be considered as the element that balances the conflicting interests of auditors, preparers and users. Persons with their principal background as auditors or preparers make up over half the board; hence auditors and preparers can be confident that their concerns will be fully taken into consideration. However this is not the case with the users. Given the limited presence of members with a background as users, the task of defending the interests of the users will fall on the professional standard-setters; that is people like Sir David Tweedie and James Leisenring, whose main activity in the last ten or twenty years has been standard-setting. In fact the development of standard-setting as a career separate from that of auditor or preparer has been one of the most striking recent developments in financial reporting. The twelve full-time members of the IASB will be a significant addition to this new profession.

Efficiency of operation

The IASB has fourteen members, which is significantly more than the FASB (seven) and the ASB (ten). The IASC's working party's report commented: 'While some might believe that a smaller sized Board would be preferable in terms of certain aspects of operating efficiency, the Working Party has come to this number (14) because of the need to have enough people to work closely with national standard-setters and the need for involvement of individuals with diverse experience.' Certainly with respect to its decision-making body, the IASB is significantly smaller than the IASC.

The expert model versus the constituency model

During 1998–99, when the new structure was being developed, the most controversial point was whether the body that had the authority to issue standards should be composed of experts (persons with a technical knowledge of accounting, financial reporting and standard-setting) or of representatives (persons representing the different constituencies, of which there was more than one dimension, for example: preparers, users and auditors, developed countries versus developing countries, Europe versus North America, the Anglo-Saxons versus the Rest). The IASC Board consisted of representatives;

thirteen of the members represented national accountancy bodies and the remainder the preparers and the users. The IASB is based on the expert model. The new constitution specifically states the Board members do not represent constituencies but should act independently in the public interest.[12] The constituencies are represented in the composition of the nineteen trustees, but only weakly as the majority of the trustees represent the public 'at large'.

Many people are unhappy with the 'expert model'. In their opinion, standard-setting is essentially a political process. Certainly it involves some technical knowledge, but in the end the ultimate fate of a proposed standard depends on political considerations. This is because financial reporting affects the distribution of wealth between individuals. Society cannot allow such important matters to be settled by the opinions of so-called experts. As was argued in Chapter 3, society considers that the appropriate way of setting the rules that affect the interests of its members is through the political processes of consultation, lobbying, bargaining, debate and in the end voting. Every standard-setting system must include the political element, if only because a standard that is rejected by important parts of society is useless. The importance of the political element is clear in the American regulatory system, where the ultimate power lies with the Congress and the SEC.[13] It is evident that the IASB's structure is modelled on the American system: the Board is the equivalent of the FASB and the trustees the Financial Accounting Foundation. However the IASB has not reproduced within its structure the political elements in the American system, Congress and the SEC. This means that the political element (which is an absolutely essential element of any regulatory system) has to be provided outside the IASB's structure. It will be provided at national level, for example the SEC has already announced (SEC, 2000) that it will vet the IASB's standards to assure itself that they are appropriate for use in the American capital market. The EU argued strongly but in vain for the new body to be based on the constituency model, as it felt that, only if the EU were represented on the rule-making body, could it ensure that no standards were issued that were contrary to its essential interests. Having failed in this attempt, the EU has set up its own body to check that the IASB's standards conform with EU law and to reject those that do not. This point is covered in more detail in Section 7.7.5 of the following chapter.

It is perhaps unrealistic to expect that the IASB could have developed within its structure a representative body which would have issued standards that all interested parties would have accepted unconditionally. That would have implied that important actors such as the SEC would have delegated authority to the IASB and, ultimately, the American government would have given up its power to set the rules for enterprises operating in the USA. For the foreseeable future the USA and other countries are unwilling to surrender these important powers to an international body such as the

IASB, which implies that there will be an important political element in the rule-making process that is outside the IASB's system. In this case, the expert model can be justified as assuring the efficient operation of the standard-setting process. But it also means that the accountancy profession in a rather surreptitious way retains control of the system since, as demonstrated in Exhibit 6.3, the majority of the experts are accountants.

6.7   Conclusions

At the start of the chapter it was remarked that the IASC suffered from two characteristics that severely limited its effectiveness: it was a private organisation and its standards had no official status or authority. This is still the case with the IASB. It has made a great effort to improve its status, notably by setting up a prestigious Board of Trustees. But it is still a private organisation. Its standards still have no authority. They will only achieve any authority if they are accepted by national authorities. This is one of the principal matters considered in the following chapters.

Notes

1. On this point, see Flower and Ebbers (2002) Chapter 1.
2. Quote from 'Preface to statements of International Accounting Standards' (IASC, 2000).
3. IOSCO stands for the International Organization of Securities Commissions. It represents the national stock exchange regulatory bodies (such as the USA's SEC and France's COB) at international level.
4. See, on this point, Section 5.2.3 of the previous chapter.
5. Robert Herz resigned in 2002 to become chairman of the FASB. He was replaced by John Smith who was almost Robert Herz's clone, being a US citizen, a professional accountant and a partner in a major US firm. Hence the author's analysis of the initial board is equally applicable to the current board.
6. On this point, See Section 6.6.
7. This information is from the IASB's website (www.iasb.org) which is a rich source of information about the organisation. The IASB's constitution is another useful source of information about the procedures that the body should follow.
8. Prior to issuing the exposure draft on share options, the IASB did reissue the discussion paper that had been published some two years earlier by the G4+1 group. However this is the exception that proves the rule, as this paper was not prepared by the IASB.
9. The head of the European Commission's Company Law Division has commented that the Anglo-Saxons should have more respect for other cultures if they wanted the IASB to be a more international organisation.
10. Quoted on the ACCA's website (www.acca.org.uk).
11. For an analysis of the composition of the European standard-setting bodies, see Chapter 13 of Flower, J. and Lefebvre, C. (1997).
12. However note the criteria (set out in Section 6.4.2) as to the background of Board members. When one of the original Board members, Robert Hertz, resigned to become Chairman of the FASB, he was replaced by John Smith. In fact both

Robert Hertz and John Smith were American citizens and partners in American accountancy firms. This can hardly have been a coincidence and illustrates the narrow distinction between acting as a representative of a constituency and having a particular professional background.

13. On this point, see Flower and Ebbers (2002) Chapter 5.

References

Biddle, G. C. and Saudagaran, S. M. (1991). 'Foreign stock listings: benefits, costs, and the accounting policy dilemma'. *Accounting Horizons* 5(3): 69–80.

Financial Times (2001). Editorial, 26 January.

Flower, J. and Ebbers, G. (2002). *Global Financial Reporting*. Palgrave.

Flower, J. and Lefebvre, C. (1997). *Comparative Studies in Accounting Regulation*. Leuven Acco.

IASC (1998). *Shaping IASC for the Future*. London, International Accounting Standards Committee.

IASC (1999). *Recommendations on Shaping IASC for the Future*. London, International Accounting Standards Committee.

IASC (2000). *International Accounting Standards*. London, International Accounting Standards Committee.

Radebaugh, L. H. and Gebhardt, G. (1995). 'Foreign stock exchange listings: a case study of Daimler Benz'. *Journal of International Financial Management and Accounting* 6(2).

SEC (2000). *Concept Release on International Accounting Standards*. Washington, Securities and Exchange Commission.

7
The EU versus the IASB versus the USA

The two preceding chapters have introduced two organisations which are involved in setting rules for the financial reporting of European enterprises: the EU through its directives and the IASB through its International Accounting Standards. This chapter introduces a third actor: the USA. It explains why the American rules (United States Generally Accepted Accounting Principles – always abbreviated to US GAAP) represent a possible alternative for the financial reporting of European enterprises. The existence of three possible sources of the rules for European enterprises makes the study of European financial reporting extremely interesting but also rather complicated. This chapter explores these complications, by analysing how the relationships between the three actors, the EU, the IASB and the USA, have developed in recent years. First it seeks to explain why the rules of a foreign country in a different continent should be of any relevance for European enterprises.

7.1 Why US GAAP is relevant for European enterprises

The principal reason why many European enterprises use US GAAP for their accounts is to gain access to the American capital market. As already explained in the previous chapter, under American law, a company whose shares are listed on an American stock exchange is obliged to file accounts that conform with US GAAP. A secondary reason is the good reputation of US GAAP; in countries other than the USA many investors prefer the shares of companies that report according to US GAAP.

7.2 US GAAP

At this point it is appropriate to set out a fuller explanation of US GAAP. Two aspects of US GAAP are considered: (1) How the rules are set. (2) The nature of its rules.

7.2.1 How the rules of US GAAP are set

A government agency, the Securities and Exchange Commission (SEC), is responsible for the regulation of the American capital market. Under the terms of the law by which it was created (the Securities and Exchange Act of 1934) the SEC has authority to set the rules that govern the financial reporting of listed companies. However the SEC has delegated the task of developing the detailed rules to a private standard-setting body, the Financial Accounting Standards Board (FASB), subject to a right of veto – the SEC reserves the right to reject a standard issued by the FASB by issuing its own countervailing rule. Hence the FASB pays very careful attention to the SEC's views in developing its standards. In its turn the SEC, as a government agency, has to consider the views of the government: both the legislator, the Congress, and the administration, headed by the president. To ensure its survival, the SEC must be responsive to the demands of these bodies. The SEC's governing body, the five commissioners, are appointed for terms of five years by the president, with the advice and consent of the Senate. The result is that the system for setting the rules of US GAAP is highly politicised. This is particularly the case when the FASB proposes a standard that could affect the interests of important elements of the US economy. Parties who consider that they may be affected by the proposed standard lobby all those involved in the standard-setting process – the FASB, the SEC, the Congress and the Administration.

The political nature of the American standard-setting process was demonstrated very clearly when in 1993 the FASB sought to strengthen the rules of US GAAP for the reporting of share options. It issued an exposure draft which proposed that the granting of an option should be reported as an expense equal to the fair value of the option at that date. This proposal led to a storm of protest which is graphically described by Zeff (1997). The opponents of the measure succeeded in portraying it as a threat to the whole practice of granting share options which were a major element of the remuneration of thousands of people. There were public demonstrations which were reported in the press and on television. The centre of the protests was 'Silicon Valley' the home of many high-tech firms whose workers received much of their remuneration in the form of share options. The high point was an employee rally described by Zeff as 'raucous' at which speakers castigated the FASB's proposal as a threat to jobs. Many Americans learned for the first time about the FASB which was represented as a sinister organisation intent on depriving true-blooded Americans of their fundamental liberties. They lobbied Congress; Congress lobbied the SEC; the SEC lobbied the FASB; in addition both Congress and the SEC threatened to intervene more directly. The result was predictable; the FASB withdrew its proposal that the cost of share options must be reported as an expense in the income statement.

This incident demonstrates clearly two important characteristics of the American system for the regulation of financial reporting:

1. It is fundamentally political. The FASB claims that standard-setting is a technical activity carried out by experts who are guided by research and basic principles. It has developed its conceptual framework to back up this claim. However these experts are only permitted to set the rules within the limits set by the politicians. Where a subject is of little political interest, the FASB is left to develop its standards following its 'due process'. But in matters that society considers to be important, the FASB has to give way. The USA is a democracy not a technocracy. Miller, Redding and Bahnson, whose book 'The FASB: the People, the Process and the Politics' (1998) is by far the best exposition of this body, ask the question 'Is the FASB a political institution?' and give the unequivocal answer 'a clear yes'.
2. Ultimate authority lies with the legislative power (Congress), subject to the veto of the president. The FASB has to acknowledge the superior authority of the SEC, a body granted this authority by a law, but, in its turn, the SEC has to consider the views of Congress in carrying out its regulatory function. The SEC was created by a law and can be abolished by a law.

Recently the FASB has renewed its efforts to issue a strengthened standard on share options and it seems very probable that this time it will be successful. However this development merely confirms the political nature of the standard-setting process, for since 1993 there has been a fundamental shift in public opinion, which, following the Enron scandal (dealt with in Chapter 9), is now very much in favour of stricter accounting for share options. Hence the Congress and the Administration, which both ultimately depend on the electorate, are now more supportive of the FASB's proposals.

7.2.2   The nature of the rules

Apart from its essentially political origin, the most remarkable feature of US GAAP is its extraordinary detail. To date the FASB has issued over 150 standards and each year adds many more to the total. However in addition there are numerous other documents that the SEC recognises as setting out elements of US GAAP; for example the SEC's own rules and the statements of the standard-setting bodies that preceded the FASB. In all, the detailed rules of US GAAP fill several thousand pages.[1] There are two reasons for this extraordinary amount of detail:

1. In essence the American government and the American public do not trust the accountancy profession and the preparers with the financial reporting of companies. There is a deep-seated distrust which has its origins in the great depression of the 1930s which most contemporary Americans

attributed at least partially to the misleading accounts issued by American companies in the boom years of the 1920s. Recent events, such as the Enron scandal (covered in Chapter 9) have tended to strengthen the public's negative attitude. Hence there is a general feeling that financial reporting should be regulated by the government.

2. The USA is a highly litigious society. It is extremely common for persons who have suffered loss to sue for damages any party that is in any way connected with the matter. Whenever a company fails or even simply suffers a loss, aggrieved shareholders will sue the auditor claiming that he has been negligent. The auditor's best defence is that, in all material respects, the audited accounts comply with US GAAP. Hence there is a great demand from the accountancy profession for detailed rules to which they can turn for justification in a lawsuit.

This brief introduction has not covered all aspects of US GAAP, for example the content of its rules. For a fuller explanation see Chapter 5 of Flower and Ebbers (2002).

7.3 The EU's dilemma

That US GAAP posed a problem for European MNEs was made very evident in 1993, when Daimler Benz applied to be listed on the New York Stock Exchange. The SEC insisted that Daimler Benz prepare and publish a statement, which reconciled its net income and equity, as presented in its German accounts according to German GAAP, with the figures for these same items calculated according to US GAAP. The preparation and auditing of this reconciliation statement was a very costly exercise, as it involved just as much work as for a full set of US GAAP accounts. More seriously the statement revealed very considerable differences between the two sets of figures (as shown in Exhibit 6.1), which clearly confused investors.

The MNEs turned to the EU to help them out of their difficulties. The EU found itself in a difficult position. Its harmonisation programme had been drawn up without giving any serious consideration to the specific needs of the MNEs. The aim of the harmonisation programme was to achieve a satisfactory level of uniformity of company accounts within the EU. What the MNEs wanted was essentially harmonisation of accounts at a global level (or at least between Europe and the USA). For the MNEs, Europe was too small.

The European Commission (1995) analysed the MNEs' problem in the following terms:

> The most urgent problem is that concerning European companies with an international vocation. The accounts prepared by these companies in accordance with their national legislation, based on the Accounting Directives, are no longer acceptable for international capital market

purposes. These companies are therefore obliged to prepare two sets of accounts, one set which is in conformity with the Accounting Directives and another set which is required by the international capital markets. This situation is not satisfactory. It is costly and the provision of different figures in different environments is confusing to investors and to the public at large. There is a risk that large companies will be increasingly drawn towards US GAAP.

In this situation, the possible courses of action that were available to the EU in 1995 may be analysed as follows:

1. *Do nothing*: One possibility was for the EU to maintain the status quo: to insist that the MNEs continue to issue accounts drawn up according to the EU's rules, which effectively condemned many of them to issue two sets of accounts. However the EU decided that the situation in which European MNEs prepared two sets of accounts was unsatisfactory and untenable in the long run.
2. *Accept US GAAP*: A second possibility was for the EU to exempt the larger European MNEs from compliance with the EU's directives and to permit them to draw up their accounts according to US GAAP. The EU came under strong pressure from the MNEs and from certain national governments to permit this. However the EU refused. To consent to this demand, would lead to a serious breach in the laboriously constructed edifice of harmonisation and, more seriously, it would mean that the rules that governed the accounts of the larger European companies would be set by a foreign power over which the EU had no influence.
3. *Mutual recognition*: The European Commission attempted to negotiate a mutual recognition agreement with the American authorities. It proposed that the USA would recognise the accounts of European companies drawn up according to the EU rules, in return for the EU recognising the accounts of American companies based on US GAAP. But the Americans showed no interest. They were not prepared to exempt European companies from the American rules. There seemed to be no necessity, given that even a company as prestigious as Daimler Benz was prepared to submit to American jurisdiction in order to secure the valuable privilege of a listing on Wall Street. Furthermore, the European Commission was in a weak bargaining position, since the more important European stock exchanges already recognised for listing purposes the accounts of American companies drawn up under US GAAP.
4. *Develop European GAAP*: The EU considered setting up a European standard-setting body which would further develop the rules enshrined in the directives with the aim of developing a 'European GAAP' that would provide the information demanded by participants on the global capital market and which would rival US GAAP in detail and in quality.

However it soon abandoned this idea as impracticable. The process of developing a European GAAP would take too long and also be too costly. Furthermore, based on the evidence of Daimler Benz's behaviour, it seemed very probable that the MNEs, if given a choice, would prefer US GAAP to the EU's rules.

All of the above alternatives had to be rejected either as impracticable or as breaching two principles that the EU regarded as inviolable:

1. that it could not permit that the rules governing the financial reporting of EU companies should be set by a body over which it had no influence – in concrete terms it could not accept that US GAAP should become the standard for the larger European companies;
2. that European companies should remain subject to EU law, at least in formal terms.

The solution that the EU ultimately adopted was to make an agreement with the IASC, the IASB's predecessor. However before considering this agreement in detail, it is necessary to bring the reader up to date with a parallel development that occurred at the IASC at this time.

7.4   The IASC–IOSCO agreement

The IOSCO (International Organisation of Securities Commissions) is the body that represents at the international level the national stock exchange regulatory bodies, such as France's COB. Probably the most important member of IOSCO is the USA's SEC. In fact many commentators believe that the SEC is the driving force behind the organisation. In 1995, the IASC made an agreement with the IOSCO, which had a profound effect on the IASC's activities and ultimately may have an equally important effect on global financial reporting. The essential points of this agreement were that:

1. if, by 1999, the IASC were to develop a comprehensive set of core standards acceptable to the IOSCO,
2. then the IOSCO would recommend to its members that the IASC's standards should be accepted for cross-border offerings and other foreign listings.

In the agreement, the IOSCO listed 14 of the IASC's standards as being acceptable and endorsed the IASC's work programme whereby new and modified standards would be developed covering those areas where the present standards were inadequate. The subjects on which new or improved standards were to be developed included financial instruments, income taxes, segmental reporting, interim reporting and provisions. The importance of the agreement was that it set a definite date at which the IOSCO would be obliged to make a decision on endorsing the IASC's standards and thus made much more concrete the possibility that the MNEs would be permitted to use the IASC's standards for their accounts. The chances of these standards becoming generally accepted around the world received a significant boost.

7.5   The IASC–EU agreement

The IASC–IOSCO agreement offered the prospect of the IASC's standards being accepted by the American authorities, for the SEC was a leading member of the IOSCO. Therefore the EU reasoned that, if it were to permit the European MNEs to base their accounts on the IASC's standards, this would largely solve these companies' problems and would certainly check the movement towards US GAAP. In November 1995, the EU announced a new policy on accounting harmonisation (European Commission, 1995). The EU declared that it intended to cooperate with the IASC with the aim of ensuring that European MNEs would in future be able to draw up their consolidated accounts in accordance with that body's standards. However the EU was determined to uphold the authority of its directives. Hence it was necessary to ensure that there were no conflicts between these directives and the IASC's standards. To achieve this, the European Commission followed a two-point strategy:

1. It announced that it was prepared to consider amending any provision in the directives that conflicted with the IASC's standards.
2. It sought to increase its influence within the IASC's organisation to ensure that its standards reflected the EU's requirements and in particular did not contain any provision that was unacceptable to the EU, notably ones that conflicted with essential articles of the directives. The European Commission expected that, by working more closely with the IASC, it would 'allow the Union progressively to gain a position of greater influence on the IASC's work, including the determination of its agenda, so that its output [would] increasingly reflect the EU viewpoint' (European Commission, 1995, paragraph 5.4).

The second point was the more significant aspect of the EU's new policy. The European Commission saw the IASC–IOSCO agreement as a threat to its power to set the accounting rules for European MNEs. The EU could not permit that in future these rules should be set by a body over which it had no influence – hence its bid to increase its influence over the IASC. In effect the EU decided that permitting European MNEs to base their accounts on the IASC's standards would be the lesser evil, compared with their choosing US GAAP, for the EU could not expect ever to have any influence over the determination of US GAAP. The EU gave up its claim to be the exclusive rule-maker for European MNEs. Instead it decided to support the IASC as the best chance of preventing US GAAP becoming the global standard.

7.6   Recent developments: the IOSCO and the IASC

For five years (1995–99) the IASC's agenda was dominated by its agreement with the IOSCO. The collaboration with the IOSCO had two major effects on the IASC's activities:

1. It led to a significant tightening and expansion of the rules laid down in the International Accounting Standards (IASs). In the first fifteen years of its existence the IASC issued some thirty IASs, but they permitted so many alternative accounting treatments that they had little impact on the diversity of financial reporting around the world. Following the agreement with IOSCO, the IASC modified a number of IASs to eliminate previously permitted alternative methods and issued new standards on matters not previously covered (for example, financial instruments).

2. It led to the IASC concentrating virtually all its efforts on standards that are relevant to the problems of the larger MNEs, that is the issues identified in the IASC–IOSCO agreement. However, according to its constitution, the IASC should have been concerned with the improvement and harmonisation of financial reporting of enterprises throughout the world, regardless of size and of country. In fact, in the past, the developing countries had been among the most loyal supporters of the IASC. Undoubtedly, in allocating virtually all its resources to the completion of the IOSCO project, the IASC neglected a major part of its constituency. Under the IASB the neglect of the developing countries has become even worse.

   In March 1999, with the issue of IAS 39 *Financial Instruments: Recognition and Measurement*, the IASC claimed that it had fulfilled its obligations under its agreement with the IOSCO. In May 2000, the IOSCO announced that it had completed its assessment of 30 International Accounting Standards (IASs) and recommended that its members (the national regulatory authorities) allow their use for cross-border listings by multinational enterprises. The endorsement was not unconditional; in its report on IASs, the IOSCO mentioned a number of points where an IAS should be supplemented by additional reconciliations, disclosures or interpretations. It is now up to each national regulatory authority to decide whether to accept the IOSCO's recommendation, which is not binding on them. Given that the IOSCO has already mentioned the need for IASs to be supplemented, it seems improbable that the national authorities will give unconditional endorsement to IASs.

7.7   Recent developments: the EU and the IASC/IASB

Since 1995, the EU has further developed its relations with the IASC and its successor, the IASB.

7.7.1 EU–IASC cooperation

In 1995, the EU accepted a position as observer on the IASC Board. Although formally it had no vote, it played a major role in the IASC's activities. It seems likely that the IASC's voting members paid careful attention to the views of the EU, since, if that body were to come out strongly against an IASC standard, it would severely undermine its acceptability. By and large the arrangement seemed to work to the satisfaction of both sides. There is evidence that the EU succeeded in its aim of gaining greater influence over the IASC's work, for example, the illustrative formats in the revised version of IAS 1 bore a remarkable resemblance to those in the Fourth Directive.[2] The IASC did not always follow the EU's suggestions, but major differences were avoided. On its side the EU kept its part of the bargain; in 2001 it amended the Fourth Directive to permit the valuation of certain assets at fair value as required by IAS 39.

7.7.2 Voluntary adoption of the IASC's standards

The EU gave a clear indication that it was satisfied with the way that its agreement with the IASC was developing when, in 1998, it encouraged the member states to amend their laws so as to permit companies to present their accounts in accordance with internationally recognised rules. The EU was quite happy to promote such a development because it made clear that a necessary condition was that the accounts must still comply with the directives. The EU had made a detailed study of the IASC's standards and had concluded that, with certain exceptions,[3] they did not conflict with the EU's directives, in that, in almost all cases, it was possible to comply with the IASC's standards by choosing the appropriate options in the directives. However, because many member states had not incorporated these options into their national law, many companies were not able to comply with the IASC's standards. Hence action by national governments was required. The governments of a number of member states enacted laws that exempted certain categories of companies from the obligation to observe national rules for their consolidated accounts, provided that they conformed to internationally recognised rules and complied with the EU's directives. The position in the three larger member states is as follows:

1. *Germany*: By a law of 1998, listed companies were permitted to adopt the IASC's standards or US GAAP for their consolidated accounts. In formal terms they were exempted from the obligation to follow the detailed provisions of the German Commercial Code (HGB), provided that the following conditions were met: the accounts complied with the EU's directives; the notes to the accounts disclosed the basis of accounting and any differences with the HGB; the information value of the accounts was at least as great as that of accounts drawn up under the HGB.

2. *France*: Under a law passed in 1998, any company was allowed to adopt the IASC's standards for its consolidated accounts, provided that they had been translated into French and approved by the Comité de Reglementation Comptable (CRC). In fact at the time of writing, the CRC has still to act, so that French companies are not yet permitted to use the IASC's standards.

3. *Britain*: This country has not changed its law. British companies are still obliged to comply with the British Companies Act and the ASB's standards.

Apart from the three larger countries mentioned above, some smaller EU member states have enacted similar laws, including Austria, Belgium, Finland and Luxembourg. However these legislative changes led to a big increase in the use of the IASB's standards by companies in only one country. According to the IASB's statistics,[4] 66 German listed companies adopt the IASs for their consolidated accounts, compared with only two in France, one in Italy and none in Britain. Of the smaller member states, only Austria (12 companies) and Denmark (11 companies) report numbers in double figures.

7.7.3   Compulsory adoption of the IASB's standards

The amendments to the national laws that have just been described were clearly a stopgap measure that suffered from a number of disadvantages:

- Not all EU member states were covered.
- In some countries, notably Germany, companies were permitted to choose between the IASB's standards and US GAAP.
- Adoption by companies was voluntary.

Hence the EU decided that more prescriptive action was necessary – that the adoption of the IASB's standards must be made compulsory. In July 2002 it enacted a regulation (EU, 2002) which provides that European companies that are listed on a European stock exchange are required to adopt the IASB's standards for their consolidated accounts for financial years commencing on or after 1 January 2005. Unlike the Fourth and Seventh Directives, which had to be transformed into national law before companies were obliged to comply with them, this regulation is directly applicable throughout the EU without any further action by the member states. In this way, many of the disadvantages of the directives were avoided – for example, late or incomplete implementation by member states. The following extract from the regulation's preamble explains why the EU felt that it could no longer base the financial reporting of listed companies on the Fourth and Seventh Directives: 'The reporting requirements set out in these Directives cannot ensure the high level of transparency and comparability of financial reporting from all publicly traded companies which is a necessary condition for building an integrated capital market which operates effectively, smoothly and efficiently.'

For the individual accounts of listed companies and for both the individual accounts and the consolidated accounts of non-listed companies, there is a provision that 'Member States may permit or require' the adoption of the IASB's standards. The word 'may' indicates that it is a member state option. The word 'permit' indicates that member states may implement this as a company option. If a member state does not avail itself of this option, national law based on the Fourth and Seventh Directives continues to apply. The various combinations are presented in Exhibit 7.1.

The regulation should certainly lead to greater harmonisation with respect to the consolidated accounts of listed companies, because there are far fewer options in the IASB's standards compared with the EU's directives. However there is a considerable danger of a reduction in the level of harmonisation in the other three quadrants of Exhibit 7.1, depending on how member states implement the available options. It would seem inconceivable that those member states where taxation is based on the individual accounts (that is, most of the countries of Continental Europe) would permit that these accounts be based on the IASB's standards. However, in the other countries (notably Britain), there is a good case for permitting companies to use the IASB's standards for their individual accounts, since the consolidated accounts are based on the individual accounts and savings can be made by using the same standards for both the consolidated accounts and the individual accounts. Hence some increased disharmony between countries in relation to the individual accounts seems probable. Furthermore there is a strong case for all countries to permit (but not require) unlisted companies to use the IASB's standards for their consolidated accounts, since some will want to prepare themselves for a possible listing and may want to make their accounts comparable with those of their listed competitors. Hence, within countries, it seems probable that some disharmony will also arise in relation to the consolidated accounts.

At the time of writing, most EU member states have still to decide how they intend to implement the options. France has indicated that, for the consolidated accounts, non-listed companies will be given the option of adopting the IASB's standards; for the individual accounts, of both listed and non-listed companies, there is no plan to allow the adoption of the

Exhibit 7.1 Use of the IASB's standards by European companies from 2005

	Consolidated accounts	Individual accounts
Listed companies	Required	Member state option to 'permit or require'
Unlisted companies	Member state option to 'permit or require'	Member state option to 'permit or require'

IASB's standards. On this latter point, the President of the Conseil nationale de la comptabilité (CNC), the French standard-setting body, commented as follows: '...taking into account the institutional context in France, the CNC's position is not to propose the application of the IASB's standards for the individual accounts. The CNC...does not envisage at this stage, a separation of the individual accounts from the tax accounts. In addition to the connection between the individual accounts and the tax accounts for the computation of taxable income, other rules of company law depend on the individual accounts, such as the determination of distributable profit, the calculation of the workers' share in a company's profits, the rights of creditors, the procedures to be followed for companies in difficulty...'[5] In contrast to France, the UK has indicated that all companies will be given the option of using the IASB's standards for both the individual accounts and the consolidated accounts.

7.7.4 EU endorsement of the IASB's standards

The brief description that has just been given of the regulation may give the impression that the EU has delegated to the IASB the task of setting the rules that govern the accounts of European companies, at least in respect of the consolidated accounts of listed companies. However this is most certainly not the case. European companies may only use an IASB standard if it has been adopted by the EU and published in the EU's Official Journal. These steps are legally necessary as it would be unconstitutional for the EU to require European companies to follow rules set by a non-EU body. Essentially the EU by adopting an IASB standard transforms it into EU law.

However this step is very much more than a legal formality. The EU may adopt an IASB standard only if it meets three important conditions:

1. that the IASB standard does not conflict with the directives' requirement that the accounts give 'a true and fair view';
2. that the IASB standard is conducive to the European public good; and
3. that the IASB standard meets the criteria of understandability, relevance, reliability and comparability required of information needed for making economic decisions and assessing the stewardship of management.

It is not self-evident that all the IASB standards will meet these conditions for a number of reasons:

1. The IASB does not put much emphasis on the 'true and fair view' requirement. The IASB's Framework contains only a brief reference to the concept and does not make it a necessary condition for accounts. Therefore there is no certainty that the IASB's standards will meet this condition.
2. The EU may decide that an IAS is 'not conducive to the European public good'. The word 'European' is intriguing. It raises the possibility of a conflict

between the EU's criterion and the 'global public good' (which is presumably the criterion used by the IASB). It also opens the door to the EU considering the economic consequences of standards; for example, the EU may decide that an IASB standard that required European enterprises to disclose certain information that is not disclosed by non-European enterprises is 'not conducive to the European public good' and therefore should not be adopted. The IASB refuses to consider the economic consequences of its standards. It considers that the function of accounts is to present the financial position and performance of an enterprise as accurately as possible and it is for those connected with the enterprise to take the appropriate decisions on the basis of the information contained in the accounts. If these decisions have a negative impact on the enterprise or on society as a whole, this is not the fault of the accountant who is simply the messenger that brings unwelcome facts into the open.

3. The EU refers to the stewardship function of accounts. The IASB gives very little weight to this function. It is mentioned briefly in its Framework (paragraph 14) but not in its objectives which refer exclusively to the information function of accounts.

7.7.5   The EU's endorsement mechanism

The EU has set up an elaborate organisation (known as the endorsement mechanism) whose function is to check whether an IASB standard meets the above conditions before it is adopted. It involves three bodies:

1. *The European Financial Reporting Advisory Group (EFRAG)*: EFRAG is a body that represents the various actors in the financial community: the preparers (industrial and commercial enterprises and financial institutions), the auditors (the national professional accountancy institutes), the users (the financial analysts) and the stock exchanges. Its principal function is to provide an assessment of the IASB's standards and interpretations. It issues a recommendation as to whether a particular standard should be adopted by the EU. Its secondary functions are to make a proactive contribution to the work of the IASB (for example by commenting on exposure drafts), to advise the EU on desirable amendments to the directives and to provide European companies with implementation guidance on the IASB's standards. Although formally EFRAG is a private body, it is recognised by the EU as its privileged advisor on technical matters relating to financial reporting. Within EFRAG, all technical matters, including the advice to be offered to the EU, are the responsibility of the Technical Expert Group, which consists of eleven members, headed by the Chairman, Stig Enevoldsen, a Danish auditor. The remaining ten members consist of a further two auditors, four preparers, two professors, one standard-setter[6] and one user. As usual with such bodies, the preparers and the auditors

are well represented and the users poorly represented. All members are part-time (20 per cent). In addition there is a full-time secretary-general, Paul Rutteman, a British auditor. Although in its literature, the EFRAG refers to its advice as being based on technical considerations, it seems inevitable that it will also reflect the opinions of the different parties in the financial community. For example, if the preparers are strongly opposed to a particular IASB standard, it seems likely that this opposition will be reflected in the EFRAG's advice, possibly couched in technical terms.

2. *The European Commission*: The European Commission is the head of the EU's executive branch, being a committee consisting of seventeen politicians nominated by the EU member states. One of its myriad responsibilities is to decide whether or not to endorse an IASB standard. After considering the advice that it has received from EFRAG, it makes a proposal to adopt or reject a standard, which it passes for approval to the third body.

3. *The Accounting Regulatory Committee (ARC)*: The ARC consists of representatives of the governments of the EU member states. It is the formal part of the EU's endorsement mechanism, being set up by an EU regulation, which defines its function as to assist the Commission. It receives the Commission's proposal to adopt or reject an IASB standard accompanied by EFRAG's technical assessment and considers any political aspects, for example whether a member state's government has any strong objections. The ARC's approval is necessary for the Commission's proposal to become law. If the ARC does not agree, then the Commission has to send its proposal to the full Council of Ministers. Basically the ARC's role is to relieve the Council of Ministers of having to make decisions on relatively minor matters.

Once an IASB standard has been adopted by the ARC and the Commission and has been published in the EU's Official Journal, it becomes part of EU law and is binding on the European enterprises covered by the EU regulation. It should be noted that although the EU has the power and the right to refuse to endorse an IASB standard, if it were to do so this would probably lead to the collapse of the whole structure of international standard-setting. Delesalle (2002) likens it to the nuclear deterrent, commenting 'for the concept of international standards only remains valid as long as all the rules are applied without exception. This weapon should be considered as a defensive tool as its use would put in question the whole reform'.

In September 2003, the EU, following the procedure outlined above, adopted most of the IASB's current standards. The exceptions were the two standards on financial instruments, IAS 32 and IAS 39. Many European banks and insurance companies objected to these standards and were supported in their opposition by the French government. The EU apparently decided that it would be prudent to put off a decision on these controversial standards, justifying its stance on the diplomatic grounds that the IASB was in the process of reviewing them. For more information on this case, see Section 8.3.3 of the next chapter.

7.7.6   The reform of the EU's directives

As already indicated in Section 7.7.3, the EU's Fourth and Seventh Directives remain in force for the consolidated accounts of non-listed companies and for the individual accounts of both listed and non-listed companies, unless a member state avails itself of the option to extend the IASB's standards to these accounts. Of the estimated five million companies registered in the EU, only a tiny fraction (some seven thousand) are listed on a stock exchange; hence, depending on how the member states implement the option, it seems likely that many million European companies will remain subject to the directives. In April 2003, the EU amended the accounting directives. It gave the following reasons:[7]

1. 'It is important that a level playing field exists between Community companies which apply IAS and those which do not.'
2. 'It is desirable that the these directives reflect developments in international accounting ... to maintain consistency between Community accounting directives and developments on international accounting standard setting, in particular within the [IASB].'

The amendments to the accounting directives are, with certain important exceptions, in the form 'Member States may permit or require' – they are member state options which a member state may implement as a company option. They cover all the provisions of the accounting directives that made it illegal for companies to apply the IASB's standards. The following are the more important points that are covered:

1. *Additional statements*: The definition of the annual accounts may be expanded to include other statements. Presumably this is to make it clear that it is legal for member states to require companies to draw up a cash-flow statement, although the term is not mentioned.
2. *Different formats*: Alternative formats for the balance sheet (to permit classification between current and non-current assets) and the profit and loss account (to permit a statement of performance) are permitted, provided that in both cases at least the equivalent information is provided.
3. *Asset valuation*: Assets may be reported at fair value and the change in value reported in the profit and loss account. Some two years earlier, the EU had amended the directives to permit companies to report financial instruments at fair value; this option has now been extended to all asset categories.

It should be emphasised that all the above points are member state options; a member state may decide not to implement them or to implement them as a company option. Hence there is no certainty that the EU will achieve one of its aims – to create a level playing field between companies that follow the directives and those that apply the IASs. Furthermore, if member states do not implement the options, companies may be unable to apply the IASB's standards.

However there are three important amendments that are not member state options:

1. *Exclusion of subsidiary*: The Seventh Directive prohibited the consolidation of a subsidiary whose activities were radically different from the rest of the group. This prohibition, which has been identified as one of the principal sources of conflict between the directives and the EU's rules, has been scrapped.
2. *Annual report*: The contents of the annual report are defined in greater detail. It is made clear that it should deal with the risks and uncertainties facing the company and with non-financial matters, such as information concerning the environment and employees.
3. *Audit report*: The contents of the audit report are also defined in greater detail. It should identify the auditing standards followed and report whether the accounts give a true and fair view and comply with statutory requirements.

The greater weight given by the EU to the annual report and to the audit is to be welcomed. These were both areas where the EU's provisions were quite inadequate. However the other amendments to the directives, since they are in the form of member state options, carry the risk that they will not forward the cause of convergence either between the EU and the rest of the world or within the EU.

7.8   The IASB and the national standard-setters

It is clear that, for the IASB's standards to achieve worldwide acceptance, they should be endorsed by national standard-setters. Two features are incorporated into the IASB's organisation in order to facilitate the achievement of this objective:

1. All the members of the board have some connection with a national standard-setter (for details, see Exhibit 6.3).
2. Seven board members have been given specific responsibility for liaison between the IASB and a named national standard-setter. Under paragraph 27 of the IASB's constitution, their function is to promote the convergence of national standards and the IASB's standards. They act as the IASB's advocate before the national standard-setter, urging it to adopt standards similar to those of the IASB, and as the national standard-setter's advocate

within the IASB, making sure that this body is fully cognisant of the national standard-setter's views on the proposed standard.

However only a limited number of national standard-setters benefit from these two elements of the IASB's organisation. Most of the world's standard-setters are left out, including all those from developing countries and countries in transition, as well as those from the EU member states, apart from Britain, France and Germany. It is clear that what interests the IASB is the endorsement of its standards by those countries that are major players in the global capital market, either as sources of capital or as the home country of MNEs: USA, Britain, Japan, Germany, France, Australia and Canada.

The IASB meets regularly with these seven national standard-setters. The report of one such meeting (House, 2001) reveals many of the problems that the IASB will have to overcome in order to achieve worldwide acceptance. The Japanese delegate complained that the IASB's proposals on business combinations did not take into account Japanese cultural attitudes. The head of the DRSC, the German standard-setter, complained that the FASB was making no effort to liaise with other countries. For its part, Jim Leisenring, a former member of the FASB and currently the IASB board member responsible for liaison with that body, complained that the UK's ASB was going it alone in starting projects on consolidation policy and de-recognition. The author of the report on the meeting commented that 'it is becoming apparent that the goal of global convergence is not going to be easy to achieve' and characterised the process as a 'rocky road'.

7.9   The IASB and the American authorities

Given the importance of the American capital market, it is clear that, for the IASB's standards to gain worldwide recognition, they must be accepted by the American regulatory authorities, that is the SEC and the FASB.

7.9.1   The IASB and the SEC

In February 2000 the SEC set out its views on the acceptability of the IASB's standards for foreign companies listed in the USA (SEC, 2000). Although the SEC did not reject the possibility, the fundamental tenor of its report was negative, notably in two respects:

1. It was very sceptical about the degree of compliance by foreign companies with the IASB's standards. It considered that many companies reported that their accounts complied with these standards when this was not fully the case. The SEC implied that a thorough overhaul of the auditing function in certain foreign countries would be necessary before it would accept accounts based on international standards.

2. It expressed certain doubts about the IASB's effectiveness as a standard-setter. For this reason, it stated that it was not prepared to adopt a process-oriented approach to the recognition of the IASB's standards. The SEC adopts a process-oriented approach with the FASB, in that, having already satisfied itself that the FASB's procedure for setting standards (its 'due process') is appropriate, it normally accepts an FASB standard as part of US GAAP and only in very exceptional cases rejects it (for example, by issuing a countervailing rule).[8] With the IASB's standards, the SEC expects to use a product-oriented approach in which it would examine each standard on a case-by-case basis. Furthermore the SEC envisages that it may have to require additional disclosures and reconciliations when an IASB standard does not provide all the information contained in US GAAP. Zeff (2000) comments: 'This proviso may go some distance toward confirming the suspicions of Europeans and others outside the US that the SEC's hidden agenda all along has been to abide IASC standards for foreign registrants only if they are so much like US GAAP as to be virtually US GAAP.'

The SEC's report was made just before the IASC was transformed into the IASB and it is possible that in the future the SEC may change its attitude. However in a public speech in October 2002, Harvey Pitt, the then chairman of the SEC, continued to be very sceptical about the SEC ever recognising the IASB's standards for foreign companies listed on American stock exchanges. After listing a number of conditions that had to be fulfilled by 2005, he stated that 'then it may be appropriate for us [the SEC] to reconsider the need for foreign private issuers from EU member countries to continue to reconcile from IAS to US GAAP' (Pitt, 2002). This statement is really very negative. Even if all its conditions were fulfilled, the utmost that the SEC is prepared to do is to possibly reconsider its present policy. The SEC does not deny the need for a single set of global standards but the author suspects that it considers that these should be US GAAP or at least so like US GAAP as to be indistinguishable.

7.9.2   The IASB and the FASB

The relationship between the IASB and the FASB, the American standard-setter, is particularly important and delicate. Relations have not always been easy. Initially the FASB seemed very sceptical. Not unnaturally it saw the IASC as a threat to its very existence, that the IASC might replace it as the principal rule-maker for American companies. It published a report listing no less than two hundred differences between its standards and those of the IASC.[9] There was a clear implication that it was the IASC which should change its standards, so that they converged on the FASB's. However, subsequently the FASB agreed that two former members of its board should become full-time members of the IASB's board. This at least demonstrates a willingness on the FASB's part to cooperate with the IASB.

In September 2002, the two bodies signed a memorandum of under-standing which committed them to use their best efforts to make their existing financial reporting standards fully compatible as soon as practicable and to coordinate their future work programmes to ensure that, once achieved, compatibility would be maintained. The agreement was neutral on the thorny question of whether the FASB's standards should converge onto those of the IASB or vice versa. The IASB's chairman, in commending the agreement, referred to changes to both US and International standards: 'by drawing on the best of US GAAP, IFRSs [IASB standards] and other national standards, the world's capital markets will have a set of global standards that investors can trust'.[10] The only thing that can be said with reasonable certainty is that the FASB has come to the conclusion that its best survival strategy is to cooperate closely with the IASB.

At present the IASB and the FASB are giving priority to differences that may be capable of resolution in the relatively short run. The thornier issues such as inventory valuation (considered in Section 8.3.1 of the following chapter) and share options are being left to be dealt with later. There have been many meetings between the two bodies but, at the time of writing, very little concrete progress (in the way of revised standards or even exposure drafts) has been made on the convergence of US GAAP and the IASB's standards, the most notable achievement being that the FASB has agreed to use the IASB's style and wording in its standards.

Some commentators are more optimistic about the likely outcome of the IASB/FASB convergence project. Jermakowicz and Gornik-Tomaszewski (2003) writes: 'The FASB has become a proponent of … a single set of standards to be used internationally and domestically. The FASB even suggests that the Board entertains the possibility that it may not be needed in the long run. Following the appointment of former IASB board member Robert Hertz as chairman of the FASB, the IASB and the FASB have agreed that convergence of IFRS and US GAAP is a "primary objective of both boards".' Certainly the public stance of both bodies (as evidenced by the statements on their websites) is very supportive of the ultimate aim of convergence.

7.10   The contest between the IASB's standards and US GAAP

As the preceding discussion has made very clear, there is no certainty that the American regulatory authorities (the SEC and the FASB) will accept the IASB as the global rule-maker, which makes it quite probable that US GAAP will remain as a rival to the IASB's standards for many years to come. Given the ambivalent attitude of the SEC and the FASB to the IASB, the present situation may be characterised as a contest between the IASB's standards and US GAAP as to which should become the global standard.

7.10.1 The case for US GAAP

There are several reasons why the national rules might converge on US GAAP:

1. American companies (which are obliged by law to follow US GAAP) make up by far the largest national contingent in the list of the world's largest companies compiled by *Fortune* magazine, being 192 of the 500 companies (*Fortune*, 2003). The second largest contingent comes from Japan, with 88 of the 500 companies. Many Japanese companies present their consolidated accounts using US GAAP as is permitted by Japanese law. Hence around half of the world's largest companies already use US GAAP. Perhaps the least costly course of action would be for the remainder to follow them.

2. US GAAP is widely regarded by the investing public as providing the most complete and rigorous set of rules for financial reporting. This is one of the principal reasons why many foreigners invest in securities quoted on the American stock exchanges: they have more confidence in the accounts of the companies listed there than they do in those of companies listed on other exchanges. Certainly this was the case until recently. It is unclear whether the recent accounting scandals in the USA, such as those involving Enron and WorldCom, have undermined investors' confidence in US GAAP. This topic is discussed in the Chapter 9.

3. Where national law gives companies a free choice between US GAAP and the IASB's standards, many choose the former. For example, the Neue Markt (the German stock exchange for smaller, technology-based enterprises) requires enterprises to present accounts based on either the IASB's standards or US GAAP. Approximately half the enterprises choose US GAAP with the proportion rising in recent years. According to Jermakowicz and Gornik-Tomaszewski (2003) in 2001 some 300 European listed companies used US GAAP compared with 275 that used the IASB's standards.

4. The American capital market is by far the world's largest and for the non-American MNEs is an important source of capital. In fact the larger an MNE grows, the greater its need to raise capital on the American capital market, as is demonstrated by the example of Daimler Benz. Essentially access to this market is regulated by the SEC, which up to now has insisted that foreign enterprises that seek an American listing must present accounts according to US GAAP or a reconciliation. If the SEC were to maintain this policy, it seems probable that an increasing number of non-American enterprises would either adopt US GAAP (where their national law so permits) or put pressure on their governments to permit them to do so.

7.10.2 The present situation

However the contest between the IASB's standards and US GAAP is by no means decided in either party's favour. Exhibit 7.2 gives an overview of the present situation concerning the standards used by the top one hundred European enterprises (those listed in Exhibit 1.4). The following very general conclusions may be drawn:

- At present, the financial statements of the great majority of European enterprises are founded on national law. In fact in only five countries are there any enterprises that use any other basis: Germany, Netherlands, Switzerland, Russia and tiny Luxembourg.
- Of the two alternatives to national law (the IASB's standards and US GAAP) there is a clear preference for the IASB. However a significant number of enterprises prefer US GAAP.

It must be assumed that, given the obvious advantages of a single set of global standards, the national rules will, in the longer run, be replaced either by the IASB's standards or by US GAAP. But, on the evidence of Exhibit 7.2, there is still a long way to go before this is achieved and it is by no means clear who will be the winner.

7.10.3   Possible scenarios

It is possible to paint four scenarios for the future development of global standard-setting:

1. *The IASB's standards prevail*: The European MNEs (which make up about half of the world's major enterprises) all adopt the IASB's standards, as required by European law. The US regulatory authorities come under pressure from American companies to change the law so as to permit the

Exhibit 7.2   Basis of the financial statements of the top one hundred European enterprises

Country	National law	IASB's standards	US GAAP
France	25		
Germany	7	10	5
UK[11]	16½		½
Netherlands	6	1	1½
Italy	8		
Switzerland	1	5	1
Spain	4		
Belgium	2½		
Sweden	2		
Russia		2	
Denmark	1		
Luxembourg		1	
Total	73	19	8

use of IASs and finally are persuaded by the argument that American MNEs are placed at a competitive disadvantage vis-à-vis their foreign competitors.

2. *US GAAP prevails*: The SEC continues to insist that foreign enterprises that seek access to the American capital market must use US GAAP. The EU comes under pressure from European MNEs to change the law so as to permit US GAAP as the sole standard. It should not be assumed that simply because European law at present requires the IASB's standards from 2005 that the law cannot be changed.

3. *The stand-off continues*: Both the US government and the EU insist on their sovereign right to set the rules for the enterprises under their jurisdiction so that the present situation where there are two sets of global standards continues for a considerable time.

4. *The IASB's standards and US GAAP merge*: The standards set by the IASB and the American authorities become increasingly similar so that in the end they are indistinguishable. There are two rather different situations in which this might occur.

   (a) *Market led*: With increasing globalisation, the conditions in capital market throughout the world become increasingly similar such that the market participants in all countries come to demand the same type of financial information. Thus the financial statements that the SEC considers to be appropriate in the American environment would also meet the needs of investors in London, Frankfurt, Tokyo and Bombay.

   (b) *American takeover*: The Americans come to dominate the IASB to such an extent that they can ensure that its standards reflect US GAAP. This could occur if the members of the IASB's standard-setting body, whilst not in the majority American citizens, came to accept the American approach to financial reporting, possibly because they had become convinced of its superiority for intellectual or cultural reasons.

Of the above scenarios, the first (IASB prevailing) seems rather unlikely. The SEC shows no signs of being ready to surrender any real powers to the IASB. The SEC sees itself as the protector of American investors and in this capacity it intends to vet the IASB's standards, no doubt rejecting some on the grounds that they assure insufficient protection for American investors and placing severe restrictions on the use of others. Hence it seems very probable that for many years, US GAAP will continue to be significantly different from the IASB's standards.

Of the remaining three scenarios, the undisguised triumph of US GAAP also seems rather improbable as the EU can thwart it by refusing to change its rules. Thus the scenario where neither prevails is a distinct possibility, but one that is clearly not in the interests of the MNEs or of those whose prosperity depends on them, that is a large part of the world's population. In the authors' opinion, the merging of US GAAP and the IASB's standards seems the most likely, with an American takeover rather more likely than a market led merge. Certainly the recent reorganisation of the IASB (described in detail in Chapter 6) has greatly increased the USA's influence in this body.

Notes

1. 'Thousands of pages' is probably an under-estimate. The FASB has issued over 150 statements, and one single statement, FAS 133, is 245 pages long! As far as the author can find out, no one has attempted to count or even list the documents that make up US GAAP.
2. In 2002, the IASB proposed revising IAS 1 to remove these illustrative formats, but, reacting to the EU's opposition, withdrew its proposal.
3. The principal exceptions were that IAS 39 required that certain assets must be reported at fair value (not permitted by the Fourth Directive) and that the EU's Seventh Directive requires that subsidiaries whose activities were very different from those of the group as a whole must be excluded from the consolidated accounts (which is not a permitted ground for exclusion in IAS 27). The EU recently amended the directives to remove these incompatibilities (see Section 7.7.6).
4. The IASB publishes on its website a list of companies that adopt its standards.
5. Antoine Bracchi quoted in Delesalle (2002).
6. The standard-setter is Allan Cook, the technical director of the UK's ASB. His background is as a preparer, but since he has been a full-time employee of the ASB for over ten years it is more accurate to describe him as a standard-setter.
7. These quotations are from the preamble to the amending directive (Directive 2003/EC of 16 April 2003).
8. For examples of the rare occasions that the SEC has overruled the FASB, see Chapter 5 of Flower and Ebbers (2002), which gives a general description of the US regulatory system.
9. For details of the report and the differences, see Cairns (2000).
10. IASB press release of 29 October 2002.
11. British companies are obliged to follow UK GAAP. The '½' in this row is the British half of Royal Dutch/Shell which is a combination of a British company and a Dutch company. The British company draws up its individual accounts according to UK GAAP. The consolidated accounts (which presumably come under no country's jurisdiction) comply with US GAAP.

References

Cairns, D. (2000). 'Waving a difference'. *Accountancy* (September).
Delesalle, E. (2002). 'Le point sur les réformes comptables en cours'. *La comptabilité en mouvement*. Paris, L'ordre des experts comptables.
EU (2002). Regulation (EC) No 1606/2002.
European Commission (1995). *Accounting Harmonization: A New Strategy vis-à-vis International Harmonization*. Brussels, European Commission.

Flower, J. and Ebbers, G. (2002). *Global Financial Reporting*. Basingstoke, Palgrave.

Fortune (2003). 'The Global 500'. *Fortune* (July 28).

House, J. (2001). 'Along the rocky road'. *Accountancy* (October).

Jermakowicz, E. and Gornik-Tomaszewski, S. (2003). The impact of international financial reporting standards on US GAAP, paper presented at the EIASM workshop on implementing IFRS, Brussels, 11–12 September 2003.

Miller, P., Redding, R. and Bahnson (1998). *The FASB: The People, the Process and the Politics*. Boston, McGraw-Hill.

Pitt, H. (2002). 'US shares common aim of one set of standards'. *Accountancy* (November).

SEC (2000). *Concept Release on International Accounting Standards*. Washington, SEC.

Zeff, S. (1997). 'Playing the Congressional card on employee stock options'. *The Development of Accounting in an International Context*. T. Cooke and C. Nobes. London, Routledge.

Zeff, S. (2000). 'What is the SEC looking for?'. *World Accounting Report* (April).

8
Convergence

The subject of the chapter is convergence, that is, the process by which the rules that are set at the national level become increasingly similar – they all converge onto a common model.

8.1 Why the IASB seeks convergence

The IASB has adopted convergence as its principal objective. It recognises that, for its standards to gain worldwide acceptance, they must be adopted by national standard-setters, for the IASB has no other means of forcing enterprises to adopt its standards. This reality is reflected in the IASB's third objective which is 'to bring about convergence of national accounting standards and International Accounting Standards...to high quality solutions'. Chapters 6 and 7 covered the elements in the IASB's organisation and processes that aim to improve cooperation with national standard-setters and hence promote the achievement of the objective of convergence. This chapter examines the convergence process at the national level, with the aim of assessing how successful the IASB is likely to be in achieving its objective. The chapter does not attempt to cover all countries in detail. Instead one country, the United Kingdom, is studied in detail, followed by a much broader review of the situation globally.

8.2 Convergence in the United Kingdom

In this section, the convergence process is studied in one particular country: the United Kingdom (UK), which has been chosen for special attention for three reasons:

1. There has been more evident progress towards convergence in the UK compared with other countries.
2. There is good information about the process in the UK, particularly in the form of the reports of British researchers that are referred to in this section.

3. The process in the UK provides a good example of how convergence may be achieved and of the attendant problems.

8.2.1 The ASB's policy

From 2005, British listed companies will be obliged to use the IASB's standards for their consolidated accounts. Up to 2004, they are obliged to comply with UK GAAP. As for unlisted companies, the British government has announced its intentions that they will be given the option of adopting the IASB's standards. However there will be no compulsion and hence there will still be a role for UK GAAP after 2005. This raises the question whether the British regulatory authorities should seek to maintain a clear distinction between the IASB's standards and UK GAAP or whether, on the other hand, they should aim for convergence.

There are two principal advantages of aligning UK GAAP with the IASB's standards:

1. For listed companies, it will ease the transition from UK GAAP to the IASB's standards on 1 January 2005. Up to then these companies are legally obliged to follow UK GAAP. However, if UK GAAP and the IASB's standards were to converge, these companies would automatically be converting to the IASB's standards without having to consider the IASB's standards. Convergence is not the only possible policy. Some commentators advocated that the UK should not amend its standards, with the consequence that on 1 January 2005 there would be a 'big bang' as listed companies changed from UK GAAP to the IASB's standards.
2. It would ensure comparability of the accounts of British companies, not only between listed and unlisted companies within the UK, but also with accounts of companies from other countries that adopted the IASB's standards, notably those within the EU.

On this matter, the Accounting Standards Board (ASB), the British standard-setting body, has a clear policy as is evident from the following quotation:

> After wide discussion with interested parties, the ASB has indicated its intention to pursue a programme of work to align UK standards with IFRS [the IASB's standards] wherever practicable. The effect of this is that the substance of IFRS will apply in the UK not only to the group financial statements of listed companies but also to individual financial statements and unlisted companies. However, the ASB will consider the option of retaining a UK standard, or modifying an IFRS in its wider application, for example if it appears likely that the cost of extending an unmodified IFRS more widely would exceed the benefits.[1]

The last sentence in the above citation suggests that the ASB feels that it is important to retain the right to set UK standards that are different from those of the IASB. No doubt it considers that at present it has the better standards in many areas and in the future it may be able to act as a pacesetter for the IASB, setting more progressive standards in areas where the IASB feels constrained to be more careful. This provides a good justification for the ASB's continued existence.

8.2.2   The magnitude of the task: the gap between UK GAAP and the IASB's standards

In 2000, the ASB sponsored a study of the differences between UK GAAP and the IASB's standards. It was undertaken by David Cairns and Professor Christopher Nobes, who together had an unrivalled knowledge of British and international financial reporting, the first being a former Secretary-General of the IASC and the second a former member of the IASC's Board. In their report (Cairns and Nobes, 2000), they point out that there are many similarities between the IASB's standards and those of the ASB, which they attributed to three factors:

1. The influence of the British members of the IASC's Board. The British profession has provided two IASC chairmen, including the first, Sir Henry Benson, and no less than three Secretaries-General, including the last, Sir Bryan Carsberg. The ASB and the IASC worked together closely to develop standards on a number of topics, notably on provisions where they adopted virtually identical standards: IAS 36 and FRS 12.
2. The reverse influence of the IASC on the ASB; for example, the ASB made extensive use of the IASC's Framework in developing its own conceptual framework.
3. Both the IASC and the ASB were influenced by a third party; for example on foreign currency translation, both IAS 21 and the ASC's SSAP 20 were influenced by the FASB's SFAS 52.

However there were also many differences between the two sets of standards, which Cairns and Nobes analysed under the headings set out in Exhibit 8.1:

Exhibit 8.1   Analysis of the differences between UK GAAP and the IASB's standards

---

A. Incompatibilities: These refer to mandatory rules in one system (IASB's standards or UK GAAP) that are incompatible with the rules of the other system, in that, if they are followed, the other system's rules will be broken.
B. Items dealt with in more detail or more restrictively by the UK, that is, UK GAAP is stricter than the IASB's standards.
C. Items dealt with in more detail or more restrictively by the IASB's standards: the IASB's standards are stricter than UK GAAP.

The categories presented in Exhibit 8.1 cover three ways in which UK GAAP can differ from the IASB's standards:[2]

A. Incompatibilities: In this case, it is impossible for a set of accounts to comply with both UK GAAP and the IASB's standards. An example is the rule set out in the British Companies Act that a proposed dividend must be shown as a liability. According to IAS 10, a proposed dividend does not meet the IASB's definition of a liability and hence must be reported as an element of equity. Since, under the rules of double entry book-keeping, it is not permitted to report the same item twice in the balance sheet, it is impossible to comply with both British law and the IASB's standard.

B. Items dealt with in more detail or more restrictively by the UK. These are less serious than incompatibilities, in that, in applying the British rules, one also complies with the IASB's rules. However the reverse is not necessarily the case. A set of accounts that complied with the IASB's rules may, in certain circumstances, not comply with UK GAAP. In terms of logic, complying with the UK GAAP, on the particular point, is a sufficient but not a necessary condition for complying with the IASB's rules. An example is the reporting of investment property. The IASB standard, IAS 40, allows offers a choice of valuation methods between fair value and cost less depreciation. The British standard, SSAP 19, requires that investment property be reported at fair value. Hence after 2005, a British company that reported investment property at cost would be complying with the IASB's standards but not with UK GAAP. However it would be possible for the British company to comply simultaneously with the IASB's rules and UK GAAP by reporting at fair value.

C. Items dealt with in more detail or more restrictively by the IASB's standards: These are of the same nature as B but the other way round: in following the IASB's standards, one automatically complies with UK GAAP but the reverse is not necessarily true. An example is the exchange rate to be used in translating a foreign subsidiary's profit and loss account. Under IAS 21 the average rate of the period must be used (in fact the standard specifies the actual rate at the date of the transaction but accepts that the average rate for the period is generally a reasonably accurate approximation); under SSAP 20 either the closing rate or the average rate may be used.

Cairns and Nobes analysed the differences between the IASB's standards and UK GAAP in November 2000 for 27 topics and classified them into categories A, B and C. Their findings are summarised in Exhibit 8.2. Overall there were 253 differences, including no less than 59 in category A (incompatibilities). The sheer number of differences gives the impression that the gap between the IASB's standards and UK GAAP is enormous and to achieve even approximate convergence would require a huge effort. However this disregards whether the differences relate to important matters (for example, having

Exhibit 8.2   Differences between the IASB's standards and UK GAAP as at November 2000

	A	B	C	Total
Context of reporting				
Objectives, substance and accounting policies	3	7	4	14
Assets and revenue				
Property, plant and equipment	5	5	3	13
Intangible assets	2	2	14	18
Investment property	2	2	5	9
Government grants	0	3	4	7
Impairment	4	4	6	14
Inventories	0	8	7	15
Construction contracts	1	1	5	7
Finance and capital instruments	4	3	2	9
Revenue	2	2	1	5
Liabilities				
Income taxes	6	1	1	8
Leases	2	4	6	12
Provisions and contingencies	0	1	0	1
Events after the balance sheet date	1	0	0	1
Employee benefits	2	8	5	15
Group accounting				
Business combinations	8	6	3	17
Consolidated financial statements	4	3	2	9
Associates and joint ventures	3	9	3	15
Foreign currencies	2	2	5	9
Presentation and disclosures				
Presentation, extraordinary items, etc.	4	8	1	13
Reporting enterprise	0	0	0	0
Cash-flow statement	1	9	5	15
Segment reporting	0	1	9	10
Related party	0	3	1	4
Earnings per share	2	4	0	6
Interim reporting	0	1	4	5
Bank disclosures	1	1	0	2
Total	59	98	96	253

a major impact on reported profits) or only to trivial matters. To answer this point in a definitive fashion would require a detailed study of all 27 topics listed in Exhibit 8.2 which is beyond the scope of this book. Instead one topic (foreign currency translation) is examined in detail with the aim of gaining an insight into the real extent of the differences in November 2000.

8.2.3   Foreign currency translation

In the area of foreign currency translation, there were, in November 2000, nine differences between the IASB's standards and UK GAAP: 2 in category

A (inconsistencies), 2 in category B (the UK stricter than the IASB) and 5 in category C (the IASB stricter than the UK). Details of these differences are presented in Exhibit 8.3.

A.1 This deals with the case when the exchange rate at which a foreign currency transaction is to be settled is fixed in the contract. UK GAAP requires that the contracted rate should be used. Cairns and Nobes claim that this is not permitted under IAS 21 and IAS 39. The author doubts whether in fact they are correct, since a transaction in which the exchange rate between the foreign currency and the domestic currency is fixed in the contract is no longer, in essence, a foreign currency transaction. Furthermore such transactions are very rare. For both these reasons, this inconsistency may be considered to be of only minor importance.

A.2 This concerns the treatment of accumulated translation differences on the disposal of a foreign subsidiary. Under UK GAAP these are retained in the balance of accumulated translation differences that is reported as a separate element of equity. Under IAS 21 they are written off as part of the gain or loss on disposal. It should be noted that both methods report the same figure for the total of net equity; they differ as to the composition of this total. More importantly, they differ as to the amount of the gain or loss on disposal and hence in the reported profit for the period when the subsidiary was sold or scrapped.

B.1 This deals with the treatment, following a devaluation, of the exchange loss on a loan used to finance an asset. Under UK GAAP this loss must be reported in the profit and loss account. In IAS 21 there is an option to add the loss to the book value of the asset.

B.2 This concerns the definition of the reporting currency. In the author's opinion the two definitions seems to have very similar meanings and thus any difference is unimportant.

C.1 This concerns the accounting for hedging transactions, including which exchange rate to use. When a foreign exchange transaction is hedged by a forward contract, UK GAAP allows that the transaction (both the expense/asset and the liability) be reported at the forward rate. This is not permitted by the IASB's standards – under IAS 21 the expense and liability should be reported at the closing rate and under IAS 39 the forward contract reported as a separate item at fair value (which initially will often be zero). The difference between UK GAAP and the IASs is largely limited to the amount of detail reported in the accounts: there is no significant difference in the figures reported for profit and net assets.

C.2 This concerns the translation gain on a long-term loan. Under IAS 21 all translation gains and losses are reported in the profit and loss account.

Exhibit 8.3 Foreign currency translation: differences between the IASB's standards and UK GAAP

Subject	UK: SSAP 20	IASB: IAS 21	Significance
A.1 Foreign currency transaction to be settled at a contracted rate	Transaction (liability and expense) translated at the contracted rate	Expense translated at current rate; liability reported at fair value	Minor
A.2 Treatment of accumulated translation differences on the disposal of a foreign subsidiary	Accumulated translation differences remain as a separate component of equity	Accumulated translation differences reported as part of the gain or loss on disposal	Moderate
B.1 Devaluation of foreign currency: treatment of exchange loss on loan used to finance an asset	Loss reported in profit and loss account	Loss added to cost of asset (alternative treatment)	Moderate
B.2 Definition of reporting currency of foreign subsidiary	The currency of its primary economic environment	The currency that reflects the economic substance of the underlying events	Trivial
C.1 Treatment of hedging transaction	Not specified in detail	Specified in detail	Moderate
C.2 Translation gain on long-term monetary items	May be deferred (alternative treatment)	Must be reported in the profit and loss account	Moderate
C.3 Treatment of long-term loan used to hedge the net investment in a foreign subsidiary	Less detail than IASB	Treatment specified in detail	Moderate
C.4 Exchange rate used to translate the profit and loss account under the closing rate method	Closing rate or average rate	Average rate	Moderate
C.5 Foreign subsidiary that operates in a hyperinflationary economy	Accounts *may* be restated before translation	Accounts *must* be restated before translation	Moderate

Under SSAP 20 these gains should be deferred in the interests of prudence, in the exceptional cases where there are doubts as the convertibility or marketability of the foreign currency. The different rules could lead to substantial differences in the reported value of assets and profits in these exceptional cases.

C.3 This deals with the hedging of a net investment in a foreign entity. Following the introduction of new hedge accounting rules in IAS 39, the IASB has tightened the conditions under which a company may report as an element of equity the translation gain or loss on a foreign currency loan that hedges its investment in a foreign entity.

C.4 This concerns the exchange rate that is used to translate the profit and loss account. Under UK GAAP, with the closing rate method, the profit and loss account may be translated at either the closing rate or the average rate. There is no such choice in IAS 21: the exchange rate at the time of the transaction must be used (the average rate for the period is often used as an approximation). Where there has been a significant change in exchange rates over the period, the difference between the closing rate and the average rate may be considerable, leading to very substantial differences in the income, expenses and profits reported under the two methods.

C.5 This deals with the translation of the accounts of an entity that reports in a currency subject to hyperinflation. Under UK GAAP (UITF 9) there is a choice of methods: either the foreign currency figures are adjusted for inflation before being translated or they are restated in terms of a relatively stable currency. IAS 21 does not permit the second method.

8.2.4 Assessment of the significance of the differences

Of the nine differences that have just been examined, the author is unsure that one (A.1) is a genuine difference and dismisses another (B.2) as trivial. In the remaining cases, there may well be differences in the profits reported under the two methods, which may be significant, depending on the magnitudes of the figures involved. However, in his opinion, none of the differences is fundamental. In effect, on the fundamental principles of translation, SSAP 20 and IAS 21 are in essential agreement:

- For the translation of transactions, the transaction should be recorded at the rate ruling at the date of the transaction; subsequently the balance sheet value of monetary items should be restated at the closing rate, with any loss or gain on translation being reported in the profit and loss account.
- For the translation of financial statements (for example those of a foreign subsidiary), the temporal method of translation is used for foreign operations that are an integral part of the parent company's business and the closing rate method for other foreign entities.

The reason for this similarity is that both SSAP 20 and IAS 21 largely followed SFAS 52. Both the ASB and the IASC made a conscious effort to preserve a degree of international harmony in this area of great importance for multinational companies.

The differences between UK GAAP and the IASB's rules are limited to details of application of the general principles, notably choices, exceptions and details of how to report hedges.

8.2.5   The causes of the differences

Cairns and Nobes (2000) analysed the reasons why the standards of the ASB and the IASC/IASB should differ. They identified six possible reasons which are presented in Exhibit 8.4.

Cairns and Nobes point out that full convergence could be achieved either by the ASB adopting all the IASB's standards or by the IASB replacing all its standards by the ASB's standards. However they do not recommend either approach. Instead they proposed that, in each case, the standard of superior quality should be chosen. Thus, of the cases in the above list, the IASB should adopt the ASB's standard in cases 1, 4 and 5. Similarly the ASB should, in case 2, adopt the IASB's standard and, in case 3, lobby for a change in the law. That leaves case 6 where there is no straightforward solution.

Applying this analysis to the differences presented in Exhibit 8.4, one reaches the following conclusions:

A.1   The difference between UK GAAP and the IASB's standards arose when, in 1998, IAS 39 introduced new rules for the reporting of hedges. Hence it is an example of case 2 and the ASB should update its standards.

A.2   Accumulated translation differences on disposal of a foreign subsidiary. The reason why the ASB and the IASB differ on this point is that they hold different views about recycling. According to the ASB, the translation

Exhibit 8.4   Reasons for the differences

---

1. The ASB's standard is more recent than that of the IASC/IASB.
2. The IASC/IASB's standard is more recent than that of the ASB.
3. The ASB was prevented by British law from issuing a standard similar to that of the IASC.
4. The IASC was prevented by the need to find a three-quarters majority from issuing a standard similar to that of the ASB.
5. The ASB was compelled to deal with an issue because of perceived abuses in the UK whereas the IASC did not feel the same compulsion.
6. Even where the IASC and the ASB were free to adopt the same standards, they reached significantly different conclusions.

differences, which were reported in the statement of total recognised gains and losses (STRGL) in the period in which they arose, may not be reported a second time (that is 'recycled') in the profit and loss account for the period when the subsidiary was sold or scrapped. The IASB does not require the preparation of a STRGL and therefore the question of reporting the difference twice does not arise. There is a fundamental difference between the ASB and the IASB on a point of principle. Hence this is an example of case 6.

B.1   Translation loss added to value of an asset. It is clear that the IASB is not happy about this provision of IAS 21. It is described as 'allowed alternative treatment' and is hedged around with many conditions: there must have been a severe devaluation, no practical means of hedging and the loan must be directly related to the acquisition of the asset. Furthermore, later the IASB admitted that the capitalised translation difference did not meet the definition of an asset in its framework.[3] The author suspects that it was only included to satisfy particular interests and is therefore probably an example of case 4. Lande (1997) presents details of a case in which a national standard-setter was pressurised into introducing this very rule.

C.1 and C.3   Hedging transactions. In both cases, the differences arose when IAS 39 introduced detailed rules on the reporting of hedging transactions in 1998. Hence they are examples of case 2.

C.2   In the author's opinion, the UK rule conflicts with the ASB's conceptual framework as the deferred gain does not meet the definition of a liability. It is possible that the ASB felt constrained by the provision in the British Companies Act (based on article 31.1.c.aa of the EU's Fourth Directive, see Section 5.7 of Chapter 5) that only realised profits should be reported. Hence this may be an example of case 3.

C.4   The difference arose when IAS 21 was amended in 1993. Hence it is an example of case 2.

C.5   The translation of the accounts of a foreign entity denominated in a hyperinflationary currency is a complex subject on which as yet there is no consensus among accountants. This would seem to be an example of case 6.

8.2.6   Removing the differences

To remove the differences between UK GAAP and the IASB's standards that were identified by Cairns and Nobes in November 2000 required action by both the ASB and the IASB. By end-2003, some three-quarters of the way towards January 2005, when hopefully full convergence will have been achieved, many of the differences had already been eliminated. This involved action by both the IASB and the ASB.

Action by the IASB

In May 2002, the IASB issued an exposure draft which set out proposed improvements to no less than 13 IASs, including IAS 21. The principal proposed changes to IAS 21 concerned the translation of the accounts of a subsidiary that operates in a hyperinflationary economy, the subject matter of difference C.5. Another major change was that the IASB adopted the American term 'functional currency' in the interests of convergence with the FASB's standard. The FASB's definition of 'functional currency' is in fact identical to the ASB's definition of 'local currency': the currency of the primary economic environment in which an entity operates and generates cash. Hence in adopting the FASB's terminology, the IASB resolved one of the differences with UK GAAP (B.2). A second difference (B.1) was eliminated when the IASB, acknowledging the conflict with its conceptual framework, decided to remove the option to capitalise translation losses. In December 2003, the IASB issued the revised version of IAS 21 which included all the changes mentioned in this paragraph.

Action by the ASB

In May 2002 the ASB issued FRED 24, which proposed an entirely new standard to replace SSAP 20. The ASB took the remarkable decision to base the text of its exposure draft on that of the IASB's exposure draft referred to in the previous section, with only very limited changes to the wording. This demonstrated a very strong commitment to convergence on the ASB's part. It proposed only minimal changes to the IASB's draft, of which only one is significant – that related to 'recycling' which is discussed further below. A second ASB exposure draft, FRED 23, dealt with the differences with the IASB concerning hedges. In this way, on the assumption that the exposure drafts will be transformed into standards, all differences between the ASB and the IASB on foreign currency translation were resolved except for that relating to recycling. At the time of writing, the ASB had not converted the exposure draft into a standard.

8.2.7   The remaining difference: recycling

The principal reason for the difference between the ASB and the IASB on recycling is that the ASB's standards require the preparation of STRGL in which a translation difference on a subsidiary is reported in the period when it arises and the ASB considers that it is incorrect to report this difference a second time in the profit and loss account when the subsidiary is sold. The IASB's standards do not require a STRGL and hence the IASB has no inhibitions about reporting the gain on disposal in the profit and loss account. The ASB has been urging the other major standard-setters to adopt its approach. In 1999 the G4 + 1 group issued a discussion paper *Reporting financial performance: proposals for change* which proposed the revolutionary idea that the profit and loss account and the STRGL should be combined in a new-style statement of performance. At the time of writing the IASB is undertaking a project on performance reporting in partnership with the ASB and it seems quite likely that this will lead to the issue of a standard that prescribes this new-style statement.

If the IASB does issue such a standard, it will resolve the conflict on recycling between its standards and the ASB's standards. This is the ASB's position, as is made clear from the following extract from FRED 24: 'The ASB is undertaking a partnership project with the IASB on reporting financial performance, the result of which may be that this practice [recycling] will be prohibited internationally.' This would be a remarkable way of achieving convergence between UK GAAP and the IASB's standards, in that both parties would be changing, although the IASB by much more than the ASB. In effect the IASB would be insisting that the world's MNEs replace the tried and trusted profit and loss account with a revolutionary new style statement of performance.

8.2.8   An overall evaluation of progress towards convergence in the UK

As has just been demonstrated, in the specific field of foreign currency translation, by end-2003, very considerable progress had been made in achieving convergence of UK GAAP with the IASB's standards, to the extent that there remained only one serious incompatibility (recycling) which the parties involved seem to think would be resolved before 2005. What is the position with the other 26 fields that are listed in Exhibit 8.2? In August 2003, David Cairns updated the earlier study.[4] His principal findings are presented in Exhibit 8.5.

Cairns identified forty principal differences between UK GAAP and the IASB's standards that remained at August 2003, on the assumption that all proposed amendments to standards set out in exposure drafts were implemented. This is a considerable reduction in the number, some 250, identified two years earlier. This suggests that very considerable progress had indeed been made, that the pattern noticed with foreign currency translation applied in other areas. An interesting finding was that some of the differences were attributable to action taken by the IASB since November 2000, notably in issuing IAS 41 Agriculture and ED 3 Business Combinations. IAS 41 requires that certain agricultural products be reported at market value, which is not (yet) permitted by UK GAAP; and ED 3 bans both the merger method and negative goodwill which are (still) permitted under UK GAAP. This suggests

Exhibit 8.5 Principal differences remaining in mid-2003

A.	Incompatibilities	11
B.	UK stricter than IASB	10
C.	IASB stricter then UK	19
	Total for all 27 topics	40

that to achieve full convergence will be a never-ending task, especially if the IASB is as proactive in issuing progressive standards as some of its supporters would wish.

8.3   The global picture

In other countries, progress towards convergence appears to be less than that achieved to date in Britain. Given the complex but essentially transitory nature of the problem, it is not proposed to make a detailed analysis of the situation in other countries, but instead to concentrate on one specific area. The area chosen is the relatively straightforward one of asset valuation and, given the great variety of assets, the analysis is limited to certain aspects of just three categories of assets: inventory, tangible fixed assets and financial instruments.

8.3.1   Inventory

The aspect of inventory valuation that is considered is LIFO, which is permitted and widely used in many countries, of which the most important are the USA, Japan and Germany. It is, however, not permitted in Britain and France. Until recently, the IASB permitted its use; however, in late 2003 it amended IAS 2 to ban the method, which, in the IASB's view, fails to represent faithfully the physical flow of inventory and could lead to a markedly distorted calculation of costs, especially when the level of inventory is reduced. However, undoubtedly the attempt to ban LIFO will meet with opposition in the USA. Under American law, companies are allowed to use LIFO for the computation of taxable profit only if they also use it in their published accounts. This condition was imposed by the American legislator in a bid to ensure that the tax benefits were kept within the company and not distributed as dividend to the company's shareholders. Hence if the IASB were to ban LIFO, it would be impossible for an American company to retain LIFO's tax benefits (which can be considerable) and, at the same time, to comply with the IASB's standards. The IASB acknowledges this dilemma: 'The board recognises that, in some jurisdictions, use of the LIFO method for tax purposes is possible only if that method is also used for accounting purposes. The board believes, however, that tax considerations do not provide an adequate conceptual basis for selecting an appropriate accounting treatment and that it is not acceptable to allow an accounting treatment purely because of tax regulations and advantages in particular jurisdictions.'[5]

The author considers that the IASB's approach is very high-minded but completely impractical. Unless there is a change in American law, American companies will never agree to give up LIFO. If the FASB were to attempt to ban LIFO, it would provoke an enormous outcry, which would almost certainly result in the American legislator intervening to override the FASB.

In attempting to ban LIFO, the IASB is in effect challenging the American Congress, a contest which, in the author's opinion, can have only one outcome.

The position is far less critical as concerns the other two major countries that permit LIFO. In both Japan and Germany, the computation of taxable income is based largely on the individual accounts. In both countries, it is permitted to base the individual accounts on the national commercial code and to base the consolidated accounts on the IASB's standards. The USA is very unusual in applying a tax rule to the consolidated accounts.

8.3.2 Plant, property and equipment

A necessary condition for convergence is that the IASB's standards should specify only one permitted treatment for any specific transaction. There should be no options or permitted alternative treatments, for then there would be no convergence in the accounts of companies that chose different options. In its last years, the IASC made a big effort to reduce the number of options in its standards, but still left much work for the IASB to do. As already mentioned, in 2002 the IASB proposed amendments to fifteen IASs, announcing that its principal objective was to reduce or eliminate alternatives. However, it has experienced difficulties in eliminating certain alternatives as exemplified in its proposed amendments to IAS 16 *Property, plant and equipment.*

Ever since it was first issued in 1982, IAS 16 has set out two permitted alternative methods for the measurement of plant, property and equipment: either historical cost or revalued amount. The reason for this choice is that there is no global consensus on this matter: in the USA, Germany and Japan, there is only one permitted method – historical cost: in the UK, France and Italy, both methods are allowed: historical cost is the normal method but revaluation is permitted in certain circumstances. The IASB, aware of these deep differences, made no attempt to remove the choice when it proposed revisions to IAS 16 in 2002. It simply stated that it was undertaking research on revaluation, which certainly gives the strong impression that convergence on this issue will not be achieved for many years or even decades. The revised version of IAS 16, unchanged from the exposure draft, was issued in December 2003.

8.3.3 Financial instruments

The valuation of financial instruments is a highly complex and controversial topic, which the IASC attempted to tackle with the issue of IAS 39 in 1999. A major problem is that, for many financial instruments, historical cost is not an appropriate measurement basis. For example, the historical cost of many derivatives is zero, but in economic terms they may represent very significant assets – or liabilities as the British merchant bank, Barings, discovered in 1995 when it was forced into bankruptcy through losses on derivatives. IAS 39 has been severely criticised on a number of points – that it is excessively rule-based, that the rules are too complex and too detailed, that it contains too many options, and that it is inconsistent, requiring certain financial instruments to be measured at fair value and others at historical cost. The particular convergence issue with financial instruments is that, in certain countries (notably in Continental Europe), financial assets are reported at historical cost, whereas, in other countries (notably the USA), there has been a tendency to report more and more financial assets at fair value.

When the IASB replaced the IASC, it adopted IAS 39 along with the rest of the IASC's standards, but, with reluctance, as it recognised IAS 39's imperfections.[6] In 2002 the IASB issued an exposure draft that proposed amendments to IAS 39. The exposure draft's remarkable length (over three hundred pages) is a vivid indication both of the unsatisfactory nature of IAS 39 and of the complexity of the problems. However the reaction to the exposure draft has made it abundantly clear that the IASB has not solved the problems. The IASB received almost two hundred comments, very few of which were wholly supportive and many of which were highly critical.[7] Respondents from Continental Europe were particularly critical. For example, EFRAG wrote that it believed 'that IAS 39 remains a complex and rule-based standard requiring further changes'. The CNC observed that 'the revised versions of the standards still raise many questions and difficulties relating to both principles and rules'. The Federation Bancaire de l'Union Européene charged 'that the exposure draft raises serious issues of due process and that the IASB Board needs to be aware of the significant harm that is being done by the conduct surrounding these standards'. The European Association of Public Banks noted that 'the revision of the standards is characterised by numerous casuistic provisions; this goes against the principle-based approach favoured by the IASB'. It should be noted that the four bodies whose comments have just been quoted represent important constituencies in the financial community.

At first the IASB dismissed these criticisms as ignorant special pleading. An unidentified staff member characterised the comment letters as being riddled with errors, the only correct point being the date. Such arrogance only served to further provoke the IASB's critics. In July 2003, the French President, Jacques Chirac, wrote to the European Commission, objecting in the strongest terms to the IASB's proposals, which he asserted 'would have nefarious consequences for financial stability'. Implied in Chirac's letter was the threat that the French government would do everything in its power to ensure that the ARC rejected the offending IASB standard (see Section 7.7.5 for the ARC's role). The European Commission urged the IASB to consult further with European banks and insurance companies with view to finding an acceptable compromise. Paul Volcker, the chairman of the IASB's trustees, publicly backed the EU's proposal. Paul Volcker's intervention was remarkable in that, in principle, the IASB's trustees should not interfere with the standard-setting process. It probably reflects his concern that the dispute between the IASB and the EU could lead to the collapse of the whole process of international standard-setting.[8] In response, the IASB modified its proposals; for IAS 39, it dropped six of its original proposed changes and introduced seven new ones proposed by commentators to the exposure draft. The revised standard was issued in December 2003. A leading British newspaper commented on the revised standard in the following terms: 'The move is likely to be the most hotly contested of all the IASB's proposals...A number of banks on the Continent, which currently value derivatives and other instruments according to how much they paid for them have opposed the reform. Politicians in France and other European countries have also criticised the proposed system, which is already widely used in America.' ('Banks called to show real risk of derivatives', *The Independent*, London, 17 December 2003). Hence it seems very unlikely that the revised standard will settle the issue, which is at heart a conflict between the Anglo-Saxon and the Continental European approaches to financial reporting. At the time of writing, the final outcome of this contest of wills is uncertain, but it seems abundantly clear that the IASB will have extreme difficulty in framing a standard on financial instruments that will achieve wide acceptance. In fact, finding a standard that would satisfy both the SEC and EU would seem to be the equivalent of squaring the circle.

8.4   Convergence with US GAAP

For the success of the IASB's mission, convergence between its standards and US GAAP is absolutely vital, given the importance of the American MNEs and the dominance of the American capital market. Jermakowicz and Gornik-Tomaszewski (2003) presents an analysis of the present differences between the two sets of standards, identifying no less than nineteen areas with major differences, ranging from business combinations (pooling is permitted by the IASB but forbidden under US GAAP) to the reporting of comprehensive income (voluntary under IAS, required under US GAAP). The current efforts of both sides to remove these differences have already been examined in Section 7.9 of the previous chapter. There have been many declarations both by the IASB and by the Americans on the subject but as yet very little concrete progress. In December 2003, the FASB issued four exposure drafts that proposed certain modifications to its standards, with the express puspose of achieving convergence with the IASB. However only relatively minor matters were covered, notaly the calculation of earnings per share, accounting for asset exchanges, the exclusion of 'idle capacity' costs from the value of inventory and the reporting of voluntary changes in accounting policies. None of the hard issues, such as those mentioned in the previous section, were covered. Hence at the time of writing, it is very uncertain that the IASB will be able to achieve convergence with US GAAP. The author is very sceptical about this ever being achieved, notably because the SEC (the more powerful of the two American bodies) is noticeably less enthusiastic than the FASB.

8.5   Conclusion

The conclusion of this brief and necessarily rather cursory analysis of the convergence process is that a considerable degree of convergence has already been achieved in the UK, as a consequence of action both by the UK's ASB and the IASB. The author attributes this progress to two factors: the sentiment among the members of the ASB that they should support the reforming efforts of their former chairman, Sir David Tweedie; and the strong British presence on the IASB which makes that body exceptionally willing to accept the ASB's position. Note that in making progress on convergence, both the ASB and the IASB have had to make concessions and to change their standards. The example of the UK demonstrates that convergence is possible. However undoubtedly the UK is a special case and it is unlikely that the same degree of convergence will be achieved globally, at least in the near future.

Notes

1. This quotation is from the preface to the ASB's exposure draft on financial instruments, FRED 23, issued in May 2002.
2. Cairns and Nobes included two further categories (D and E) relating to disclosure. They are not considered here, because they are less fundamental as they do not impact the figures reported for profit and net equity.
3. See paragraph A.20 of the IASB's exposure draft for the revision of IAS 21.
4. See Cairns (2003).
5. This citation is from the exposure draft's basis for conclusions.
6. One member of the IASB's board (Professor Whittington) did not vote for the adoption of IAS 39, because of the standard's lack of principles. Apparently the other board members were more swayed by practical considerations – the chaos that would have resulted from the withdrawal of a promulgated standard.
7. The following citations are all from the comments which may be viewed on the IASB's website (www.iasb.org).
8. For further details of this incident, see the *Financial Times* of 12 and 29 July 2003.

References

Cairns, D. (2003). *Convergence Handbook Update*. London, ICAEW.

Cairns, D. and Nobes, C. (2000). *The Convergence Handbook*. London, Institute of Chartered Accountants in England and Wales.

Jermakowicz, E. and Gornik-Tomaszewski, S. (2003). The impact of international financial reporting standards on US GAAP, paper presented at the EIASM workshop on implementing IFRS, Brussels, 11–12 September 2003.

Lande, E. (1997). 'A comparative study of the normalization process in France and Spain'. *Comparative Studies in Accounting Regulation in Europe*. J. Flower and C. Lefebvre. Leuven, Acco: 431.

9
The Impact of Enron

This chapter examines recent events in the USA and assesses their impact on financial reporting in Europe.

9.1   The scandals in the USA

In recent years, the USA has been rocked by a series of business scandals involving the collapse of a number of major companies which previously had been highly respected and much admired, of which the most notorious was Enron.[1] The common feature of these scandals was that, in each case, the company's financial statements for past years, which had been audited by a leading accountancy firm and which had reported high profits and a sound financial position, were revealed as being seriously faulty and misleading. The reaction of the American public and government was to heap most of the blame on the accountants. This led very quickly to the collapse of Andersen, the major accountancy firm that had audited many of the companies involved, and subsequently to a series of government measures aimed at reforming the practice of accountancy and auditing. At present the impact of these measures largely affects only American companies and foreign companies that do business in the USA. However the aftermath of these scandals is certain to be felt in Europe, for at least two reasons: first the European authorities, both national governments and the European Commission, have expressed alarm that the American scandals have revealed the inadequacy of much current accounting and auditing practice and are examining what action should be taken to prevent similar problems in Europe; secondly the USA is such an important actor on a global scale, both in business and in accountancy, that in the end Europe is bound to be affected by what happens there.

This chapter analyses the present crisis. It starts with an account of what went wrong at the American companies involved, with the emphasis on Enron and only brief references to other firms. It then analyses those aspects of American accounting and auditing that have been considered as being responsible, at least partially, for the problems. This leads to an account of the measures that the American administration has taken or is proposing to take to reform American accounting and auditing, with the aim of preventing similar scandals in the future. Finally the impact on Europe is analysed.

9.2   What went wrong at Enron

9.2.1   Enron: the business

Enron was formed in 1985 with the merger of Houston Natural Gas with InterNorth. At that time, it was a rather boring business providing a useful but not very profitable service: the marketing and transportation of gas. The company's CEO, Kenneth Lay, wanted something better. He hired McKinsey & Co to assist in developing a more profitable strategy. McKinsey assigned a young consultant, Jeffrey Skilling to the engagement. Skilling came up with a revolutionary idea: he proposed that Enron create a 'gas bank' in which the company would buy gas from a network of suppliers and sell it to a network of customers, contractually guaranteeing both the supply and the price, and assuming the associated risks. It would go further than simply matching demand and supply. It would offer customers a variety of gas contracts, including those normally associated with financial instruments, such as futures, options and swaps. In effect Enron would create a market for gas. The company would be transformed from a utility to a financial intermediary with gas derivatives as its principal product. Lay was so taken with the idea that in 1990 he created a new division and hired Skilling to run it. The new division was a great success and soon came to dominate the gas market with more suppliers and more customers than any of its competitors. Enron earned very high profits, based in part on its knowledge of supply and demand which enabled it to predict future prices with remarkable accuracy. With this development, Enron was transformed from a boring gas transportation utility earning normal profits to a gas trader and financial intermediary, earning super profits. Over the years, Enron expanded into other fields, such as electricity and broadband communications. The company became ready to create a market for anything that could be traded, for example derivatives in coal, paper, steel, water and even the weather. In 1999 it set up Enron Online, a commodities trading website, which immediately attracted much business, handling trades of $335 billion in 2000.

Enron came to be regarded as one of the most admired and respected companies in the USA – a company that was able to exploit the opportunities offered by the Internet to earn exceptional profits. For six consecutive years, 1996–2001, it was named by *Fortune* magazine as America's most innovative company. On the stock exchange, Enron's shares climbed ever higher, reaching an all-time high of $90 in August 2000.

However Enron's success was not based on solid foundations. During the 1990s two essentially temporary factors helped Enron to earn exceptionally high profits:

1. It was the first company to offer energy derivatives and therefore was, for a short time, in a quasi-monopoly position. However, as competitors entered the market in the later 1990s, inevitably Enron's profit margins declined.
2. During the 1990s there was a remarkably protracted boom in the American economy with GNP growing year after year. In fact certain economic commentators were unwise enough to suggest that, with the development of telecommunications, the Internet and other elements of the 'knowledge economy', the USA had entered a new phase in which the shortcomings of the old economy with its booms and recessions no longer applied. In this situation, Enron came to expect and to rely on continuous growth in its business. However, if the American economy were to fall into recession, then Enron would be unable to achieve the continuous growth on which its business plan and its share price were based. In fact, at the start of 2001, the American economy entered recession.

A further factor increased Enron's vulnerability. Enron's principal business was that of a trader and supplier of derivatives. It was essential that those who entered into contracts with Enron should have absolute confidence in its creditworthiness, that Enron would be able to honour its commitments when they fell due. Any suggestion that Enron's financial position was anything other than completely sound would have a most deleterious effect on its business. In fact for the reasons given above, Enron's profitability began to decline in the late 1990s with a consequent impact on its financial position.[2] However, as is explained in the following section, this was not reflected in Enron's financial statements.

9.2.2   Enron's financial statements

It is now known that Enron's financial statements for the financial years 1997–2001 were seriously misleading, overstating profits and equity and understating liabilities. In October and November 2001, Enron announced a series of corrections to its past accounts, which cumulatively had the effect of reducing both its reported profits and its equity by over $1.5 billion. The effect of these announcements was to destroy the confidence of trading partners and investors in the company. In December 2001, Enron declared itself bankrupt – at that time the largest bankruptcy in American history.

Enron's special-purpose entities

Central to the manipulation of Enron's accounts was the use that the company made of special-purpose entities (SPEs). An SPE is a business entity (partnership, corporation or trust) set up by a company (its sponsor) for a specific limited purpose. According to Hartgreaves and Benston (2002), SPEs had originally been developed in the early 1980s to permit banks and financial institutions to securitise their receivables. The bank would set up the SPE and arrange for it to issue debt and equity capital. With the proceeds the SPE would purchase receivables from the bank. If the equity capital was provided by an independent third party, the bank did not control the SPE and therefore did not include the receivables or the SPE's debt in its consolidated balance sheet, in this way improving its reported financial position.

Enron's SPEs, in common with those of most other American companies, had the following characteristics:

- They were not formally controlled by Enron in that a majority of their equity was provided by independent parties. If Enron had owned the equity, then according to US GAAP the SPE's assets, liabilities, income and expenses would have had to be integrated in full in Enron's consolidated accounts.
- The SPEs were highly geared. The majority of their finance consisted of debt, mostly bank loans, which were generally guaranteed by Enron.
- The proportion of the SPE's total funds that was provided by independent third parties was very small, generally 3 per cent.

The rules of US GAAP relating to SPEs have been described as 'confusing' and 'convoluted' (Hartgreaves and Benston, 2002). They are set out principally in a statement of the FASB's Emerging Issues Task Force (Issue No. 90–15). Although formally this statement applied only to SPEs formed to own leased assets, it came to be applied to all SPEs. The most important provision was that the independent third party must have a substantial residual equity investment in the SPE. Although Issue No. 90–15 provided no quantitative guidance on this matter, the SEC indicated that an investment equal to at least 3 per cent of the SPE's total assets would normally be necessary. On the basis of this statement, a consensus developed among company accountants and their auditors that SPEs were not consolidated if a third party controlling equity interest financed at least 3 per cent of the total assets. In effect what the SEC had considered to be the minimum outside equity investment became the norm. In fact Issue No. 90–15 specified a further condition, that the company has divested itself of substantially all the risks and rewards of ownership of the assets and liabilities transferred to the SPE. However it seems that Enron generally ignored this condition, perhaps because it was not expressed in quantitative terms. For example, in many cases Enron guaranteed an SPE's debt but did not consolidate its assets and liabilities, even though it still bore substantial risks.

The senior officer at Enron who was the driving force behind its SPEs was Andrew Fastow, who joined Enron in 1990 and was promoted to Chief Financial Officer in 1998. The two Enron officers above Fastow (Lay and Skilling) both claimed after the debacle that they were not aware of the significance of Fastow's activities with the SPEs. Fastow used SPEs to manipulate Enron's financial statements in a number of highly imaginative and complex ways. In most cases they involved transactions between Enron and an SPE that Fastow was able to effect because in fact the SPE was under his control, as in most cases either Fastow himself or a subordinate was the manager. The following are some of the ways in which Fastow used SPEs to manipulate Enron's accounts. The Annex to this chapter presents a hypothetical example that illustrates how the accounts may be manipulated.

Reporting debt as equity.   In many cases Enron issued its own shares to an SPE. In most cases the SPE paid for the shares with the proceeds of bank loans, which Enron guaranteed. In its consolidated balance sheet, Enron reported the shares issued (increase in equity) and the cash received (increase in assets). In reality the source of the cash was the bank loan which would have been clear if the SPE had been consolidated. By not consolidating the SPE, Enron was able to report as equity what was in effect debt, thus improving its debt–equity ratio. In some cases the SPE paid for the shares that it received not in cash but with a promissory note. Enron reported the promissory note as an asset in its consolidated balance sheet, which is contrary to US GAAP which requires that it should have been deducted from equity, on the grounds that the note may not be paid. This incorrect treatment increased Enron's equity and assets by $172 million in 2000 and $828 million in 2001, in total an overstatement of $1000 million.

Reporting a profit on assets sold to an SPE.   Enron could generate instant profits by selling an asset at an inflated price to an SPE. For example in December 1999, Enron sold to LJM2, an SPE formed and controlled by Fastow, a 75 per cent interest in a company which owned a power plant under construction in Poland, for $30 million, recording a gain of $16 million on the deal.

'Marking to market'.   Enron valued most of its investments in other companies and all of its derivatives (both assets and liabilities) at market value, as is permitted and, in many cases, required under US GAAP. In some cases the market value was easy to establish, for example when a company's shares were quoted on the stock exchange. But in very many cases, there was no easily available market value. In this situation, Enron had to use estimates. In many cases, the basis for the estimated figures was a transaction with an SPE. For example, in September 1999, Enron sold to LJM1, a second Fastow SPE, a 13 per cent interest in a Brazilian company, Empresa Productora de Energia (EPE). The price paid by LJM1 was used by Enron to justify reporting a gain of $65 million on the rest of its investment which was reported as an asset in its balance sheet measured at market value.

Hiding unprofitable investments.   Thomas (2002) speculates that Enron used SPEs to 'park' troubled assets that were falling in value. In this way, these assets and the associated losses could be kept off the consolidated accounts.

Hedging Enron's investments.   As mentioned before, Enron recorded most of its investments in other companies at market value, reporting as income any increase in value. Of course any subsequent decrease in market value had to be reported as an expense. In order to protect itself from such losses, Enron often bought a put option on the company's shares; if the shares fell in value the profit on the put option would cancel the loss in market value and Enron would suffer no loss. However in many cases Enron bought the put option not from a bank, which would have been the normal procedure, but from one of its SPEs – which was anything but normal and which in reality offered Enron no protection at all.

For example, in 1999 Enron bought a put option on its investment in a broadband company, Rhythms, from LJM Swap Sub, a third Fastow SPE. Enron paid for the option, which was valued at $104 million, by transferring to the SPE $168 million of Enron shares; the SPE gave Enron a promissory note for the difference of $64 million. In fact, as the market value of both Enron's and Rhythms' shares fell in value, it became clear that the SPE (whose principal asset was Enron shares) did not have sufficient assets to meet its commitments under the hedge contract. However, even if the SPE had been able to meet its commitments, Enron's shareholders would not have been protected from the fall in value of Rhythms shares, in that the market value of their Enron shares would fall, reflecting that, in order to redeem the option, the SPE would have been obliged to sell its Enron shares. In November 2001, Enron's auditor decided that the SPE should have been consolidated; this led to corrections to Enron's reported profits of $95 million for 1999 and $8 million for 2000. Benston and Hartgreaves (2002) comment: 'All along, though, Enron was really hedging itself with itself – which, of course, is of no economic value to Enron's stockholders. Nevertheless, until it was reversed, it served to keep the decline in Rhythms stock off Enron's financial statements.'

This was only one of many hedges that Enron entered into with its own SPEs. Benston and Hartgreaves (2002) estimate that in this way Enron was able to hide from its shareholders losses on its investments totalling over $1077 million.

Reporting profits on own shares.   US GAAP does not permit a company to report as income the increase in the market value of its own shares. However Enron did just this in connection with a company called JEDI. As originally set up, JEDI was a 50/50 joint venture of Enron and CalPERS; at that time Enron quite correctly accounted for its interest in JEDI using the equity method. In 1997 Enron decided to acquire CalPERS's interest, which would have the effect of converting JEDI into a 100 per cent owned subsidiary.

To avoid having to consolidate JEDI, Enron arranged for CalPERS's 50 per cent interest to be acquired by an SPE, Chewco, which, as with most of Enron's SPEs, was effectively controlled by Fastow. Enron therefore claimed that JEDI was not a subsidiary and continued to account for it with the equity method, taking 50 per cent of JEDI's profits into its consolidated income statement. JEDI owned 12 million Enron shares and reported as income the increase in their market value. Enron included 50 per cent of JEDI's income in its own consolidated income statement, thus effectively taking credit for the increase in value of its own shares, which is quite contrary to US GAAP. To add insult to injury, when Enron's shares declined in market value in the first quarter of 2001, Enron did not record its share of the loss.

US GAAP attempts to ensure that the readers of the accounts appreciate the significance of transactions with SPEs by requiring the company to give information in the notes. Enron did include such notes with its financial statements. But it is doubtful whether it helped the readers. One analyst, quoted by Thomas (2002), remarked of Enron's notes, 'The notes just don't make sense and we read notes for a living!'. One wonders whether Enron's motive in drafting the note was to confuse rather than to provide information.

Other techniques

Not all the techniques used by Enron to inflate its profits involved SPEs. Two are considered here: the general use of 'mark to market' and sham trades.

'Mark to market'. The general use of 'mark to market' for the valuation of derivative contracts offers unscrupulous managers opportunities for manipulating profits. The following extract from Benston and Hartgreaves (2002) points out the dangers: 'US GAAP requires energy trading contracts to be stated at fair values that may be determined by estimated present values. This calculation involves managers in estimating future cash flows and applying a discount rate to obtain present (fair) values. Such procedures allow managers who want to manipulate net income to make "reasonable" assumptions that give them the gains that they want to record.' The greater part of Enron's reported profit came from 'marking to market'. Singleton-Green (2002) estimates that 78 per cent of Enron's reported profit for the year 2000 ($763 million of $979 million) came from 'marking to market' its derivative contracts.

An example of how Enron used 'mark to market' is its reporting of its partnership with Blockbuster Inc. In 2000 Enron entered into a joint venture with Blockbuster to develop a company (Braveheart) that would offer customers access to Blockbuster videos through Enron's fibre-optic lines. According to a report in the *Wall Street Journal* (Smith, 2002), 'Enron assigned the partnership a value of $124.8 million based on its projections of the revenue and earnings potential of the Blockbuster venture . . . for the fourth quarter of 2000, Enron claimed its ownership of Braveheart resulted in a $53 million profit, even though the Blockbuster venture was only two weeks into its pilot programme and not generating any profit at all . . . In the following quarter, Enron claimed an additional $57.9 million in revenue from Braveheart.' The partnership with Blockbuster was a failure and was dissolved in March 2001. In October 2001, Enron had to reverse the $110.9 million profit that it had claimed earlier. In May 2003, the SEC charged five former Enron executives with fraud in connection with this overstatement of profits.

Sham trades.   Another way to inflate profit is to engage in sham trades with a friendly company. This technique may be illustrated by the following hypothetical example based on Fusaro and Miller (2002):

> You and your friend are both running antiques businesses and that at the end of the year you find that both of you are losing money and you don't want your wives to find out that your businesses are doing so poorly. Each of you take Chippendale chair that you had bought earlier in the year for $500 and agree to sell it to the other for $2500. By merely swapping the two chairs, you could each appear to have made a profit of $2000.

Of course the transaction has not generated any additional cash or any real profit. All that has happened is that you have increased the value of an item of inventory by $2000. Accountants attempt to guard against overvaluation of inventory by insisting that it be valued at the lower of cost and market. However, where there is no ready market for an item, it may be difficult to estimate the market value. In the above example, the fact that an identical chair has just been 'sold' for $2500 provides 'objective' evidence that the market value is not less than $2500.

It would seem possible that Enron engaged in similar trades to boost its revenues and its profits. Fusaro and Miller (2002) refers to a report that the SEC was investigating a $500 million broadband swap between Enron and Qwest, the telecommunications company, in September 2001. It should be noted that such a trade will always inflate revenue but will only inflate profits if the capacity ceded is reported as a sale and the capacity acquired is treated as capital expenditure.

9.2.3   The failure of Enron's corporate governance

After the Enron scandal broke, many people asked how a major company was able to manipulate its accounts in such a flagrant matter, given the many safeguards that, according to American law and practice, should have been operating. In American corporations, the two most important control organs are the board of directors and the auditor.

The board of directors

Under American law and practice, the function of the board of directors of a corporation is to monitor the management. In most American companies, the board is made up mainly of 'outside' directors who are not employees, with a minority of senior officers such as the chief executive officer and chief financial officer. Most boards meet at regular intervals to receive reports from the management. A major responsibility of the board is the review and approval of the corporation's financial statements. However often much of the detailed work is done by board committees, of which the most important is the audit committee.

Benston and Hartgreaves (2002) review the membership of Enron's audit committee and come to the conclusion that it was exceptionally well qualified, with the Professor of Accounting at Stanford University Business School as chairman. Furthermore the main board seems to have appreciated the risks associated with the SPEs for it assigned to the audit committee an expanded duty to review transactions with them. However it carried out this review only in a cursory way, as is made clear in the following extract from the Powers report,[3] 'The board had agreed to permit Enron to take on the risk of doing business with its CFO (Fastow), but had done so on the condition that the audit committee review Enron's transactions with the LJM partnerships. These reviews were a significant part of the control structure and should have been more than just another brief item on the agenda...lasting ten to fifteen minutes.' The lesson seems to be that it is insufficient for the members of the audit committee to be well qualified; in addition they must carry out their duties conscientiously. But this raises the question 'Quis custodet custodes?' – who audits the auditors? A principal function of the audit committee is to monitor the performance of the corporation's control system. Is it necessary to have a further committee to monitor the audit committee, and yet another to monitor that one and so on ad infinitum?

The auditors

The well-known firm of Arthur Andersen (AA) audited Enron's financial statements since 1985 and in each year gave an unqualified audit opinion, the last being for the year 2000. AA worked with Fastow in setting up the SPEs to make sure that they were organised in such a way that they did not have to be included in Enron's consolidated accounts. AA's principal concern seems to have been that Enron did not violate the letter of codified GAAP. It did not appear to have realised or been concerned that the substance of GAAP was violated. However, according to Benston and Hartgreaves (2002), Enron's accounts did not comply with the substance of GAAP is at least the following respects:

1. The Fastow SPEs should have been consolidated as they were not independent.

2. Profits and 'mark to market' gains that were based on transactions with SPEs should not have been included as they were not supported by trustworthy evidence.
3. Enron's obligations in respect of its guarantees of the SPEs' debt were not reported in its balance sheet as a liability or even in the notes as a contingent liability.
4. The put options written by the SPEs on certain investments (for example, Rhythms) were of little or no economic value and therefore could not be used to justify not reporting the decline in value of the investments in Enron's balance sheet.
5. The accounts should have included a full explanation of the transactions between Enron and Fastow, as there is a requirement to disclose related party dealings.[4]

AA did not survive the Enron debacle, not because of its audit failures, but because it was found guilty of the criminal offence of obstructing justice in destroying documents relating to the audit. The firm was fined $500,000 but the real punishment was much more severe. The SEC suspended it from acting as the auditor of public companies. AA's larger clients discovered that their audit reports were practically worthless, as the investing public had lost all confidence in AA's audits. As a result AA gave up auditing and has virtually ceased to exist as a separate firm, most of its staff joining other accountancy firms.

9.3   Other scandals

Enron was only the most spectacular of many business scandals that have rocked the USA in recent years. Most had two common features:

1. manipulation of the financial statements by a management keen to present performance as better than it really was;
2. failure of the auditor to prevent the issue of misleading accounts.

Both errors were factors in the travails of the three companies that are analysed in this section.

9.3.1   WorldCom

In June 2002, just six months after Enron filed for bankruptcy, the USA was struck by another scandal. WorldCom, America's second largest telephone operator and a company which, on most measures, was considerably larger than Enron,[5] announced a $3.8 billion error in its accounts for the two previous years. Two months later, it announced a further correction of more than $2 billion. The company filed for bankruptcy, surpassing Enron as the largest bankruptcy in American history (so far!).

The manipulation of WorldCom's accounts involved techniques that were far simpler than those used by Enron. There were two principal methods:

1. *Capitalisation of expenses*: The first correction of $3.8 billion related to expenditure that had been capitalised as improvements to WorldCom's network but which in fact related to repairs and maintenance.
2. *Release of provisions*: The second correction of $2 billion related to the undisclosed release into revenue of provisions that had been set up during past acquisitions. The process involves the setting up of excessive provisions on the occasion of some exceptional event, such as an acquisition, and later using these provisions to boost profits by releasing them covertly to the profit and loss account.

As with Enron, the principal actor in the manipulation of the accounts was an energetic and ambitious chief financial officer, Scott Sullivan, who was subsequently charged with fraud. The company's auditors, Arthur Andersen (AA), the same firm that audited Enron, had issued unqualified audit reports for the relevant years. AA claimed that it had been misled by Scott Sullivan who had withheld important information.

Most commentators considered that AA was seriously at fault in not detecting the improper capitalisation of expenses that clearly belonged in the income statement. However the author is not so certain. Most of the expenses related to the maintenance of telephone lines and network connections. In almost all cases, this activity resulted in an improvement in the asset: for example a longer life and increased capacity. In these circumstances, it is permissible under GAAP to capitalise some part of the expenditure. The difficulty is in deciding how much. It seems clear that the proportion capitalised by WorldCom was excessive; if they had been less greedy no one would have complained.

9.3.2 Waste Management

In the 1990s, Waste Management was the largest waste haulage and disposal company in the USA. In the 1980s it had been a favourite growth stock of American investors, its share price increasing more than twentyfold in that decade. However in 1998 it shocked the stock market, when it announced that its previous accounts had overstated profits and assets by $3.5 billion – an enormous figure. All years since 1992 were affected; for example, in 1996 Waste Management had reported a profit of $192 million, the corrected figure was a loss of $39 million, a reduction of $231 million. The SEC (2002) analysed the accounting errors that led to this enormous adjustment as follows:

1. The useful lives of fixed assets were systematically increased in order to reduce the depreciation charge; for example, whereas the standard industry practice was to depreciate trucks over eight to ten years, in the early 1990s

when the management sought to boost profits, the useful life was stretched a further two to four years.

2. In calculating depreciation, high salvage values were assumed, whereas standard industry practice was to assume no salvage value.

3. The values of landfill sites (a major part of the company's assets) were not written down as they were filled with waste (on the unwarranted assumption that they could be extended) and the costs of unsuccessful projects were not written off.

4. Inflated provisions were established in connection with acquisitions, which subsequently were set off against unrelated operating expenses without this being disclosed.

5. Some operating expenses were improperly capitalised (although not to the same extent as in WorldCom).

6. Insufficient provision was made for deferred taxes and other expenses.

Basically what Waste Management did was to err consistently on the side of optimism in making the estimates on which the financial statements are based, for example, in the calculation of depreciation, the useful life and the salvage value. This is exactly the opposite of the normal approach of accountants which is based on prudence. The error in each individual case may have seemed not significant, but for Waste Management, a company with very substantial fixed assets (not only trucks and landfill sites, but also recycling plants and water treatment facilities), the accumulated effect was a very significant misstatement of the depreciation charge.

Yet again, Arthur Andersen (AA) was the accountancy firm involved. It gave Waste Management unqualified audit reports for all of the years covered by the correction, which subsequent events showed to be completely without justification. In retrospect the breaking of the scandal in 1998 was a clear sign that there was something very wrong with the firm's approach to auditing and it can be considered to be the beginning of the end. The SEC investigated the affair; its report which gives a fascinating account of AA's failings has been analysed by Brandt (2001). It reveals that, right from the beginning in 1992, AA's audit staff noted the problems and reported them to AA's senior management. However the latter decided that, although the misstatements in that year totalled $93.5 million, they were not material and decided to issue an unqualified audit report. The next year the same thing happened. As the accumulated error grew ever larger, AA proposed that it should be written off in instalments over future years – which is clear proof that AA was aware that the accounts were wrong.

The SEC found AA guilty of improper professional conduct in that it knowingly or recklessly issued materially false and misleading audit reports. AA agreed to pay a civil penalty of $7 million, at that time a record amount for an accountancy firm. AA also paid more than $240 million to settle suits brought by aggrieved shareholders. The SEC was able to document so clearly what went wrong with AA's audit, because it had access to AA's working papers and internal communications, such as Emails, going right back to the early years. The author suspects that AA's bad experience of being found guilty on the basis of its own documentation was a major factor in its fateful decision to destroy documents relating to the Enron audit, an action which led to the firm's demise.

9.3.3   Xerox

However not all the American companies that were implicated in the recent accounting scandals were audited by Andersen. Xerox, the last company to be considered in this section, was, at the relevant time, audited by KPMG. Xerox was a major manufacturer of office equipment, particularly photo-copiers. A major part of its output was leased to customers, typically for periods of three to four years, which covered the greater part of the equipment's useful life. Typically the lease contract also provided for Xerox to service the equipment and provide financing. The recognition of revenue from such medium-term lease contracts is not a straightforward matter and gives opportunities for management to overstate profits (at least in the early years of a lease) by making over-optimistic assumptions. Under US GAAP, revenue from the provision of the equipment may be recognised at the beginning of the lease, but revenue from the servicing and financing elements has to be recognised over the course of the lease.

The SEC investigated Xerox's accounting for leases and discovered that, without disclosing the fact, the company had deliberately changed its accounting methods so as to shift revenue from the financing and servicing elements of leases to the equipment element. For the years 1997–2000, the SEC calculated that in this way Xerox improperly boosted its revenue by $6.1 billion and its profits by $1.9 billion. The company also used approxi-mately $1 billion from various accounting credits to artificially improve its operating results without disclosing the fact. The credits included 'big-bath provisions' and the improper recognition of a one-time gain. The SEC found that by not disclosing the changes in its accounting methods and the offset-ting of various gains against operating expenses, Xerox created the impression that it was earning much more from its sales of equipment than was actually the case.

The SEC required Xerox to pay a $10 million civil penalty and to reclassify $2 billion of revenue for the years, 1997 to 2000. Early in 2003, the SEC charged KPMG, Xerox's auditors, with fraud.

9.4   The faults in the American financial reporting system

The business scandals that have just been described revealed a number of shortcomings in the American financial reporting system. In this section, these shortcomings are analysed under three headings: US GAAP, the accountancy profession and the regulatory system.

9.4.1   US GAAP

A noticeable feature of all these cases is that there were very few clear-cut breaches of US GAAP. The most obvious was that Enron reported as an asset a promissory note that it received for an issue of its shares whereas it should have deducted it from equity. Also Enron was clearly wrong in reporting as income the increase in the market value of its shares held by an associated company. However these clear breaches of GAAP were comparatively minor factors in the overstatement of Enron's assets and profits. Clear and unambiguous breaches of GAAP were also largely absent from the other cases. Apparently, in the case of Waste Management, Andersen considered that the 1993 accounts did not comply with GAAP, for it set out a series of 'action steps' to be taken in respect of future accounts. Also, in the case of all three companies, the SEC came to the opinion that the accounts did not comply with GAAP. However the non-compliance with GAAP did not arise, in most cases, from a clear breach of specific rules. Rather the misleading nature of the accounts arose from three circumstances:

1. The reporting of complex transactions in a way that was arguably in accordance with the detailed rules of GAAP but which resulted in misleading accounts. This was particularly the case with transactions involving Enron's SPEs which seem to have been constructed with a view to artificially inflating reported profits.
2. The use (or rather abuse) by management of the degree of discretion permitted by the GAAP rules so as to report excessive profits. For example under GAAP, the amount of depreciation that is charged in the income statement is based on estimates of the relevant asset's useful life and salvage value. Management should make the estimates in good faith using the best available evidence. The SEC concluded that in the case of Waste Management this did not happen and that therefore the accounts did not comply with GAAP.
3. The disclosure of the accounting methods used (and of changes to these methods) was insufficient. This was particularly the case with Xerox, which, if it had made full disclosure both of its change in its reporting of leases and of its offsetting exceptional gains against operating expenses, would probably have escaped serious censure from the SEC. Enron reported its transactions with its SPEs in footnotes, but in such an opaque way that even the experts could not fathom what was going on.

The above analysis suggests that the scandals would not have been avoided if the detailed rules of GAAP had been different. It seems probable that a sufficiently determined and imaginative chief financial officer will always be able to find ways of getting round a specific rule so that the accounts comply with the detail of the rule but not its spirit. Three reforms would seem to be required to prevent similar debacles in the future:

1. Better disclosure of accounting policies and of significant transactions.
2. Better control of how management exercises its discretion in making the estimates that are an unavoidable feature of financial reporting.
3. A change in the character of GAAP from rules that attempt to cover every possibility in detail to rules that are based on general principles.

Benston and Hartgreaves (2002) compare Enron's approach to complying with GAAP with that of a company that seeks to minimise its tax liability. With tax, it is perfectly acceptable that a company should exploit every loophole in the tax rules so as to avoid paying taxes. Enron adopted the same approach with the application of GAAP. It followed the letter of GAAP but not the spirit. The reaction of society to the Enron debacle suggests that, whereas such an approach may be permitted for tax, it is not acceptable for financial reporting.

9.4.2 The accountancy profession

There can be no doubt that, in all the cases that are discussed in this chapter, the auditor failed the investing public in that he issued an unqualified audit report on accounts that were subsequently shown to be seriously misleading. However, it would seem that, in general, no blame can be attached to the audit firms' junior staff who performed the detailed checking and in fact detected most of the problems. What went wrong was that, when the senior staff were informed of the problems, they came to the wrong conclusion. A very clear example is to be found in the SEC's report on Andersen's audit of Waste Management (SEC, 2001). In respect of the 1993 accounts, the auditors discovered misstatements totalling $128 million (about 12 per cent of income). The audit team informed the responsible partner who consulted widely within the firm, including with the firm's managing partner. The partners determined that the misstatements were not material and that Andersen could issue an unqualified audit report. The same thing happened in the three following years. The SEC on the basis of the same facts came to the conclusion that the misstatements were material and that Andersen's unqualified audit report was materially false and misleading.

The SEC suggested two principal reasons why Andersen's senior partners were unwilling to qualify the audit report:

1. *Andersen was too involved in the management of the company*: Until 1997 every chief financial officer and every chief accounting officer had previously worked as an auditor at Andersen. During the 1990s some fourteen former Andersen employees worked for Waste Management, mostly in key

financial and accounting positions. It seems probable that the Andersen audit staff identified themselves with the company and were reluctant to take any action that might imply criticism of their former colleagues or jeopardise their own prospects of a similar job.

2. *Andersen was too dependent on Waste Management*: The SEC claims that Andersen regarded the company as a 'crown jewel client'. Andersen earned very high fees from Waste Management. Between 1991 and 1997, the company paid Andersen $7.5 million in audit fees and $11.8 million in other fees. It also paid a related entity, Andersen Consulting, $6 million, of which $3.8 million was for a strategic review on which the audit partner worked. Andersen's audit partner for Waste Management was also the marketing director of Andersen's head office and was responsible for the cross-selling of non-audit services to audit clients. In setting his compensation, Andersen took into account total billings to Waste Management for audit and non-audit services.

In the author's view, Andersen's fault was that it regarded its client as the management and that, as auditor, its principal task was to help the management to improve the company's performance, whereas the proper client was the body of shareholders and Andersen's task was to report objectively on the accounts, in this way helping the shareholders to monitor the management.

9.4.3   The regulatory authorities

A government agency, the Securities and Exchange Commission (SEC), has been responsible for the regulation of the American capital market ever since it was set up under the Securities Exchange Act of 1934. In the field of financial reporting, two aspects of its work are of particular interest:

1. The setting of the accounting rules.
2. The supervision of the audit profession.

The setting of the accounting rules

Under the Securities Exchange Act, the SEC has the responsibility and authority to set the rules that govern the financial reporting of listed corporations. However, right from the onset, it decided to delegate the task to a private body, initially the Committee on Accounting Procedure and currently the Financial Accounting Standards Board (FASB). The SEC retained a right of veto, which however it has used very sparingly.[6] In general it seems to have been satisfied with the standards that the FASB has set. In the case of accounting for SPEs, the SEC closely associated itself with the FASB's work through its observers on the FASB's decision-making bodies. Following the Enron debacle, there was general agreement that the FASB's inadequate rules relating to the reporting of SPEs permitted Enron to present accounts, which, as the SPEs were excluded, presented a thoroughly misleading picture of Enron's financial position and performance. The SEC must bear the ultimate responsibility for the inadequacy of the rules; not only did it fail to exercise forceful oversight over the FASB to ensure that it issued proper rules, but also it publicly endorsed the inadequate rules that the FASB set.

Supervision of the audit profession

The SEC failed to ensure that the audits of public companies were effective. The SEC has the power to discipline auditors for 'improper professional conduct', which is defined to include wilfully or recklessly attesting to financial statements that violate the provisions of GAAP or GAAS (generally accepted auditing standards). However, as with setting of accounting rules, the SEC delegated much of the task of monitoring and disciplining the auditors to the private sector. To fulfil this function, the American accountancy profession set up the Public Oversight Board, which, in view of its failure to prevent the recent scandals, lost the confidence of the public. *The Economist* (2001b) criticised it (after the Enron scandal broke) as lacking independence from the accountancy profession (which funds and staffs it) and having insufficient disciplinary powers. The SEC retained the right to take action and in fact fined Andersen $7 million for its failings in the audit of Waste Management (see Section 9.3.2 above). However this was its first successful action against an auditor for fraud in more than twenty years (*Economist*, 2001a) and, coming as it did only in 2001, it can be described as 'too little and too late'.

9.5   The reform of the American regulatory system

9.5.1   The Sarbanes-Oxley Act

American investors were shocked by these scandals. Very many lost large sums of money, in some cases their entire savings, with the collapse of the share price of Enron and others. With the breaking of the Enron scandal in September 2001, shares on the New York Stock Exchange fell by over 20 per cent wiping billions of dollars off the value of investors' wealth. Although the whole of this fall cannot be blamed on the accounting scandals, the loss of investor's confidence in corporate financial reporting was a major factor. Fearing that other corporations were manipulating their accounts, investors both reduced their estimates of future profits and increased the discount rate used to calculate present values – a 'double whammy' that led to a fall in the market value of equities in general; even the shares of such highly respected companies as GE and Microsoft were not spared from the general disdain.

Stung by their losses, the American investing public demanded that the government take action. The legislature was under great pressure to do something and, in July 2002, passed the Sarbanes-Oxley Act (named after its principal sponsors) which sought to tackle many of the shortcomings in the

American system of financial reporting that the scandals had revealed, notably in respect of the supervision of the auditing profession, the rules for auditor independence and corporate governance.

9.5.2   The supervision of the auditing profession

The most important provision of the Sarbanes-Oxley Act was the establishment of a new body to supervise the American auditing profession. Previously this function had been performed by the Public Oversight Board, a private body that had been set up and funded by the profession. However this body had clearly failed to prevent the audit failures at Enron and elsewhere and was generally regarded as lacking both independence from the profession and the will and the power to take the strong action that many considered would be necessary to reform the profession. In fact the Public Oversight Board voluntarily disbanded itself in a fit of pique when the government proposed setting up an alternative body.

The new body that was set up under the Sarbanes-Oxley Act carries the title the Public Company Accounting Oversight Board (PCAOB). Formally it is a private body, although subject to direct and substantial oversight by the SEC, which appoints its members and arranges for its funding (principally through a levy on audit firms and listed corporations). The PCAOB's functions are:

1. To maintain a register of firms that are authorised to audit the accounts of companies that are subject to SEC supervision (principally listed corporations).
2. To establish the rules and standards relating to the conduct of audits. Previously this function had been performed by the profession's Auditing Standards Board. Although the PCAOB has the authority to adopt rules set by another body, it decided not to do so but instead to set up its own rule-making procedure. This involves an advisory group consisting of auditors, preparers and investors. The PCAOB has stated that it 'expects that the advisory group will have fairly equal representation among these broad groups and that no one group will dominate' (PCAOB, 2003). Hence the auditors will be in a minority which implies that, in future, audit standards may be set against the opposition of the experts in the field, a truly remarkable eventuality which vividly illustrates the American public's distrust of the audit profession in the wake of Enron.
3. To conduct regular inspections of registered audit firms – annually for firms that audit more than 100 SEC supervised companies (that is the 'Big Four') and at least once every three years for other firms. The aim of these inspections is to check that the firms respect the board's rules and thus assure a high standard of audits. Previously the profession had monitored audit quality through a system of peer review – audit firms had checked each other. The recent audit failures had highlighted the

weaknesses of this system and there was a general feeling that the accountancy profession could no longer be trusted to regulate itself.
4. To conduct investigations and disciplinary proceedings, and to impose appropriate sanctions to enforce compliance with its rules.

The effective establishment of the PCAOB was delayed by difficulties over the appointment of the chairman. The first nominee, William Webster, was forced to withdraw after it was revealed that he had been the chairman of the audit committee of a company under investigation by the SEC for fraud. In May 2003, the SEC appointed William McDonough as the PCAOB's chairman. He is a well-known and influential figure in the financial community, being President of the Federal Reserve Bank of New York and, significantly, not a professional accountant.

It is too early to make a definitive judgement of the PCAOB's impact. However it is clear that the American accountancy profession has lost the battle to control how it is governed. The profession lobbied strongly against the proposal to set up the PCAOB, characterising it as a 'de facto government takeover of the accounting profession'.[7] It lost. The profession's influence over the new board will be far less than it was over its predecessor, the Public Oversight Board. Only two of the five members of the new board are CPAs and, in order to ensure their independence, they are obliged to refrain from any other business or professional activity whilst serving.

9.5.3 Auditor independence

In the opinion of many commentators, a contributory factor to the audit failures at Enron and elsewhere was that the auditor's independence had been compromised. The auditors were unwilling to take a stand against the management and to insist on corrections to the accounts for a number of reasons:

1. The audit firm earned high fees from supplying non-audit services (such as consultancy and tax advice) to the client, which would be at risk if the auditor took a too independent stance; for both Enron and Waste Management, the fees that Andersen earned from non-audit work exceeded the audit fees. Beattie and Fearnley (2002) report on an American study that examined the fee income of the Big Five in 1999: of total fee income 44 per cent came from consultancy, 22 per cent from tax services and only 34 per cent from accounting and audit, with the last figure presumably including some non-audit services. These figures suggest that the Big Five had become principally consultancy firms, with the attendant danger that they might neglect the audit function and be reluctant to put their consultancy fees at risk by being too strict with their audit work.
2. In many client companies important management positions were filled by former employees of the audit firm. This tended to limit the effectiveness

of the audit as the auditors were often unwilling to take a firm stand on contentious issues for two reasons: this might embarrass their former colleagues and it might prejudice their own chances of future employment with the client.
3. Within audit firms, the remuneration and promotion of senior staff was often determined by their success in selling non-audit services to clients but rarely took account of their efficiency as auditors.

The Sarbanes-Oxley Act mandated the SEC to issue rules that governed the independence of auditors. The SEC issued these rules early in 2003 (SEC, 2003a). They are extremely detailed, taking up no less than 126 pages – a telling commentary on the course that the regulation of financial reporting is currently taking in the USA in the wake of Enron. The principal features of the independence rules are:

Prohibition of non-audit services

An accountant is prohibited from providing a whole range of non-audit services to the corporation of which he is the auditor. In deciding on which services to prohibit, the SEC followed three basic principles, violations of which would impair the auditor's independence:

1. an auditor cannot audit his own work;
2. an auditor cannot function in the role of management; and
3. an auditor cannot serve in an advocacy role for the client.

The SEC could have limited itself to laying down these principles and have left to the individual auditor the application of these principles in specific cases. This would have been appropriate if the SEC had had confidence in the professional integrity of accountants. However the SEC did not do this. Instead it set out a long list of non-audit services that an accountant may not provide to an audit client:

- book-keeping services;
- design and implementation of financial information systems;
- appraisal and valuation services;
- outsourcing of internal audit;
- management functions;
- human resources functions, such as selection and development;
- legal services;
- expert services.

The rationale for most of these prohibitions is based firmly on the three basic principles. For example, in respect of book-keeping services, the SEC (2003a) states: 'If, during an audit, an accountant must audit the book-keeping work performed by his accounting firm, it is questionable that the accountant could, or that a reasonable investor would believe that the accountant could, remain objective and impartial. If the accountant found an error in the book-keeping, the accountant could well be under pressure not to raise the issue with the client if raising the issue could jeopardize the firm's contract with the client for book-keeping services or result in heightened litigation risk for the firm.' Note, in the above citation, the SEC places emphasis on the appearance of independence, that a reasonable investor should believe that the auditor acts independently.

In respect of legal services, the SEC (2003a) writes: 'We have long maintained that an individual cannot be both a zealous legal advocate for management or the client company, and maintain the objectivity and partiality that are necessary for an audit. The Supreme Court has agreed with our view. In the United States v. Arthur Young, the Supreme Court emphasized, "If investors were to view the accountant as an advocate for the corporate client, the value of the audit function might well be lost." ' Note, in the above citation, both the SEC and the Supreme Court seem to consider that the auditor's principal client is the body of shareholders and not the corporation.

The SEC also considered prohibiting accountants from providing taxation services to their audit clients. In fact taxation services are a major source of income for most audit firms, making up about a fifth of total fees (Beattie and Fearnley, 2002). Unsurprisingly the accountancy profession lobbied very hard against the prohibition of tax services. The SEC yielded to this pressure and decided to continue to permit auditors to provide tax services which has been characterised as a victory for KPMG (IHT, 2003). In the author's view, the first basic principle (that an accountant should not audit his own work) implies that the accounts should be prepared by the management without the assistance of the auditor, whose task is to provide an independent judgement on the figures. However, if the auditor has provided tax advice, then he is not able to make a fully independent and objective judgement on a major figure in the accounts (the tax provision). This would seem to imply that the exclusion of tax advice from the list of prohibited services is based not on principles but on the need to satisfy an influential lobby.

Rotation of audit staff

It is often claimed that many audit failures would be prevented by periodically changing the auditors. The argument is that, if the same person has audited a company for many years, he ceases to maintain an objective approach to the audit, for example he becomes too closely associated with the management and begins to adopt its viewpoint. Hence, from time to time, the proposal is made that there should be a limit to the number of years that a particular accountancy firm may act as auditor for a particular company. The accountancy profession has always vigorously resisted these proposals. The author suspects that the principal reason for the profession's opposition is that it would weaken the competitive position of the established firms (which have the most influence within the profession). However there are more respectable arguments against the proposal, notably that it would increase the costs of audit, because the new auditor would have to spend time in familiarising himself with the company's accounting system and that there is no evidence that audit failures are less common in those countries which practise compulsory rotation of audit firms. Under Italian law, an auditor is appointed for a term of three years and may be reappointed twice. Consequently after nine years, a different audit firm must be appointed. However most commentators do not consider that auditing in Italy is noticeably better compared with other countries.

The SEC seems to have been persuaded by these arguments and did not propose the compulsory rotation of audit firms. The only requirement is that the individual within the audit firm who is responsible for the audit (the lead partner) should be changed every five years. However the question of audit firm rotation (as opposed to audit partner rotation) has not been forgotten, as the SEC will continue to study it.[8]

Other measures

The new rules contain a number of further measures that are designed to improve auditor independence. Thus there is a requirement that a member of the audit team who wishes to join the management of a client must serve a 'cooling-off' period of one year and another that audit partners may not be remunerated for selling non-audit services to a client. Both rules are clearly aimed at malpractices uncovered in the Waste Management case. In the author's opinion, they are the equivalent of 'shutting the stable door after the horse has bolted' and show up the poverty of the SEC's practice of prescribing detailed rules to cover specific malpractices rather than of relying on broad general principles.

On the question of principles versus detailed rules, the author strongly supports the position of FEE (the body that represents the European accountancy profession) as set out in the following quotation:

> FEE supports a principles-based approach to financial reporting, independence and other standards, rather than detailed rules...By focussing on the underlying aim rather than detailed prohibitions, the principles-based approach combines flexibility with rigour in a way that is unattainable with a rule-based approach. In particular, it:
>
> – allows for the almost infinite variations in circumstances that arise in practice;
> – it can cope with rapid changes in the modern business environment;
> – prevents the use of legalistic devices to avoid compliance ...

In a rapidly evolving modern global economy, it is impractical to comprehensively list all possible threats to independence. In fact, such an approach is open to the danger of ignoring threats not specifically mentioned or detailed in the rules. (FEE, 2003)

9.5.4 Corporate governance

The Sarbanes-Oxley Act deals with three matters in the general field of corporate governance

1. *Audit committees*: The Act gives an enhanced role to the audit committee of a corporation's board of directors, which must be composed entirely of independent directors, who may not receive any remuneration from the company apart from directors' fees. The committee has to pre-approve all contracts with the audit firm for audit and permitted non-audit services. It is directly responsible for the appointment, compensation and oversight of the accountancy firm that is appointed as auditor. The auditor must report directly to the audit committee and inform it of a number of matters relating to the conduct of the audit, with particular reference to problems encountered. However, curiously, there is no obligation on a board of directors to set up an audit committee – if none exists, its function is performed by the entire board, which in that case must be composed entirely of independent directors.
2. *Attestation of accounts*: The Act requires that the chief executive of an SEC-supervised company has to certify an oath before the SEC that the accounts are accurate, making the individual criminally liable if subsequently the accounts are shown to be incorrect. This provision has caused considerable anguish to many chief executives, notably those of European companies that are listed in New York. It is reported (Accountancy, 2002) that the German carmaker, Porsche, put off plans to list its shares in New York because its chief executive did not want to commit himself by taking an oath. In the author's opinion, any provision that brings home to management its ultimate responsibility for the accuracy of the accounts is highly desirable.
3. *Internal control report*: The company must include in its annual report an assessment of the effectiveness of the internal control procedures for financial reporting. The auditor is required to attest to the management's assessment. Accordingly the auditor will be required to attest to portions of the company's annual report that fall outside the financial statements, a significant increase in the auditor's responsibilities.

9.5.5 Changes to US GAAP

The recent scandals revealed a number of inadequacies in certain of the detailed rules of US GAAP. The Sarbanes-Oxley Act made no fundamental changes to the American standard-setting system under which the standards are set by the FASB subject to the oversight of the SEC. The SEC (2003b) has reaffirmed its policy towards the FASB, whereby it recognises that body's standards as 'generally accepted'. The Sarbanes-Oxley Act set out certain conditions that the standard-setting body should meet, notably that it should consider, in adopting accounting principles, 'the extent to which international convergence on high quality accounting standards is necessary or appropriate in the public interest and for the protection of investors' (SEC, 2003b). Hence the FASB now has a duty to consider 'international convergence' but only within the context of the (American) public interest and the protection of (American) investors. In fact, the Sarbanes-Oxley Act rather strengthened the FASB's position by giving it statutory recognition and by putting the body's finances on a more solid basis. The FASB acted quickly to tighten the rules governing the consolidation of SPEs, requiring them to be consolidated if the third party equity investment was less than 10 per cent of total assets (the previous rule was 3 per cent) or if it is probable that the sponsor would be obliged to pay out on a guarantee of the SPE's debt. However the author is sceptical that these changes will solve the fundamental problem which is US GAAP's emphasis on detailed rules rather than on broad principles.

The Sarbanes-Oxley Act required that the SEC study the feasibility of basing US GAAP on a principles approach. In July 2003, the SEC presented its study (SEC, 2003c). It provides an excellent analysis of the weaknesses of the rule-based approach, arguing that 'rules-based standards can provide a roadmap to avoidance of the accounting objectives inherent in the standards ... This can result in financial reporting that is not representative of the economic substance of transactions and events. In a rules-based system, financial reporting may well come to be seen as an act of compliance rather than an act of communication.' However it also points out the disadvantages of the other extreme which it terms a 'principles-only' approach, notably a loss of comparability because of management and auditor discretion in the application of the principles and a greater difficulty in restraining 'bad' actors. Hence the study recommends a compromise between the two extremes which it terms 'objective-oriented' standard-setting. Standards should set out the accounting objective 'at an appropriate level of specificity' with 'an appropriate amount of implementation guidance'. The author is very sceptical about this proposal. What is 'appropriate' to one person may be seen as excessive to a second and inadequate to a third. Hence, to the author, the approach is not operational.

9.5.6   Principles-based rules: comparison with the UK

British accountants claim that their approach is superior as it puts more emphasis on principles. Under British law, the auditor must certify that the accounts give a true and fair view. Furthermore, if the effect of following a specific legal provision or standard would be that the accounts do not give a true and fair view, then that law or standard must be disregarded – the general requirement to give a true and fair view overrides the particular rule. In the USA, the auditor must certify that the accounts 'present fairly in accordance with GAAP'. There is a fundamental difference between the British and the American rules – in the USA the particular rules of US GAAP override the general 'present fairly' rule.

A good example of the British rule is the reporting of SPEs. The ASB's standard, FRS 5 *Reporting the substance of operations* (the title is very revealing) requires that 'quasi-subsidiaries' be treated in the consolidated accounts in the same way as ordinary subsidiaries; it defines a 'quasi-subsidiary' as an entity or 'vehicle that, though not fulfilling the definition of a subsidiary, is directly or indirectly controlled by the reporting entity and gives rise to benefits for that entity that are in substance no different from those that would arise were the vehicle a subsidiary'. Note that the rules for the reporting of 'quasi-subsidiaries' do not rely on legal definitions but on the reporting of the substance of the situation. What is remarkable about this rule is not so much that the ASB promulgated it but that it worked, in that from then on all British companies consolidated all the various entities, including SPEs, that they had previously set up to raise off-balance sheet finance. It is clear that British auditors take very seriously their obligation to follow the ASB's standards, even when they are based on general principles. A major factor in this matter is the effective enforcement of the ASB's standards through the Financial Reporting Review Panel.

The author is very sceptical that a similar approach can be implemented in the USA, given the highly litigious character of the US business environment. Law suits by investors against directors and auditors for damages arising from alleged faulty accounts are very common. The threat of being sued causes all those connected with financial reporting (directors, accountants, auditors and lawyers) to demand clear-cut rules to which they can appeal when accused of failing to obey the law. Hence there must be a fundamental change in the nature of the American legal system before one can expect a change in the character of US GAAP from a rules-based approach to a principles-based approach.

9.6 Impact on Europe

The impact on Europe of Enron and the other scandals is analysed here from three viewpoints: European companies, European audit firms and European regulatory authorities.

9.6.1 European companies listed in the USA

European companies that are listed in the USA, principally on the NYSE and NASDAQ, are subject to the SEC's jurisdiction and hence have to obey the new rules set by the Sarbanes-Oxley Act, for example the requirement that the chief executives swear an oath on the accuracy of the accounts.[9] Most European companies accept this as the part of the price of an American listing.

9.6.2 European audit firms

Very many European audit firms are caught by the provisions of the Sarbanes-Oxley Act, not only the auditors of European companies that are listed in New York but also the auditors of the much more numerous European subsidiaries of American companies. In principle all these firms (which include many relatively small firms) have to register with the PCAOB and be subject to that body's inspection and disciplinary regimes. These firms are concerned that this will make their work more complicated and more costly. In fact there may be occasions when the American rule conflicts with a legal requirement imposed by a European government; for example, a Belgian auditor is required by law to provide a report on the value of an asset contributed to the company which would be considered to be a prohibited non-audit service under the SEC rules. European audit firms resent very strongly the increased regulatory burden imposed on them by the SEC and have been actively lobbying their governments and the EU to get the American authorities to offer exemption. The EU (2003) has written to the PCAOB, setting out in detail its objections. It listed four principal reasons why regulation of European audit firms by the American authorities was undesirable:

1. It was unnecessary, because the EU already had an effective system of regulation of audit firms, based on the Eighth Directive.
2. It would lead to conflicts between American law and European law, particularly in that, in many EU member states, there is a legal prohibition against auditors transferring confidential information to third parties (in this case, the PCAOB).
3. It would lead to a further concentration in the supply of audit services, as smaller firms (unwilling to incur the costs of registering with the PCAOB) withdrew from the audit of US listed companies and their subsidiaries.
4. It represented an unwarranted attempt to extend American jurisdiction into Europe.

The EU requested exemption for European audit firms from the provisions of the Sarbanes-Oxley Act and threatened retaliatory action (requiring American firms to register in Europe) if this was not forthcoming.

9.6.3 Action by European authorities

The first reaction of the European accountancy profession to the American scandals was that 'it couldn't happen here!'. Although in recent years a number of European companies have admitted irregularities in their previously published accounts, none of the companies involved were as important as

Enron or Worldcom. However in March 2003, the Dutch company, Ahold, the world's third biggest food retailer and the 43rd largest European company (see Exhibit 1.4) announced that it had overstated its profits over the previous two years by more than €450 million by such accounting tricks as reporting the gain on a sale-and-leaseback deal as profit. To some observers, this suggested that Europe was not immune to 'Enronitis'; however others noted that most of the accounting irregularities occurred at Ahold's American subsidiary (which had been audited by the US arm of one of the 'Big Four') and concluded that the Ahold case was simply confirmation that the problem was largely confined to the USA.

However in December 2003, the European financial community was shocked by the sudden collapse of Parmalat, an Italian dairy product manufacturer and distributor, which was generally considered to be financially sound, on the basis of a balance sheet that reported a substantial cash balance. However it transpired that this cash balance did not exist. For many years the company's management had concealed a deteriorating financial position by falsifying the financial statements through the inclusion of a fictitious bank account held by a subsidiary located in the Caymen Islands. The auditors did not detect the falsification because they were deceived by a forged document, which purported to certify that the subsidiary held a balance of €3.9 billion in an account with the Bank of America. Although Parmalat was not nearly as large as Enron or WorldCom[10], in terms of the amounts involved in the falsification of the accounts, the cases are comparable; for example, the two corrections to WorldCom's balance sheet totalled $5.8 billion (about €4.5 billion). The Parmalat case was similar to the American cases in two respects: (1) It involved the falsification of the financial statements by a management intent on showing the enterprise's performance as better than it really was; (2) There was a clear failure of the control organs: the directors and the auditor. However the Parmalat case differed in that it involved a much more straightforward, even blatant, fraud. The Parmalat case tended to strengthen the general view that the problems revealed by the American scandals also existed in Europe.

The European regulatory authorities had never had any doubts. Frits Bolkestein, the member of the European Commission with responsibility for financial markets, was very frank: 'We are not naïve or complacent. Enron could have happened in Europe' (Bolkestein, 2002). He set out a set of measures that the EU planned to take with the aim of restoring investors' confidence in the financial reporting of companies. They included the tightening up of accounting standards, both their content and, more importantly their enforcement; proposed recommendations on auditor independence and audit quality, a new code of corporate governance and steps to assure the integrity of financial analysts and credit rating agencies.

The reaction of the European regulatory authorities to Enron was to increase their level of surveillance over the financial reporting and auditing of companies. Their main effect was to accelerate the long-term process whereby the regulation of the accountancy profession has been taken out of the hands of the profession itself and entrusted to bodies representing the public interest in which the influence of the profession is very much reduced.

9.7   The impact on international standard-setting

Chapter 7 analysed briefly the contest between the IASB's standards and US GAAP to become the dominant standard for the world's MNEs. Before the Enron scandal, it seemed likely that this contest would be won by US GAAP for the reasons given in Section 7.10.1:

- About half of the world's largest MNEs are already obliged under their national law to use it.
- Investors seem to prefer it.
- Where companies have a free choice between US GAAP and the IASB's standards, many preferred he former.
- The MNEs want access to the American capital market.

However the Enron scandal made a big dent on the reputation of US GAAP. Investors were shocked that Enron's accounts which had been certified by a reputable auditor as complying with US GAAP could be wrong to the extent of billions of dollars. The confidence of investors (both in the USA and elsewhere) in US GAAP was severely shaken. Such a development must surely weaken the position of the FASB and the SEC in their efforts to prevent the IASB's standards becoming accepted first for foreign companies listed on US stock exchanges and ultimately for American companies. In the author's opinion, it makes it more probable that the SEC and the FASB will be prepared to reach some form of agreement with the IASB.

9.8   The impact on theory

It seems probable that the scandals at Enron and other American companies will have a negative impact on the readiness of the financial community to accept two theories favoured by many academics: the efficient market hypothesis and fair value.

9.8.1   The efficient market hypothesis

The efficient market hypothesis holds that the market price of a company's shares is determined by market traders, who take into account all information about the company that is publicly available, irrespective of the source. Applying this theory to accounting, it should make no difference to the market price of a company's shares whether an item of information is published in the accounts proper (the balance sheet and the income statement) or in the notes to the accounts. However in the public comments on the recent scandals, particularly by journalists and politicians, the emphasis was always on the fact that the accounts proper were incorrect – that the published figures for profits and assets were overstated – and not that the disclosure in the notes was insufficient. The author takes this as an indication that, for the public, the accounts proper are important and that it is insufficient that relevant information is disclosed only in the notes. This does not mean that the efficient market hypothesis is disproved – rather that it has limited relevance to the practice of financial reporting.

9.8.2   Fair value

Many academics consider that balance sheets should report assets at their fair value rather than at their historical cost. In recent years, there has been a clear movement on the part of standard-setters towards requiring more and more categories of assets to be reported at fair value. Fair value is defined under both US GAAP and the IASB's standards as the amount for which an asset could be exchanged or a liability settled between knowledgeable willing parties in an arm's length transaction. For example, IAS 39 requires many financial assets, including all derivatives, to be reported at fair value and, under US GAAP energy contracts must be marked to market. Where an asset has a readily available market price, it is simple to establish its fair value and thus provide information in the accounts that is both relevant and reliable. However for many assets there is no readily available market price and the management has to use judgement in establishing fair value; for example, the asset may be reported at present value, which requires that estimates be made of future cash flows and at the appropriate discount rate. In the case of Enron, it was discovered that, for many assets, the market values established by the management were excessive, being based on overly optimistic estimates of future cash flows and discount rates. This demonstrated that often the reported fair values of assets are highly subjective and cannot be considered as fulfilling the criterion of reliability. The impact of Enron's misuse of 'fair value' is likely to be that the financial community (standard-setters, preparers and investors) will have second thoughts about whether 'fair value' is such a good idea. Benston *et al.* (2003) have already come to this conclusion: 'Enron used fair-value accounting to report income of doubtful validity, thereby giving the appearance of superior performance that, in fact, did not exist. If accounting standard setters want to reduce the likelihood of future Enrons, they should abandon current efforts to rely further on fair values in financial reports.'

9.9   Conclusions

In the author's opinion, the Enron affair is one of the most significant events in accounting in the last hundred years. It is a striking confirmation of the theory that change in accounting comes about in discrete jumps as a result of scandals and not in a gradual and orderly fashion. It would seem that normally the rest of society (including the government, investors and the general public) has little interest in accounting and is content to let the specialists (the auditing profession, the standard-setters and the company accountants) get on with their job. However, from time to time, a scandal jerks the general public out of its complacency and the public outcry forces the government to take action. The author is profoundly sceptical that this is the most efficient way to achieve reform in accounting.

Annex: How a special-purpose entity may be used to manipulate the accounts

On 1 December 2003, the XYZ Corporation set up an SPE which is to be managed by XYZ's chief financial officer, who personally contributed the SPE's equity of €300,000. The remaining 97 per cent (€9,700,000) of the SPE's funds are provided through a bank loan, which is guaranteed by XYZ. Exhibit 9.1 presents the balance sheets after these transactions of:

- The XYZ Corporation
- The SPE
- The consolidated balance sheet of XYZ plus SPE.

Note that Enron did not consolidate the SPEs that were controlled by its CFO and for which a minimum of 3 per cent of the funds were provided by persons other than Enron. Hence its accounts would be like those of XYZ. Under the new rules introduced by the FASB after the Enron affair, the SPE in this example would have to be consolidated. The manipulation of the accounts depends critically on the SPE not being consolidated, as can be seen by comparing XYZ's unconsolidated balance sheet with the consolidated balance sheet.

On 2 December 2003, XYZ issues 9700 ordinary shares to the SPE for cash at an issue price of €1000 per share. Exhibit 9.1 presents the updated balance sheets. In the consolidated balance sheet, the issue of XYZ shares is not reported because it is to a group member; the shares in the SPE balance sheet are set off against the equity in XYZ's balance sheet. Note that, if the SPE is not consolidated, the XYZ's debt–equity ratio is reported as misleadingly low, because what is effectively XYZ's debt (it is guaranteeing the bank loan) is reported as equity.

On 3 December 2003, XYZ sells one half of its holding of ABC shares to the SPE for €4 million, reporting a profit of €1.5 million on the deal. The SPE values these shares at their acquisition cost. Note that, in the consolidated balance sheet, no profit is reported on this transaction as it is between members of the group; the ABC shares held by the SPE continue to be

Exhibit 9.1 How an SPE may be used to manipulate the accounts

XYZ Corporation		SPE		Consolidated	
Balance sheets at 1 December 2003 (after bank loan)					
Assets					
Shares in ABC	5.0			Shares in ABC	5.0
Cash	0.0	Cash	10.0	Cash	10.0
less debt	1.0	less debt	9.7	less debt	10.7
Net assets	4.0	Net assets	0.3	Net assets	4.3
				Minority interest	0.3
Equity	4.0	Equity	0.3	Equity	4.0
Balance sheets at 2 December 2003 (after issue of XYZ shares)					
Assets					
Shares in ABC	5.0	Shares in XYZ	10.0	Shares in ABC	5.0
Cash	10.0	Cash	0.0	Cash	10.0
less debt	1.0	less debt	9.7	less debt	10.7
Net assets	14.0	Net assets	0.3	Net assets	4.3
				Minority interest	0.3
Equity	14.0	Equity	0.3	Equity	4.0
Debt/equity ratio	1:14		9.7:0.3		10.7:4.0
Balance sheets at 3 December 2003 (after the sale of half the ABC shares)					
Assets					
Shares in ABC	2.5	Shares in ABC	4.0	Shares in ABC	5.0
Receivable	4.0	Shares in XYZ	10.0		
Cash	10.0	Cash	0.0	Cash	10.0
less debt	1.0	less debt	9.7	less debt	10.7
		less payable	4.0		
Net assets	15.5	Net assets	0.3	Net assets	4.3
				Minority interest	0.3
Equity	14.0	Equity	0.3	Equity	4.0
Profit	1.5	Profit	0.0	Profit	0.0
Debt/equity ratio	1:15.5		13.7:0.3		10.7:4.0
Balance sheets at 4 December 2003 (after the revaluation of the other half of the ABC shares)					
Assets					
Shares in ABC	4.0	Shares in ABC	4.0	Shares in ABC	5.0
Receivable	4.0	Shares in XYZ	10.0		
Cash	10.0	Cash	0.0	Cash	10.0
less debt	1.0	less debt	9.7	less debt	10.7
		less payable	4.0		
Net assets	15.5	Net assets	0.3	Net assets	4.3
				Minority interest	0.3
Equity	14.0	Equity	0.3	Equity	4.0
Profit	3.0	Profit	0.0	Profit	0.0
Debt/equity ratio	1:17		13.7:0.3		10.7:4.0

reported at their original value. Essentially the consolidated balance sheet is unchanged by the deal.

On 4 December 2003, XYZ revalues the remaining half of its holding of ABC shares at €4 million, on the grounds that this is the market value as evidenced by the sale to the SPE. It reports a further profit of €1.5 million. No profit is reported in the consolidated balance sheet. Note that for this manipulation to be successful, XYZ should value its investment in ABC at market value and that no objective market value should be available (for example a stock exchange quotation).

Notes

1. Other American companies that were hit by scandals include WorldCom, Waste Management, Xerox, Adelphia Communications, Tyco International, Global Crossing, and HealthSouth. Of these, the first three are covered later in the chapter.
2. Palepu and Healy (2003) identify a third reason for the decline of Enron's profits in the late 1990s – that the profitability of the other markets into which it expanded was lower than in its core gas market. They write: 'Enron's gas trading idea was probably a good response to the opportunities arising out of deregulation. However, extension of this idea into other markets and international expansion were unsuccessful.' In effect Enron failed because it attempted to grow too quickly. There is some evidence to support this thesis. Certainly some of Enron's ventures into broadband communication were a failure, for example the joint venture with Blockbuster, which is referred to later.
3. Late in 2001, after the resignations of Lay and Skilling, the Enron board of directors set up an investigative committee. The committee's report, known as the 'Powers report', after its chairman William Powers, is a most useful source of information about the whole affair. Its text (all 218 pages!) can be viewed on the web page Findlaw: http://findlaw.com/hdocs/docs/enron/sicreport/index. html.
4. There seems to be some disagreement among commentators as to whether these breaches in the substance of GAAP as opposed to the letter of GAAP should be considered as breaches of the law. Benston seems to think so. However the examiner in bankruptcy, the court official appointed to examine whether Enron's actions broke the law, reported that 'Enron's managers used technical compliance with an aggressive application of GAAP rules to avoid the substance of those rules' (quoted in Benston *et al.*, 2003).
5. The relative figures are (1) Assets: WorldCom $104 billion, Enron $63 billion. (2) Revenue: WorldCom $35 billion, Enron $138 billion. (3) Employees: WorldCom 85,000, Enron 15,000. Enron reported higher revenues as it treated sales imbedded in derivatives as revenue.
6. For an analysis of the relationship between the SEC and the FASB and of the rare occasions when the SEC has exercised its veto, see Flower and Ebbers (2002) Chapter 5.
7. Quoted in *Economist* (2002).
8. Benston *et al.* (2003) point out that there are good grounds for insisting on the rotation of audit partners rather than audit firms. The audit partner may be unwilling to take a firm stand against an audit client, as he would suffer a drop in income if the client were to go elsewhere. On the other hand he may not be

deterred by the threat of fines for negligence during the audit, as these would be paid for by the firm as a whole.
9. The SEC's rules also apply to the European subsidiaries of American companies.
10. According to the author's calculations (based on the method outlined in the Annex to Chapter 1) Enron was over three times the size of Parmalat and World-Com over four times.

References

Accountancy (2002). 'UK companies fearful of Sarbanes-Oxley obligations'. **130**(1309), September.

Beattie, V. and Fearnley, S. (2002). *Auditor Independence and Non-audit Services: a Literature Review*. London, ICAEW.

Benston, G. J. and Hartgreaves, A. L. (2002). 'Enron: what happened and what we can learn from it'. *Journal of Accounting and Public Policy* **21**: 105–27.

Benston, G. J., Bromwich, M., Litan, M. and Wagenhofer A. (2003). 'Following the money: the Enron failure and the state of corporate disclosure'. *AEI-Brookings Joint Center for Regulatory Studies*. Washington.

Bolkestein, F. (2002). Speech at the American Enterprise Institute, 29 May 2002, published on the EU's website, europa.eu.int/comm/internal_market/en/speeches/spch-02-240.htm.

Brandt, R. (2001). 'The crown jewel client'. *Accountancy* (October).

Economist (2001a). 'Andersen's fairy tales'. June 21.

Economist (2001b). 'Who fiddled what?' December 20.

Economist (2002). 'House of correction'. June 20.

EU (2003). *Letter to the Chairman of the SEC*. Brussels, European Commission.

FEE (2003). Comment letter to SEC on auditor independence, FEE.

Fusaro, P. C. and Miller, R. M. (2002). *What Went Wrong at Enron*. Hoboken, New Jersey, Wiley.

Hartgreaves, A. L. and Benston, G. J. (2002). 'The evolving accounting standards for special purpose entities'. *Accounting Horizons* **16**(3): 245–58.

IHT (2003). 'SEC adopts "softened" regulations for auditors'. *International Herald Tribune*.

Palepu, K. and Healy, P. (2003). The fall of Enron. Harvard NOM research paper no. 03–38, Harvard University, Cambridge.

PCAOB (2003). *Statement Regarding the Establishment of Auditing and Other Professional Standards*. Washington, PCAOB.

SEC (2001). Press release 2001–62.

SEC (2002). Press release 2002–44.

SEC (2003a). *Strengthening the Commission's Requirements Regarding Auditor Independence*. Washington, SEC.

SEC (2003b). *Reaffirming the Status of the FASB as a Designated Private-sector Standard setter*. Washington, SEC.

SEC (2003c) *Study Pursuant to Section 108(d) of the Sarbanes-Oxley Act of 2002 on the Adoption by the United States Financial Reporting System of a Principles-based Accounting System*. Washington, SEC.

Singleton-Green, B. (2002). 'Enron – how the fraud worked'. *Accountancy* (May).

Smith, R. (2002). 'Braveheart'. *Wall Street Journal* (January 17).

Thomas, C. W. (2002). 'The rise and fall of Enron'. *Journal of Accountancy* **193**(4).

10
Europe's Contribution to Financial Reporting

This chapter rounds off the book by evaluating Europe's contribution to financial reporting.

10.1 Europe's past achievements

In the field of accountancy and financial reporting, the achievements of Europe have been immense but two, in particular, stand out: the invention of double entry book-keeping and the development of the accountancy profession.

10.1.1 The invention of double entry book-keeping

Accounting did not originate in Europe. Its most probable birthplace is the valley of the Tigris and Euphrates in what is now Iraq. It was here that archaeologists have unearthed what they consider to be the earliest accounting records, clay tokens and tablets that record the assets of a primitive agricultural society: cattle, sheep, wool and so on. Some of these tokens have been dated to 3500 BC or even earlier, which implies that accounting (the keeping of accounting records) may have even developed before writing.[1] At that time most of Europe was untouched by civilisation being covered in impenetrable forests and swamps.

However, Europe has contributed mightily to the development of accounting. Its most lasting achievement has been the invention of double entry book-keeping. Luca Pacioli, the Italian friar who has already been mentioned in the Foreword, is often regarded as the inventor of double entry, but in fact his contribution was to write the first book on the subject, Summa de Arithmetica, Geometria, Proportioni et Proportionalita, which was published in Venice in 1494. In fact by that time the techniques of double entry had already been practised by the merchants of the city states of Northern Italy for some two hundred years. The earliest accounts based on double entry are claimed to be those of the Farolfi company, a firm of Florentine merchants, for the years 1299 and 1300 (see Lee, 1977). However, it is probable that double entry developed simultaneously in a number of Italian cities (Siena, Genoa, Milan and Venice, as well as Florence) around the end of the thirteenth century. Numerous examples of double entry accounts from the fourteenth and fifteenth centuries have survived, mostly from Italian merchants from the above-mentioned cities but with interesting examples from their branches in other European cities such as London (see Nobes, 1994). They demonstrate that the techniques of double entry had been substantially perfected by the time that Luca Pacioli came to write about them in 1494. The eminent historian, Raymond de Roover, characterises the fourteenth and fifteenth centuries as 'perhaps the most brilliant and progressive period in the history of accounting' (de Roover, 1956), and it all took place in Europe!

Although Luca Pacioli did not invent double entry, he was instrumental in the spread of the technique throughout Europe. He was fortunate in that the technique of printing with movable type had been invented only a generation earlier by Johannes Gutenberg of Mainz. Hence his book was reproduced in far larger quantities than would have been the case fifty years earlier and it reached a wide circulation not only in Italy but in neighbouring countries. It was widely read and copied. Within a generation of Luca Pacioli's death in 1515, his book had been translated into French, German, Dutch and English. By the end of the sixteenth century, double entry book-keeping, known as the 'Italian method' after its inventors, had become established throughout Western Europe as the most modern and efficient way of recording commercial transactions. However for some three hundred years its use was limited to the more progressive firms and it was not until the nineteenth century that the technique became widely adopted in business.

The spread of double entry to the other continents followed in the wake of European traders and colonisers: to the British and French colonies in North America, Asia and Africa, and to Spanish and Portuguese colonies in South America and Asia. The story of how double entry reached Japan is particularly well documented as it occurred relatively recently (see Cooke, 1994; Nishikawa, 1956). The British (or rather the Scots), the French and the Germans all contributed to the transformation of the accounting of Japanese enterprises from traditional single entry methods to modern double entry book-keeping. Undoubtedly the role played by Europe in this matter in other parts of the world was equally important but, as this occurred earlier, it is not so well documented.

10.1.2 The accountancy profession

Europe's second great contribution to financial reporting is the development of the accountancy profession. The Scots claim to be the creators of the profession with the foundation in 1853 of the world's first association of accountants, the Society of Accountants in Edinburgh. This claim is contested by the Italians who point to the Collegio dei Rasonati of Venice founded in

1585. However the Collegio ceased to exist when the Venetian Republic was dissolved in 1797, whereas the Edinburgh society, after having merged with two other Scottish bodies in 1951 to form the Institute of Chartered Accountants of Scotland, can claim a continuous existence since 1853.

The foundation of the first professional societies in Scotland was followed half a generation later by the first foundations in England. Between 1870 and 1877, professional bodies were formed in London, Liverpool, Manchester and Sheffield. In 1880 these bodies merged to form the Institute of Chartered Accountants in England and Wales, which is today by far the largest professional accountancy body in Europe. Over the next generation many more professional bodies were founded in Britain, including the Institute of Chartered Accountants in Ireland (1888), and, in 1904, the London Association of Accountants, the forerunner of the present-day Chartered Association of Certified Accountants. The second half of the nineteenth century was an extremely productive period during which the foundations were laid down not only of the British accountancy profession but also, as will be shown, of those of other countries. All the British societies had the common characteristics that they were formed as private associations of individuals which only subsequently received official recognition in the form of a royal charter. For this reason the British societies were self-regulating; in particular they retained control over the process whereby new members attained the qualification through apprenticeship with an existing member and examinations set by the association.

On the continent of Europe, only the Netherlands followed the British example. According to Zeff, van der Wel and Camfferman (1992), the Nederlands Instituut van Accountants which was founded in 1895 was modelled on the Institute of Chartered Accountants in England and Wales which had been founded some fifteen years earlier. The Dutch even borrowed the term 'accountant' from the British as there was no Dutch term that adequately described the activities performed by the new professionals.

Italy had its own tradition of professional accountancy which developed quite independently of that of Britain. Although the original 'Collegio dei Rasonati' of Venice had been dissolved in 1797, similar bodies were later set up in several cities on the Venetian model. Following the reunification of Italy, the Accademia dei Ragionieri (Academy of Accountants) was established in Milan in 1868 (Zambon, 2001). Over the next forty years the Italian profession continued to grow in numbers and status, culminating in the Collegio dei Ragionieri being given official legal recognition in 1906. At that time, as now, the Italian accountancy profession was second only to the British in Europe in terms of size.

The dominance at this time of the British and Italian accountancy professions can be gauged by some figures quoted by Foreman-Peck (1995). In 1900 there were around 11,000 professional accountants in the world as a whole; of these one half were in the British Isles and one quarter in Italy, leaving only one quarter for the rest of the world combined including the USA, Canada, Australia, the Netherlands and the other countries of Continental Europe. However, notwithstanding its size, the Italian profession played almost no part in the development of the accountancy profession in other countries, as its influence outside the borders of Italy has been virtually non-existent. This is in sharp contrast to the Italian influence over the development of double entry, which, as shown in the previous section, was enormous. By contrast the British accountants and the British accountancy bodies were the driving force behind the development of the accountancy profession in many countries. These countries may conveniently be divided into three groups.

Canada, Australia, New Zealand and South Africa

These countries were all members of the British Empire, which had been colonised largely by emigrants from Britain and in which English was the dominant language. Initially accounting and auditing services were provided by qualified professionals sent from Britain. However the local accountants soon saw the advantages of setting up their own associations and when they did so they followed the British model of a self-regulating body. Some even copied the British title of 'chartered accountant'.

India and other British colonies in Asia and Africa

These countries were also members of the British Empire but differed from the first group in that British immigrants formed only a tiny governing class. These countries had not set up their own professional bodies before they became independent of Britain after the Second World War. Instead most professional accountants in these countries were members of a British professional association who had gained their qualification not in Britain but through working and studying locally. The British societies set up centres in these countries where local students could take the examinations and obtain the British qualification. One British body in particular has been very active in this field: the Association of Certified Accountants.

In effect this body exported qualifications whereas, in Canada and the other countries mentioned above, the British chartered bodies exported the idea of associations.[2] The Certified Accountants (since 1984 under the grander title of the Chartered Association of Certified Accountants) have continued to be the principal means by which British professional accountancy is spread around the globe. In 2002, of its 95,000 members half were located in countries outside Britain. However, following their independence from Britain, many of these countries set up their own professional accountancy bodies on the British model. The prime example is the Institute of Chartered Accountants of India, the world's fourth largest professional association with 96,000 members,[3] which was founded in 1949 after India gained its independence. The use of the term 'Chartered Accountant' is a clear indication of the prestige of the Institute of Chartered Accountants in England and Wales, whose members were the first to call themselves 'Chartered Accountants'. There are no less than eighteen other professional associations outside the British Isles that include the words 'Chartered Accountant' in their title.

The USA

The development of the American accountancy profession has been deeply influenced by British accountants, but in a rather different way from the countries mentioned previously. The first qualified accountants in the USA were all immigrants from the British Isles, who were instrumental in setting up the first American firms. All of the 'Big Four' American firms can trace their origins to British accountants. Thus the 'Young' in 'Ernst & Young' refers to Arthur Young a Scotsman from Glasgow. The three names in Pricewater-houseCoopers (the megafirm created by merger in 1998) are all English: Samuel Price was born in Bristol, Edwin Waterhouse was born in Liverpool and Arthur Cooper was a member of the first council of the Institute of Chartered Accountants in England and Wales. The initials KPMG stand for Klynfeld Peat Marwicke & Goerdeler of whom two were British: William Barclay Peat, who helped found the London Institute of Accountants in 1870, and James Marwicke, a Scottish chartered accountant, who emigrated to Canada. In the case of Deloitte Touche Tohmatsu, William Welch Deloitte was a member of the first council of the Institute of Chartered Accountants in England and Wales in 1880 and George Alexander Touche was a Scottish Chartered Accountant. It is noteworthy that the roots of Arthur Andersen & Co., the major American firm which failed to survive its involvement in the Enron scandal, were exclusively American. It is tempting to surmise that a contributory factor in the firm's demise was its lack of a British origin!

Although British qualified accountants played a central role in establishing the first American firms, the American professional association, the Institute of Certified Public Accountants, was not modelled on the British institutes in one vital respect. The American qualification is bestowed not by the professional body but by an official licensing authority, which is generally the State government. An idea of the way in which the accountancy profession started in Britain and subsequently spread to the USA is given by the fact that in 1900 there were some 5000 professional accountants in Britain compared with only 500 in the USA, many of whom were British immigrants.

In those parts of the world not covered by the three above sections 'Canada, Australia, New Zealand and South Africa', 'India and other British colonies in Asia and Africa' and 'The USA', the influence of the British accountancy profession was far less marked. These countries include Continental Europe (other than the Netherlands), Latin America and much of Asia and Africa. The weak British influence has had two consequences: first the professional associations in these countries were generally founded much later than those in the countries previously mentioned and, compared with the British bodies, the state exercised far greater influence. Consequently the accountancy profession in these countries is far weaker both in numbers and in influence. This is clearly the case in Europe as is demonstrated by the figures in Exhibit 4.5: the British and Italian bodies dominate the European accountancy profession, making up more than three quarters of the members.

The importance for a country of a strong and flourishing accountancy profession is in the improved quality of its financial reporting created by the efforts of a well-trained and highly skilled body of men and women specialised in the theory and practice of accountancy. Thanks to Europe (and in particular to Scotland and its southerly neighbour) many countries throughout the world now enjoy these benefits.

10.2 The European approach to financial reporting

The past achievements of Europe are remarkable. But what of the present? Do Europe's achievements lie all in the past? What is Europe's present importance? In particular is there a specifically European approach to financial reporting, superior to that of other continents and countries?

10.2.1 The great divide: the British approach versus the Continental approach

It is noteworthy that of Europe's two great contributions to accountancy, the first (double entry book-keeping) originated on the continent of Europe and the second (the profession) in Britain. This is symptomatic of the great schism in accounting matters that divides Europe between, on the one hand, the British Isles and on the other hand the other countries of Western Europe. In discussing the question whether there is a specifically European approach to financial reporting and, if so what are its characteristics, one must at once admit that there is not a single European approach. There are at least two fundamentally different approaches: the British approach and the Continental European approach. The characteristics of these two approaches are summarised in Exhibit 10.1.

The table compares the distinguishing characteristics of financial reporting in Britain with those of the Continental European countries. The differences have been painted with a very broad brush and therefore, in interpreting this table, two words of caution are in order:

1. It is simplistic to portray all Continental European countries as having exactly the same approach to financial reporting. In particular, the approach in the Netherlands and in much of Scandinavia incorporates certain aspects of the British approach. And within the other Continental countries there are often significant differences in approach on particular matters.

Exhibit 10.1   Approaches to financial reporting: Britain versus Continental Europe

	The 'idealised' British approach	The 'idealised' Continental European approach
The principal driving force	The Accountancy Profession	The State
The objectives of financial statements		
Primary	To provide information for the capital market	To regulate distributions to stakeholders
Secondary	To assist shareholders in controlling the enterprise's management	To constrain the enterprise's management in the interests of stakeholders
What should be measured by the financial statements?	The profitability and solvency of the enterprise	'Efficiency' of the enterprise from the viewpoint of society
The most important qualitative characteristic of financial statements	Relevance	Reliability
The predominant manifestation of this characteristic	Substance over form	Prudence
Preparers' discretion	May use professional judgement	Must adhere to the rules
Flexibility versus uniformity	Flexibility (adaptation to the needs of the individual enterprise)	Uniformity (e.g. charts of accounts)
Prevalent abuse	Creative accounting	Secret reserves
Expression of this characteristic	'A true and fair view'	'A picture according to the facts'

All that Exhibit 10.1 gives is an indication of the approach in Continental European countries in general.

2. The differences have been presented in the form of stark alternatives: for example, in the first row of Exhibit 10.1, the principal driving force behind financial reporting in Britain is stated to be the accountancy profession and on the Continent, the State. However in fact the State has considerable influence in Britain, as has the accountancy profession on the Continent. Exhibit 10.1 should be interpreted as indicating that, in Britain, the accountancy profession has more influence than the State and, on the Continent, the reverse is the case.

In effect what is presented in Exhibit 10.1 is an idealised form of the approach to financial reporting in both Britain and the Continent, in which the differences between the two approaches are generalised and exaggerated, in order to make them more evident. The degree to which Exhibit 10.1 represents the current reality is discussed later. The first row of Exhibit 10.1 has already been discussed. The remaining rows are now considered, starting with the objectives of financial statements. Exhibit 10.1 presents both a primary objective and a secondary objective.

The primary objective

Readers will not be surprised at the objective attributed to the financial statements under the British approach, which is to provide information for the capital market. The objective attributed to the financial statements under the Continental approach (to regulate distributions to stakeholders) has been considered earlier in Chapter 2. However the concept of stakeholders needs further explanation; it covers not only the shareholders but all groups with an interest in the enterprise, including notably creditors, employees and the government. The financial statements serve the function of facilitating the division of the enterprise's wealth and income among these groups. Essentially these groups are in competition with each other. For example, if the enterprise's funds are depleted through the payment of excessive dividends to shareholders, this will increase the danger of the enterprise being unable to repay its debts to creditors. Hence an important function of financial statements is to limit the amount that may be distributed as dividend so as to protect the position of creditors. Another important stakeholder is the government. In most European countries the government may be considered to be a partner in the enterprise alongside the shareholders, a partner who is entitled to receive about a third of the profits by way of tax. The proper division of the profits between the shareholders and the government is clearly a matter of supreme importance to both parties and the financial statements form the essential factual basis for this division. A further important stakeholder is the enterprise's work force. The workers are interested in the continued viability of the enterprise, which can most effectively be assured by limiting distributions to other stakeholders.

The secondary objective

For the British approach the secondary objective is to enable the shareholders to control the enterprise's management. For the Continental approach, it is to constrain the enterprise's management in the interests of stakeholders. These objectives may seem very similar but there are two important differences. The first is straightforward: the British give priority to the shareholders, the Continental Europeans to the wider group of stakeholders. The second difference is rather more subtle. In Britain the role of the financial statements is to provide information that assists shareholders in controlling management; for example, if the income statement reveals that profits are unsatisfactory, the shareholders may decide to dismiss the present management. On the

Continent, the financial statements do of course provide information that is useful for control purposes but in addition the financial statements *in themselves* act as a constraint on management, preventing it from acting in ways that would be contrary to the interests of particular stakeholders. An example is the common rule that a grant from the government to the enterprise must be credited to a non-distributable reserve, thus ensuring that the money is not dissipated in dividends to shareholders and bonuses to management, which might occur if it were to be credited to income. A weaker form of the constraining influence of financial statements is when a powerful stakeholder (generally the government) insists that the financial statements provide information on the enterprise's activities that are important for that stakeholder; for example, the government may be concerned about the total spent on research or the amount of investment in disadvantaged regions. Disclosing this information both motivates the management to take action to ensure that the figures are satisfactory and alerts the government that intervention is necessary if they are not.

What should be measured by the financial statements?

The shareholder versus stakeholder conflict shows itself in the answers to this question. In Britain, the financial statements should measure the profitability and solvency of the enterprise; profitability is the prime measure but it needs to be backed up by a measure of solvency since it is possible for a profitable enterprise to become bankrupt. Naturally profitability is measured from the viewpoint of the shareholder. In Continental Europe a wider view is taken; the financial statements should measure the 'efficiency' of the enterprise from the viewpoint of society as a whole. The term 'efficiency' is used in the sense of the degree to which the enterprise meets the objectives of society. This concept of 'social efficiency' permeates the work of two very influential Continental accounting theorists: Eugen Schmalenbach and Theodore Limperg.[4] For Schmalenbach, the enterprise's contribution to the welfare of the community was measured by its profit, because profit is the increase in the total value of goods and services resulting from the enterprise's activities. The enterprise takes in certain goods and services and transforms them into different goods and services; if the value of the outputs exceeds that of the inputs then society has benefited from the enterprise's activities. For Schmalenbach, profit was a measure of 'social efficiency'; he was not at all interested in profit as a measure of the reward to shareholders.

The primary qualitative characteristic of financial statements

With the British approach, the emphasis is placed on relevance; with the Continental approach, more emphasis is placed on reliability. The conflict between relevance and reliability has been evoked several times in previous chapters. An example of the different approaches is that the British use the percentage of completion method for measuring the profit on a long-term contract, whereas the Continental Europeans prefer the completed contract method. The different emphasis placed on relevance and reliability can be traced to the different objectives attributed to financial statements: the capital market requires information that is relevant for investment decisions; on the other hand, to regulate distributions to stakeholders, it is absolutely essential that all parties accept that profit and other elements of the accounts are measured in an objective fashion; top priority is given to preventing the management manipulating the figures to the advantage or disadvantage of a particular party.

The next five rows of Exhibit 10.1 present various consequences of the decision to give priority to relevance or to reliability.

The predominant manifestation of this characteristic

In Britain the emphasis is on substance over form, as it is the reality behind the legal form that gives value to the enterprise. On the Continent, the emphasis is on prudential valuations in order to limit the danger of the enterprise making excessive distributions; once funds have been distributed, they cannot easily be recouped.

The discretion allowed to preparers

In Britain preparers may use their professional judgement in drawing up the accounts; in certain circumstances they can ignore the rules in order to present the most relevant information; on the Continent the preparers must follow the rules. This is also an aspect of the relative importance of the accountancy profession and the state, as indicated in the first row of the table.

Flexibility versus uniformity

In Britain, preparers may adapt the general rules to the specific requirements of the individual enterprise, so that, for each enterprise, the most relevant information is provided. This flexibility is enshrined in the 'true and fair view override'; the specific rule should be disregarded when this is necessary to present a true and fair view of the individual enterprise. On the Continent such flexibility is not permitted. Not only must preparers obey the rules, but the rules are devised in the interests of society as a whole and not of the individual enterprise. The most obvious example of this preference for the collectivity over the individual is the imposition of uniform charts of accounts in many Continental countries. This is also an application of the principle that what is measured is the 'social efficiency' of the enterprise and not simply the profit earned for shareholders.

Abuses

The emphasis of relevance or reliability (or rather the neglect of the other quality) can lead to abuses. The prevalent abuse with the British approach is 'creative accounting'; that is preparers use their freedom to draw up accounts that present an unjustifiably favourable picture. On the Continent, the abuse is to carry the prudence principle to an extreme with the result that assets are seriously undervalued and liabilities grossly overstated leading to the creation of secret reserves.

Expression.   The British approach may be summed up in the expression 'a true and fair view' which is achieved through the professional account-ant's efforts (using her skill and judgement) to present the substance of the position of the individual enterprise. The Continental approach may be summarised in the phrase 'a picture according to the facts';[5] the facts must be reported, there is no place for judgement or discretion, the same rules should be applied by everyone.

10.2.2   The reality

However, Exhibit 10.1 paints too stark a picture of the differences between Britain and Continental Europe. It depicts 'idealised' approaches; the reality is rather more complicated, in respect of both Britain and the Continent.

Britain

There are two important points to be made about the 'idealised' British approach.

1. This approach has never been applied by the great mass of small and medium-sized companies that are not listed on the stock exchange. For these companies, the principal objective of the financial statements is and always has been the regulation of distributions, particularly the computa-tion of tax payable to the state. Hence the financial reporting of these companies places more emphasis on reliability than on relevance.
2. However even for listed companies, Exhibit 10.1 is, in some respects, rather out of date as it depicts the situation of a generation ago. In the last thirty years, two important developments have had a profound influence on financial reporting in Britain: the implementation of the EU Directives and the establishment of a powerful standard-setting body. As a result of these developments, the position of the accountancy profession as the driving force behind financial reporting has been seriously weakened; many rules are now laid down in the law or in standards, whereas previously they were considered as a matter for the judgement of the professional accountant. There is greater uniformity than before, resulting notably from the impact of the EU Directive's prescribed formats. However it is prob-ably still true that in respect of all these matters there is still a significant difference between Britain and most Continental countries, although the differences are less than they were thirty years ago.

Continental Europe

Two rather similar points may be made about the 'idealised' Continental European approach.

1. As in Britain, this approach applies most strongly to the financial statements of small and medium-sized enterprises. However it also applies to the individual accounts of larger listed enterprises (which is not the case in Britain). The approach is least marked in the consolidated accounts of listed enterprises.

2. Recent developments have tended to weaken certain aspects of the Continental approach as regards the consolidated accounts of the largest listed enterprises. Responding to the challenge of globalisation, these enterprises have begun to adopt for their consolidated accounts certain aspects of the British approach, notably the objective of providing information for the capital market and the primacy of relevance as a qualitative characteristic. This development has been facilitated by the recent changes in the law in Germany and other continental countries that permit certain large enterprises to draw up their consolidated accounts according to IASB or American standards. The EU's decision that European listed companies should, from 2005, adopt the IASB's standards, is a further manifestation of a weakening of the Continental approach.

Furthermore it would be wrong to portray all Continental European countries as having the same homogeneous approach to financial reporting. As has already been mentioned, the Netherlands and, to a lesser extent, the Scandinavian countries are in some respects more similar to Britain than to the other European countries; the biggest difference is that these countries put more emphasis on the 'social efficiency' of the enterprise than on its profitability. What is presented in Exhibit 10.1 as the 'idealised' Continental European approach is essentially that of Germany. The other Continental European countries follow the German approach, some more closely than others.

The result of recent developments has been that Britain and Continental Europe have moved closer together in terms of their approach to financial reporting. The consolidated accounts of the large European multinational concerns (such as Total and Metro) are becoming almost indistinguishable, as to their form and the standards applied, from those of their British counterparts (such as BP and Tesco). By contrast, small and medium-sized enterprises in Britain have always based their financial reporting on the Continental approach. Perhaps in the future the divide within Europe will be between the large multinational enterprises and the rest, and not between Britain and the Continent.

10.2.3 The advantages of diversity

In the Foreword it was claimed that the predominant characteristic of Europe is its diversity. This diversity clearly applies in financial reporting as amply demonstrated in Exhibit 10.1. Such diversity adds greatly to the interest of the study of the subject, but, in respect of the diversity of approaches to financial reporting within Europe, a rather more significant claim may be made: that diversity is an advantage – that because of its diversity Europe is able to find better solutions to the problems of financial reporting than it would do otherwise, that the quality of European financial reporting is higher because it is founded on a variety of traditions and approaches. This claim is based on the following argument.

When the impartial reader examines the columns of Exhibit 10.1, she soon comes to the conclusion that neither the British approach nor the Continental approach is completely correct, that neither offers the single 'true' solution to the problem of how to report the enterprise's activities. This becomes clear when one considers the abuses that arise under both approaches. 'Creative accounting' occurs under the British approach because of excessive reliance on judgement; to avoid this abuse, judgement must be tempered by rules. On the other hand, secret reserves are made possible through the unjustified application of the prudence principle; to avoid this abuse, the application of the prudence principle must be constrained in some way, perhaps by insisting that the end result does not misrepresent the substance of the position. It would seem that the 'ideal' solution would draw elements from both approaches. Consider the question of whether the state or the accountancy profession should be the strongest influence in determining the rules and practice of financial reporting. Clearly there are strong arguments for the state, as it represents the whole of society and not simply one sectional interest. However there are dangers in the excessive domination by the state, as demonstrated by the way that the Nazi regime in Germany in the 1930s subjugated financial reporting to the task of building up its military might.[6] Hence it is highly desirable that the state's power be tempered by a strong and independent accountancy profession. But the accountancy profession should not be allowed to determine the rules on its own, because it represents only one party of the many that are affected by financial reporting. The interests of these other parties (which includes the whole community) should also be taken into account and the most effective way of achieving this is by the participation of the state. Hence the ideal way to set the rules of financial reporting is through a balance of power between the state and other parties. However this is precisely the direction in which the countries of Europe have been moving. In Britain, where previously the accountancy profession was the dominant source of the rules, an increasingly important role is being played by both the preparers and the state. With the setting up of the Accounting Standards Board, the accountancy profession has had to share the task of standard-setting with the preparers, and, over the last twenty years, the state has intervened in enacting a number of laws that regulate financial reporting to an unprecedented degree. But in Germany the reverse process has occurred: with the establishment of the Deutsche Rechnungslegung Standards Committee,[7] the state has surrendered powers to other parties: Both Britain and Germany are moving (from opposite extremes) towards the best compromise.

10.2.4 The best compromise between flexibility and uniformity

How does this argument apply to the rules that govern financial reporting? For example, how does one resolve the conflict between the interests of the individual enterprise and those of society as exemplified in the question of flexibility and uniformity? The imposition by the EU's directives of standard formats has had a marked impact on the uniformity of financial statements throughout Europe. However the EU's attempt to introduce a degree of flexibility for the individual enterprise through the 'true and fair override' must be considered a failure, because very few individual enterprises have made use of this opportunity. Perhaps the French idea of insisting on uniformity in the balance sheet and the profit and loss account and using the notes to present the information peculiar to the individual enterprise suggests a better way in which progress may be made. In the author's opinion, the ultimate solution has not yet been achieved but some progress has been made towards that goal.

10.2.5 The objectives of financial reporting: shareholders versus stakeholders

But does the argument that diversity is an advantage apply to the objectives of financial reporting. On this question, the Europeans seem to have reached a pragmatic compromise that, for the larger multinational enterprises, the consolidated accounts should adopt the British objective and the individual accounts the Continental objective. However, in the author's opinion, the compromise is unsatisfactory and will not last, because the needs of all stakeholders for information about the enterprise are not met either by the consolidated accounts or by the individual accounts. The consolidated accounts are deficient because they are designed to meet the needs of only one social group – the shareholders; the individual accounts are inadequate because they do no present the picture of the group as a whole. The author rejects the IASB's argument that the needs of all social groups are met by providing the information that meets the needs of shareholders.[8] In effect a compromise on this point is not possible: a decision has to be made as to whether the financial statements are prepared for the shareholders or for the wider group of stakeholders.

In Britain the shareholder is king. This is even clearer in the USA. In that country academic research in accounting is dominated by the quest to establish a relationship between the accounts and the market price of the enterprise's shares. The other stakeholders are virtually ignored. The FASB adopts this approach. For this body, the users of the accounts are the shareholders and their advisors, the financial analysts.

For the author, this approach is wrong. The shareholders are just one of the many social groups that contribute to the enterprise's prosperity and in turn depend on it for their well-being. They are not even the most important group in their particular field of providing capital for the enterprise, as is proved by some remarkable research conducted by Mayer (1988). Between 1970 and 1985 shares made a negative contribution (–4 per cent) to the finance of physical investment by enterprises in Britain, compared with a positive contribution (+5 per cent) by loans. The figures for Germany were +1 per cent (shares) and +37 per cent (loans). The claim that the shareholders are the most important source of the enterprise's finance does not stand up in the face of these figures. In the author's opinion, the present domination of the shareholder interest in Britain and the USA is not based on an objective assessment of the relative importance of the different stakeholders but rather reflects the political and economic power of the shareholder interest.

10.2.6   The impending triumph of the British approach

In Section 10.2.3, it was claimed that the diversity of financial reporting practice in Europe was a source of strength. Europe is able to make progress through the reconciling of two quite different approaches to financial reporting because both approaches are living forces supported by powerful advocates who ensure that the arguments in favour of their position are not neglected. The tension between the two approaches leads to the best compromise which draws the best from both sides. This argument is logical and seems to apply to the development of the national regulatory system, as evidenced by events in Britain and Germany. However, in the other areas of financial reporting, the likely outcome seems to be that a compromise solution will not be achieved but rather that one approach will come to dominate the other, more specifically that the British approach will triumph over the Continental approach.

This is especially the case with the development of the rules for the financial reporting of larger enterprises, where at the moment the British approach is carrying all before it. The last ten years has witnessed a continuous decline in the influence of the Continental approach. The EU's directives were based on the concept of a compromise between the two approaches. They must be judged to have failed, for in 1995 the EU decided to turn to the IASB as the source of the rules for the financial reporting of the European multi-national enterprises. However, the IASB is dominated by the Anglo-Saxons, who ensure that this body's standards embody the essential features of their approach, notably information for the capital market and the primacy of shareholder interests. It seems that the Continental approach (with its emphasis on information for society as a whole and on the primacy of wider stakeholder interests) has no longer any influence over the financial reporting of the larger European enterprises. In fact the major unresolved issue in this field is whether, in the future, the rules will be based not on the IASB's standards but on US GAAP, which in no way embodies the Continental approach and which differs from the British approach only in minor details. It would appear that, in the future, in Europe (including Britain) the Continental approach will be limited to the financial reporting of small and medium-sized enterprises.

10.3 Europe's current contribution

At present the major contribution of Europe to financial reporting on the global scale is that it provides the driving force behind the IASB. Eight of the IASB's fourteen members are citizens of European countries, including the chairman, Sir David Tweedie, whose forceful personality has had a marked impact on the nature of the IASB's output. However the IASB, as it is currently constituted and operated, manifests only one aspect of European financial reporting, the British approach, and thus the IASB's approach can in no sense be considered to be representative of Europe as a whole. The characteristics of financial reporting to which Sir David Tweedie attaches the greatest importance are information for the capital market, relevance and substance over form, all of which are elements of the British approach. The three IASB members from Continental European countries seem to have little influence; they are outnumbered by the five British citizens, who are also supported by the five other members from 'Anglo-Saxon' countries, whose approach to financial reporting is much closer to that of Britain than to that of the Continent.

The aspect of the IASB's current approach that the author finds most regrettable is the emphasis on providing information for shareholders and the consequent neglect of the needs of other stakeholders. No heed is taken of the long experience of the countries of Continental Europe in reporting to these other stakeholders.

10.4 The future

In assessing how financial reporting in Europe will develop in the future, a distinction should be drawn between the major European enterprises of an international character, such as the European top one hundred presented in Exhibit 1.4, and the great mass of small and medium-sized enterprises, whose horizons are limited to their home countries.

1. The European multinationals. It seems clear that the impact of globalisation will result in the accounts of multinational enterprises throughout the world (not just those in Europe) becoming increasingly similar. Hence, for these enterprises, a specifically European approach to financial reporting will cease to exist, being merged with a global approach. Whether the model will be the IASB's standards or alternatively US GAAP has still to be decided. However both models have been strongly influenced by Europe and hence, in an indirect fashion, a European approach to financial

reporting will persist at the global level. The author regrets that both models are based on reporting to shareholders and neglect the other stakeholders. However he is convinced that the present obsession with shareholders' values is almost certainly a passing phase, but only time will tell whether it will last a decade, a generation or a century. It is to be hoped that, when eventually the global rule-makers appreciate their error, they will draw on the accumulated wisdom of the counties of Continental Europe in developing standards that meet the information needs of all stakeholders.

2. Small and medium-sized enterprises: The forces of globalisation which will lead to the disappearance of a specifically European approach to accounting for the multinational enterprises should have little impact on the great mass of small and medium-sized enterprises. It is to be expected that, for the accounting of these enterprises, a specifically European approach to financial reporting will survive, including that most characteristic feature of European financial reporting – the remarkable diversity in financial reporting practice.

The author is sure that, in the future, financial reporting in Europe will be marked by the two main narratives of this book: for the larger European enterprises, the search for a global model, and for the rest, the continued diversity of national practice. This should ensure that, in the future, the study of European financial reporting will remain the fascinating subject that it is today.

Notes

1. For an exposition of the origins of accounting see Mattesich (1994).
2. See R. H. Parker (1994) 'Importing and Exporting Accounting' for further reflections on this theme.
3. The three larger associations are the American Institute of Certified Public Accountants (330,00 members), the Chinese Institute of Certified Public Accountants (127,000 members) and the Institute of Chartered Accountants in England and Wales (120,000 members).
4. For an analysis of the ideas of the two 'accounting heroes' see Flower (1996).
5. This phrase is in fact the English translation of the phrase in the German version of the Fourth Directive which in the English version is rendered as 'a true and fair view'.
6. For the Nazi's approach to financial reporting see Flower and Ebbers (2002) page 31.
7. See Chapter 4, Section 4.2 for more about this committee.
8. The IASB's approach is set out in its Framework (paragraph 10): 'As investors are providers of risk capital to the enterprise, the provision of financial statements that meet their needs will also meet most of the needs of other users.' The IASB presents no evidence to support this assertion, which the author considers to be completely unwarranted.

References

Cooke, T. E. (1994). 'The evolution of financial reporting in Japan'. *Accounting History: Some British Contributions*. R. H. Parker and B. S. Yamey. Oxford, Oxford University Press.

de Roover, R. (1956). 'The development of accounting prior to Pacioli'. *Studies in the History of Accounting*. A. C. Littleton and B. S. Yamey. London, Sweet & Maxwell.

Flower, J. (1996). 'Three "Accounting Heroes" of Continental Europe'. *Essays in Accounting Thought*. I. Lapsley. Edinburgh, ICAS: 201.

Flower, J. and Ebbers, G. (2002). *Global Financial Reporting*. Basingstoke, Palgrave.

Foreman-Peck, J. (1995). 'Accounting in the industrialization of Western Europe'. *European Financial Reporting: A History*. P. Walton. London, Academic Press.

Lee, G. A. (1977). 'The coming of age of double entry'. *Accounting Historians Journal* (Autumn).

Mattesich, R. (1994). 'Archeology of accounting and Schmandt-Besserat's contribution'. *Accounting Business and Financial History* 4(1).

Mayer, C. (1988). 'New issues in corporate finance'. *European Economic Review* 32: 1–23.

Nishikawa, K. (1956). 'The early history of double-entry book-keeping in Japan'. *Studies in the History of Accounting*. A. C. Littleton and B. S. Yamey. London, Sweet & Maxwell.

Nobes, C. (1994). 'The Gallerani Account Book of 1305–8'. *Accounting History: Some British Contributions*. R. H. Parker and B. S. Yamey. Oxford, Clarendon Press.

Parker, R. H. (1994). 'Importing and exporting accounting: the British experience'. *Accounting History: Some British Contributions*. R. H. Parker and B. S. Yamey. Oxford, Clarendon Press.

Zambon, S. (2001). 'Italy'. *European Accounting Guide*. D. Alexander and S. Archer. Aspen, Gaithersburg, New York.

Zeff, S., van der Wel, F. and Camfferman (1992). *Company Financial Reporting*. Amsterdam, North-Holland.

Index